I0759475

TRAITOR

TRAITOR

The LIFE & ASSASSINATION of JOHN DUNN HUNTER, AMERICAN RADICAL

ANDY DOOLEN

JOHNS HOPKINS UNIVERSITY PRESS BALTIMORE

Printed in the United States of America on acid-free paper
2 4 6 8 9 7 5 3 1

Johns Hopkins University Press
2715 North Charles Street
Baltimore, Maryland 21218
www.press.jhu.edu

Library of Congress Cataloging-in-Publication Data is available.

ISBN 978-1-4214-5328–6 (hardcover)
ISBN 978-1-4214-5329–3 (ebook)

A catalog record for this book is available from the British Library.

Special discounts are available for bulk purchases of this book. For more information, please contact Special Sales at specialsales@jh.edu.

EU GPSR Authorized Representative
LOGOS EUROPE, 9 rue Nicolas Poussin, 17000, La Rochelle, France
E-mail: Contact@logoseurope.eu

In memory of David Bogan. Nobody could tell a story quite like him.

DIED
JOHN DUNN HUNTER

This individual, who rendered himself so well known in Europe and America, by the publication of his singular book, and by the imputations which were thrown upon him by several gentleman of the first respectability, of being an impostor, and of having deceived the English public by a relation of the adventures, which he never experienced, was lately cut off by two Indian assassins not far from Nacogdoches, in the province of Texas.

—*Richmond Enquirer*, June 8, 1827

CONTENTS

A NOTE ON TERMINOLOGY

I USE THE TERM *Native peoples* to refer generally to the many different Indigenous communities and nations living in North America. Whenever possible, I use tribal names to refer to specific communities and nations, which acknowledges that they are distinct and sovereign peoples with their own histories, traditions, and practices.

At times I refer to *Indian tribes*, an established phrase in historical scholarship, but only when appropriate to the context or the source. There are also occasions when I use the problematic term *Indian*, but I do this only to convey the broad perspective of white Americans during the period and emphasize how this fictitious term was fundamental to the articulation of settler ideology and power. I sometimes use the term *Indigenous* for referencing Indigenous peoples worldwide and their common history of being the original inhabitants of a land prior to colonial invasions. Finally, the term *American* appears throughout this book in a very parochial sense, for referring to the United States and the nationality of its people, even as I recognize that the term, in the larger context of the Americas, can be applied to various nations and peoples in the Western Hemisphere.

PROLOGUE

A TRAVEL-WEARY MAN WINDS up the hilly road to Thomas Jefferson's Monticello in the fall of 1822. Tucked in his satchel are letters of introduction and the latest draft of his manuscript about the manners and customs of some of the Indian tribes west of the Mississippi. Around twenty-one years of age and on a break from his medical studies in Philadelphia, he is a surprising new voice on the Indian world.[1] He had been taken captive as a boy by the Kickapoos on the Illinois frontier and then traded to several tribes before ultimately settling into a happy home with an Osage family who raised him as one of their own.

His name is John Dunn Hunter, and he is one of the great mysteries of his era. The manuscript he hopes to discuss with Jefferson will, in two short years, be a widely acclaimed book in its third edition and translated into several languages. He will take London by storm. Royalty and aristocrats will seek his company, philanthropists and reformers will ask for his advice on saving the "poor Indian" from extinction, and poets will worry that the siren song of his former life will lure him back to the dangerous freedom of the wilderness. Their prophecy will come true.

This book tells the life story of John Dunn Hunter. Sitting across from the living legend that day at Monticello, Hunter was the embodiment of Jefferson's Enlightenment belief in universal equality: If human beings are born equal, regardless of social station, then even Native peoples, widely assumed to be less advanced in their social development, could climb the ladder of progress, provided they gave up their savage habits and accepted civilization. Hunter, raised by Native peoples on the wild frontier, seemed to prove the validity of the theory. However, during this era of westward expansion Jefferson's fellow citizens had grown highly cynical about sufficient progress happening anytime soon, if ever. Native peoples were being condemned for clinging to their homelands, standing in the way of American settlements, and spurning the nation's supposedly generous efforts to turn them into farmers and Christians. After so many Indian tribes chose to fight alongside the British during the War of 1812, American attitudes became even more hostile toward Native peoples. In the American mind, they seemed fixed in a state of savagery and incapable of improvement, let alone gratitude for a peaceful and enlightened nation that had invested such hope and capital in their progress and salvation.[2]

The great immigration of American settlers across the Appalachian Mountains after the War of 1812 hardened these attitudes and fueled a growing impatience with the very presence of Native peoples within the United States. Expansion was drastically transforming the continental interior. American settlers were building cabins, barns, and farms; forming towns, counties, and cities; establishing post offices, banks, churches, and schools; creating transportation, communication, and trade routes; starting factories, distilleries, newspapers, and forges; and founding the new states of Indiana, Illinois, Missouri, Alabama, and Mississippi. The breathtaking speed of expansion inspired a supposedly humane solution to the "Indian problem": All Indian tribes who refused treaty agreements and assimilation into an American way of life would be removed to west of the Mississippi, where they would be free to change at a slower pace. It was said to be a mercy to remove Native peoples from what seemed to be for them the destructive path of progress.[3]

This book is only the second biography of John Dunn Hunter, and the first in over fifty years.[4] It traces his rise to fame as one of the era's most unusual frontier heroes, and then his sudden fall from grace. For a thrilling moment, the acclaimed author, raised in the wilderness by Indians, embodied the myth of the triumph of civilization over savagery with the same bravura as his more well-known contemporaries: Daniel Boone blazing a path from Virginia through the Cumberland Gap and founding the commonwealth of Kentucky; Meriwether Lewis and William Clark, and their successors, Zebulon Pike and Stephen Long, plunging into the lands beyond the Mississippi and claiming the West for the United States; Governors William Henry Harrison and Lewis Cass bringing law and order to the frontier and securing massive land cessions from Indian tribes; General Andrew Jackson subduing the defiant ones and making the Southeast safe for American settlement. Alongside these iconic figures, many others, including pioneers in covered wagons, rough-looking trappers, scientists, missionaries, naturalists, and artists, were also celebrated at the time for their heroic roles in the rise of the American West.

The realm of culture did what it must inevitably do in every settler society by helping the newcomers rationalize their taking the place of the Indigenous peoples being ethnically cleansed from the land.[5] In American culture, the frontier hero's double, his tragic reflection, was the doomed Indian. In the Leatherstocking Tales of James Fenimore Cooper, in the poetry of William Cullen Bryant and Henry Wadsworth Longfellow, in the historical novels of Lydia Maria Child and Catharine Maria Sedgwick, and in stage dramas such as *Pocahontas* and *Metamora*, the picturesque noble savage is vanishing from the continent. Without exception, the Indian figure exists in the remote or recent past, at turning points when the ripples of white settlement began appearing on the coasts and in the valleys and the proud savage, recognizing the arrival of a superior people, voluntarily retreats deeper into the frontier. By the 1820s, the expectation that Native peoples would inevitably disappear from the land calcified into, in the words of historian Brian Dippie, a "habit of thought."[6] Expressing concern and grieving for the poor Indian became an early form of virtue signaling, and much more. The acts of remembrance in novels, poetry, and the arts inspired this first generation of Americans to see themselves as the rightful heirs to a continent won not only by revolution but also by the divine laws of nature.

Hunter became a cultural phenomenon because he represented a new age of possibility for the American nation. He was considered a remarkable exception to an ancient rule: White people who had lived among Native peoples, a phenomenon that had been occurring for over two centuries, were widely viewed with suspicion, fear, and loathing. According to historian Colin Calloway, "These renegades had a reputation as degenerate outcasts who found in Indian society the freedom to give full vent to vicious natures and homicidal tendencies. They surpassed their Indian friends in savagery and cruelty."[7] However, there were special individuals, such as Boone and Hunter, who had pulled off the nearly impossible feat of "going native" without becoming a savage or suffering any major debilitating effects. They were not reviled as the "scum of the frontier," as Calloway observes. Even in captivity, they had never forgotten their Americanness, lost their moral compass, or otherwise been degraded by living with Native peoples. As evidenced by their metamorphoses on the frontier, they knew how to make the most of their inheritance, taking only the noblest of Indian qualities and fusing those with a new national consciousness focused on the American continent rather than on Europe.

Boone and Hunter were held up as role models for a settler democracy.

I was initially drawn to Hunter because we so rarely encounter white men like him during this age of expansion and colonization. I remember being slightly confused the first time I read him. His writings about Native peoples and communities were unlike anything I had ever seen from the period (a belief shared by some of his contemporaries). Here was a young white man whose knowledge, feelings, and hopes were clearly based in personal experience. He had not gleaned any of that knowledge from libraries or from a short tour of the frontier. He wrote with joy and admiration for the Native peoples who had raised him and whom he missed terribly. He respected Indigenous sovereignty, ceremonies, and land rights. It became his life's ambition to help Native peoples adapt to the demands of the settler nation, and he had shared this with Jefferson in his library.

Nobody during the period epitomized the new American more than Hunter—that is, until his pro-Indian views and criticism of the United States suddenly made him a public enemy. If officials in the War Department had not accused him of being an imposter, John Dunn Hunter might still be remembered today as an iconic figure of the nineteenth century. Two of the nation's leading experts on Native peoples, Lewis Cass, the governor and superintendent of Indian affairs in Michigan Territory, and Thomas McKenney, the head of the new federal Office of Indian Affairs, had taken notice of Hunter after British reviewers praised his book for being, among other things, an impassioned and informed critique of the ongoing mistreatment of Native peoples. Cass and McKenney were particularly concerned that British plaudits for Hunter could spark criticism in the United States and possibly imperil a landmark bill on Indian removal coming before the next Congress. McKenney struck the first blow, anonymously mocking the British in the *National Intelligencer* for gullibly believing Hunter; then Cass set to work on a more extensive plan for discrediting Hunter and humiliating his British admirers.

Cass spent weeks combing through Hunter's book for any information that could be used against him. He read passages to his agent Henry Rowe Schoolcraft as their flotilla of canoes traveled down the western coast of Lake Michigan on their way to a treaty conference at Prairie du Chien. He reviewed War Department reports on Indian depredations from around the time Hunter said he had been taken captive by the Kickapoos. He attempted to verify the identities of individuals mentioned by Hunter in his book and consulted philologists with the aim of finding mistakes in the Osage lexicon compiled by Hunter and included in his book. He traveled to St. Louis to confer with the explorer William Clark, who was superintendent of Indian affairs for the West. With his help, Cass interviewed several fur traders, asking them if they had ever encountered a white child in the Osage villages fifteen or twenty years earlier. By signed affidavit, they swore they had not. Then Cass returned to Detroit before the ice set and got to work on his screed against Hunter.

In January 1826, just before the opening session of Congress, his unsigned article appeared in the important and widely read *North American Review*.[8] Cass, hiding behind his anonymity, accused Hunter of being an imposter and the author of an elaborate hoax. As a young man Cass had once ridden the Ohio circuit as a prosecutor, and he knew well enough how to insinuate guilt and raise doubts about a defendant's veracity. His disparaging ad hominem attack on Hunter consisted of personal accusations and insults, innuendos about Hunter's secret motives, and a host of unsubstantiated charges of fraud. There will be much more to say in this book about Cass's effort, which eventually involved even more people in the

Department of War and the Department of State. For now, it is enough to acknowledge that Cass succeeded in discrediting Hunter. If he is remembered at all today, it is as the mysterious white man who was not who he claimed to be.

Cass was saved by Hunter never having the opportunity to defend himself. A few months before Cass's article was published, he had disappeared from public view after crossing the Mississippi to build his farm in Arkansas and assist the Quapaws in transitioning as quickly as possible to American-style agriculture; he believed—with good reason—this was their only hope of fighting off the efforts to expel them from their homeland. However, in the seven years since he had last seen the Quapaws, they had lost most of their land to white settlers and been nearly annihilated. He wandered for months through the Ozarks in search of the Quapaws, finally picking up word that they had headed toward the Red River, making an exodus to the Mexican province of Texas, along with other Indian refugees from the United States. Hunter decided to follow them.

Hunter followed the Quapaws across the Red River and into what had become a haven for thousands of Native people displaced from the United States. Their villages in the hills and valleys outside of Nacogdoches were surrounded by pastures of cattle and horses and fields of corn, beans, pumpkins, squash, and melons. The more numerous Cherokees headed a loose confederacy in the region of around twenty bands and tribes, including Quapaws, Choctaws, Miamis, Kickapoos, and Delawares. They traded with each other, celebrated some of their feast days together, and acted as good neighbors. They enjoyed a short period of relative peace and security, but it was swiftly coming to an end by the time Hunter came to live among them.[9]

American settlers were also coming across the border in larger numbers and receiving enormous land grants from Mexico, which had won its independence from Spain in 1821.

Previous attempts by the Cherokees to obtain a land grant had failed, but the growing size of their confederacy encouraged them to make one final attempt. The chiefs on the council recognized that Hunter's background might make him an effective advocate, so they chose him to go to Mexico City and present their case to the government. Over the spring of 1826, Hunter sought supporters in the capital and tried to change perceptions of the Native people settling in Texas, painting a picture of peaceful, civilized, and thriving Indian immigrants, but he ultimately could not sway President Guadalupe Victoria to give them a land grant. When Hunter returned home a few months later with the bad news, there was dismay and anger among the chiefs and warriors and calls for a war movement against the government.

As it turns out, they were not the only settlers in the region furious with the Mexican government. After a group of Americans had their land grant revoked, they took up arms and overthrew the municipal government in Nacogdoches. This rebel faction, wanting their Indian neighbors on their side, held talks with a delegation consisting of a venerable Cherokee chief named Richard Fields, three other Cherokee chiefs, and Hunter. They quickly found common ground in their grievances against Mexico and decided to secede and establish their own nation. They declared their independence in the name of the Fredonian Republic, dividing it into a northern region for "red people" and a southern region for "white people," both sides bound together in a body politic based on the principles of universal equality and freedom. Their founding treaty stipulated that trade would flow across open borders and property rights would be sacrosanct. They pledged to defend each other from external attack. After the signing ceremony, the Fredonian flag, lined with bars of red and white, was raised above the stone fort where they were meeting.[10]

Almost two centuries later, the Fredonian Rebellion is widely seen as exclusively a white settler event. It was immediately and ever after pronounced a fiasco caused by a group of vainglorious white men, who were part of the long history of filibustering raids in Texas and Mexico. Although they would be partially rehabilitated as precursors to the Texas revolutionaries, their rebellion always has been understood as inconsequential, even embarrassing, and about the only people who know much about it are aficionados of Texas history. The rebellion eventually became lodged in collective memory as a farce after the Marx Brothers gave the name Fredonia to the autocratic, riotous fictional country in their 1933 film *Duck Soup*. It is hard for Hunter not to look scandalous and slightly absurd in this context.

One thing this book does is overturn the misconception that the Fredonian Rebellion was solely a white settler event. Hunter's story brings to light an overlooked history of Indigenous resistance at a watershed moment in North America. The Fredonian agreement was a rare example of a cross-cultural alliance on the frontier, utopian in its aspirations and positively futuristic in the way Indigenous peoples sought to control their own lives and destinies.

This vision never got off the ground because of a disagreement about strategy. The Cherokee council had instructed their delegation to Nacogdoches to explore their options with the American settlers, but that delegation decided on its own authority to enter a formal alliance with the settlers. After debating the wisdom of the alliance for several days, the Cherokee council could not accept it and ultimately decided to remain loyal to Mexico; Hunter and Fields, unwilling to break their word, and tired of broken promises from Mexico, assembled a faction to join the settlers and fight for their land. The uprising initially caused a frenzy of activity in Texas, but because the

Cherokee confederacy kept its warriors out of the fighting, Mexican troops marched easily toward Nacogdoches, sending the rebels fleeing toward safety in the United States.

Hunter did not make it that far. Mexican authorities had offered the Cherokees a deal: In exchange for the lives of Hunter and Fields and for crushing the breakaway faction, the government would forgive the coup attempt. Cherokee warriors tracked Hunter down and shot him off his horse in the shallows of a river west of the Louisiana line. Fields was killed around the same time. A few weeks later, in Nacogdoches, the Cherokee chiefs, their warriors, and delegations from the other Indian immigrants made a solemn procession to the stone fort, where 300 state militia were waiting for them. If one of the chiefs held a red stone pipe aloft, the traditional gesture of peace and loyalty among their people, it would have seemed redundant. They possessed the only token of peace and loyalty that mattered at that moment to the government: Hunter's rifles and the Fredonian flag, taken from Fields's house.

The suspicion in the United States that Hunter was a traitor and dangerous imposter colored the few spare lines on his ignominious death appearing in frontier newspapers during the spring of 1827. Cass's article in the *North American Review* had clearly hit its mark. The manner of his death in Texas, disgraceful in the eyes of his contemporaries, indelibly tainted him and settled the debate over his identity. His name thereafter was synonymous with scheming, deception, and mystery. The "delusion" that led him to play the part of a war chief and lead a band of savages into battle, which is how people understood his decision and actions, further sullied his name as a race traitor, as much a pretend white man as a pretend Indian.

As an author, Hunter faced a fundamental problem of representation: There was no adequate literary form—certainly not the Indian captivity narrative or the Christian conversion narrative—for relating his exceptional life story.[11] Two of his

Figure 1 Drawing of John D. Hunter by Charles Robert Leslie. Frontispiece of the 1824 edition of *Memoirs of a Captivity*. Charles Robert Leslie, an American artist based in London, created this side-view portrait of Hunter, which appeared in the second and third editions of the book.
Source: https://archive.org/details/memoirsacaptivi00huntgoog/page/n8/mode/2up

contemporaries faced the same problem when telling the stories of their ambiguous, "mixed" identities: Mary Jemison and John Tanner, who also were born into white families, were taken captive as children, and spent much of their lives as adopted members of Native families, absorbing their beliefs, habits, and traditions. Their autobiographies, like Hunter's, were distinctive precisely because they subverted the captivity genre, the narrative form that had defined the "Indian" and ideas of Indianness for centuries. Seeing themselves as fully integrated into their Native communities, Hunter, Jemison, and Tanner did not write from the perspective of captives held against their will and yearning to be reunited with their white countrymen. They did not demonize Native peoples as "savages," ridicule Native beliefs and traditions, or describe their return to white society as a providential triumph over an inferior civilization. They cared deeply for the people who had raised them and given them a home.[12] Perhaps this explains why the word *captivity* did not even appear in the title of the first Philadelphia edition of Hunter's book, which emphasized the main topic, his ethnographic study of Native life west of the Mississippi. It was the London publisher, looking to capitalize on the popular captivity genre, that released the book under a new title: *Memoirs of a Captivity Among the Indians of North America, from Childhood to the Age of Nineteen.*

Paying closer attention to the form and the content of Hunter's life story is the first step toward understanding him and his world. His life story, like Jemison's and Tanner's, has much in common with the autobiographies of Native peoples, such as those by Samson Occom (Mohegan), William Apess (Pequot), George Copway (Ojibwe), John Norton (Mohawk), and Black Hawk (Sauk).[13] As will become clear in the pages ahead, Hunter's *communal* sense of self is one of the most relevant similarities between his autobiography and those by Native authors. His self-identification as an adopted son of the

Kansas and the Osages, his pride in becoming a provider for his family and a protector of his people, bound him to their cultures, traditions, and histories.[14] Hunter was as purposeful and selective as Apess or Copway in sharing stories about his childhood that might vindicate Native peoples, freeing them from the ugly discourse on Indian savagery and perhaps changing the hearts and minds of his white readers. That he succeeded is evident not only in the accolades he received from his peers but also in the powerful impact his words continue to have on readers today—a fact I have witnessed firsthand in the classroom, where my students are often deeply moved when encountering his work for the first time. For instance, Hunter pointedly remembered that the accident of his birth did not diminish his standing in the Kansa or Osage communities, nor did it make him feel like he never belonged with them. He recalled his devoted Kansa family reassuring him that his white ancestry would never block him from pursuing his dreams with them: "I might become an expert hunter, brave warrior, wise counsellor, and possibly a distinguished chief of their nation."[15] His story carries a political edge that continues to resonate with readers today. He suggests that by accepting him as an equal and nurturing his communal sense of self, the Kansas embodied the democratic spirit currently being betrayed by the Americans as they pushed Native peoples off their land. This sort of dissident critique is a common trait in Native American autobiographies from the nineteenth century, but it is highly unusual to find it in the work of a white American author from the 1820s.

As this book tells the story, Hunter's extraordinary life mirrors the rapid and fractious growth of a settler democracy in the United States. The first part of the book moves chronologically from Hunter's captivity as a boy to his painful parting from the Osages as a young man. It weaves together the memories documented in his personal narrative, from the bustling

Kansa villages on the Kansas River, wars against the Pawnees, feast days with neighboring villages, his naming ceremony, and an epic hunting trip across the Rocky Mountains to the rising flood of fur traders, missionaries, and whiskey peddlers into Indian country, Tecumseh's scorching eloquence as he called for his Osage brothers to join the resistance, the shocking sight of valleys littered with skinned buffalo carcasses, and Hunter's fateful decision to warn an American trading party about an impending attack by a party of Osage warriors. It follows Hunter to a mixed French and American hamlet on the White River, where he treated the sick with Osage herbal remedies and learned that there might be a place for him in America. He picked up some English, hired himself out as a trapper, and worked the Mississippi as a boatman. On the levee in New Orleans, he told his story for the first time and soon became known as the "white Indian."

The book's second and third parts chronicle his new existence as a public figure and successful author. They reconstruct his life in Philadelphia and New York by picking up a documentary trail that leads to major figures such as the botanist David Hosack, who invited him to his weekly gatherings of scientists and intellectuals; the Yale geologist Benjamin Silliman, who hoped to publish Hunter in his *American Journal of Science*; the educator Samuel Akerly, who watched him staring in wonder at the students speaking in signs at the Institution for the Instruction of the Deaf and the Dumb; the French philologist Peter DuPonceau, who transcribed his Osage grammar in a notebook; the inventor Edward Clark, who helped him prepare his manuscript for publication; and, in London, the Duke of Sussex, who enjoyed strolling with him in Kensington Garden; the US ambassador Richard Rush, who took a professional interest in getting to know his famous countryman; the American artist Chester Harding, who praised his friend as one of the most remarkable men he ever knew; the agricultural innovator Thomas

William Coke of Norfolk, who introduced him to the latest farming practices; the Romantic poet Felicia Dorothea Heman, who implored him in verse not to return to the frontier; the American novelist John Neal, who was a fellow boarder in Charing Cross; and the socialist reformer Robert Owen, one of the most famous men in Europe and the founder of New Harmony in Indiana, who mentored Hunter and learned about the frontier from him.

The final part also uncovers much more than was previously known about Hunter. It follows him back across the Atlantic to carry out his mission of assisting his Quapaw friends in transitioning to an agricultural life. In a change of plans that was good for posterity (and for this book), Hunter ended up traveling west with Owen, who was headed to Indiana to purchase New Harmony. The dutiful journal keepers in the party, Owen's son William and Captain Donald Macdonald of the Royal Engineers, provide an illuminating account of their journey with Hunter over the new National Road as they dodged droves of squealing hogs on their way to eastern markets, made the acquaintance of General Andrew Jackson, and then headed a thousand miles down the Ohio River, past cotton mills, shipyards, blast furnaces, and busy towns with church spires overhead. At the mouth of the Wabash River, Hunter bade the others farewell and continued down the Ohio and Mississippi Rivers with dreams of a better future for himself and the Quapaws.[16]

Hunter may have met a tragic end, but he was not a tragic figure. He did not die in vain or without hope, because his legacy was never his alone. This book concludes by placing him at the beginning of a resistance movement that spans generations and is alive today. The outlines of this legacy begin to appear in 1839 as the Cherokees were forced out of the new Texas Republic; some of the Cherokees, refusing to relocate to Indian Territory in present-day Oklahoma, kept up a guerilla war for several years in the hopes of recovering their homes. This legacy becomes even more visible as the Cherokees began using the law to fight for their rights and their stolen land. From the 1850s to the 1960s, the Cherokee Nation repeatedly sued and petitioned the state and federal governments for reparations. There were always defeats, but also an important victory. Archival documents and oral testimony from a 1963 hearing forced the state of Texas to concede that the Cherokee Nation once occupied 1.6 million acres north of Nacogdoches. If historical precedent is our guide, then do not bet against this legal action being renewed one day.

This is the afterlife of the rebellion that killed Hunter. It is a rebellion for a democratic society not limited by the exclusion of Indigenous rights and humanity. Today Native peoples stand out as the true inheritors of the American experiment. Over 3 million strong, from over 570 federally recognized tribes, they are leading democratic movements for self-determination, political equality, human rights, and climate justice. They continue to organize and fight for their land, water, resources, and civil rights, and they continue to win huge settlements against the federal government for broken treaties and mismanaged annuities. It is what democracy looks like in the twenty-first century. Even when Native peoples have been defeated in the courts, in the legislatures, or in public opinion, the legacies of the past are a haunting precedent. Hunter's ghost, among many other ghosts from that bygone era, is alive and well and reminding us about our nation's unfinished revolution.

TRAITOR

PART I

Rise of a Freeman

CHAPTER ONE

First Years with the Kickapoos

THE TRAUMA OF HIS KIDNAPPING never left Hunter. Even twenty years later, the memory of being dragged through the prairie grass by Kickapoo warriors could suddenly materialize to torment him. He saw the stricken faces of two other white children, the girl sobbing uncontrollably until a warrior suddenly bludgeoned her to death and then gestured toward him with the bloody tomahawk, an unmistakable order: "If I cried, he would serve me in the same manner."[1] They marched and ran for days on end before splitting up, one group darting upriver with the other boy, the "last I saw or heard of him," Hunter later wrote. He was weak with hunger and too terrified to cry. His "fear of being left behind" somehow kept his legs churning and ultimately saved his life.

He remembered only snippets about how he came to live with the Kickapoos. He knew that the story of his life should not begin this way. "In works of this kind," he wrote, the author was expected to have a very detailed recollection of the important events of their childhood, but so many of his earliest memories flickered through his mind "like the imperfect collection of a dream."[2] He often tried to sift through the fragmented memories of his trauma. He could still feel the "smoky and peculiarly gloomy appearance" of the forests before reaching the Kickapoo village.[3] He could still feel the heat of the forest ablaze on his cheeks, see the smoke rising from the ground, smell the burning leaves. Writing it all down in 1823, he made use of his imperfect memories in a way that brought some order to the broken story of his childhood. A rough timeline marking his kidnapping and his violent passage into this new world was important to him. The smoky forests led him to believe that he was taken captive in the autumn months, when the Kickapoos burned fallen leaves "to facilitate the collection of nuts for their consumption during the approaching winter."

Writing about these days filled him with heartbreak and confusion. He lamented that minor details stuck in his mind, while more important memories were lost forever. The smell of burning leaves could instantly transport him back to the terrifying scene of his kidnapping, but it was maddening that he had trouble remembering any details about his mother and father. Their faces, his mother's touch, and his father's voice were "faint traces" in his mind. He did not understand why the smell of burning leaves was still fresh in his mind while his beloved parents "should have nearly or quite escaped my memory." He confessed he would not recognize them if he saw them, if by some miracle they were still alive.

He was staggering with exhaustion by the time they reached the Kickapoo village on the banks of a large river. Given the events that follow and the geographical clues in the text, the village was probably located along the Sangamon, which winds its way 250 miles through central Illinois. That night began a celebration that lasted for several days. He was vaguely aware of huddling together with a few other frightened captives, all of them white, then being pushed before a howling crowd that poked and grabbed them. The warriors yelled in triumph, some thrusting the scalps of their enemies into the air, as the young and old women, including a strange "white woman attired in the Indian costume," danced around them and cried out in appreciation. The terrifying sight of this white woman, chanting and dancing more wildly than anyone else, lodged in his mind forever. Hunter was too young to have grasped everything that was happening around him. It was the custom in victory celebrations among the Kickapoos, Delawares, Shawnees, and other Algonquian peoples for the returning warriors to tell the stories of their exploits from the raids and recognize those brave brothers who had distinguished themselves by stealing a horse, taking a scalp, or capturing a prisoner. The spoils of the raid, including the prisoners, whose fates could be grim, would be divided and distributed among the people. Prisoners often suffered gruesome torture and were put to death unless they had value as ransom. They were relegated to slavery and servitude, and their experiences ranged from being badly mistreated and viewed as dangerous outsiders to being humanely treated and assimilated into the community. The fortunate ones, usually women and children, were spared death and slavery.[4] While we never learn the fate of his fellow prisoners, it was the first of three times in his life that Hunter would be captured.

He was given over to the care and protection of a woman, who fed him, sang to him at night, and tried to ease his suffering. As he settled into his new life, she became a mother to him and ushered him into the Kickapoo world, where he spent his early childhood until the age of approximately seven years. He would have been raised like every other boy in his village, passing the days ranging through the woods with his playmates, practicing with his sycamore bow, and gathering roots, berries, and firewood for his mother and grandmothers. He remembered competing with the other boys in footraces, throwing contests, and wrestling matches. Sometimes these competitions were a reality check for him, reminding him that he was a little different from the other boys. To test him and gauge his toughness, they would "upbraid me with being *white*," their insults raining down upon him as he struggled to break free from his opponent's hold and as his lungs slowly caught fire and his body ached for a surrender he steadfastly refused. Boys at play can be cruel, but they gave him the strength to stay on his feet and off his back.[5] "I sometimes came off victorious," he wrote.

Their play was intense because the boys were the next generation of hunters and warriors. The games developed their physical skills, built their character, and instilled courage. They had to prove themselves and earn each other's respect and trust; this was especially so for a boy with white skin. Their elders took the games very seriously, cheering the boys on, always pushing them to do better. Even losers were applauded if they showed some grit. The future of their people was always at stake, he explained, which was why "instances of cowardice are seldom discovered among them after the age of puberty."

Originally from the western shores of Lake Erie, the Kickapoos had migrated in the 1600s to what today is southern Wisconsin, then continued moving farther south before settling along the Illinois, Sangamon, and Wabash Rivers.[6] Like other Algonquians, they farmed in the summers, living near their fields in large villages along the rivers, and hunted in the winters, setting up smaller encampments in the woodlands and prairies. When the French began appearing in the Illinois country in the late 1600s, there emerged a "middle ground" between them and around a dozen Indian tribes in the region. While there were inevitably conflicts, the guiding value of that middle ground was mutual respect for one another's independence and territory, which lasted for a century until collapsing under the weight of American expansionism. Of all the Algonquians, the Kickapoos were a notable exception when it came to interacting with the French, the British, and, later, the Americans.[7] They had proven themselves to be fiercely independent and deeply suspicious of the values of the middle ground. They especially resented the arrogance of the American officials who expected them to welcome the droves of settlers coming into the region. When the United States faced Kickapoo defiance for the first time in the summer of 1791, the army was deployed to force them to submit to the Treaties of Fort Stanwix and Fort McIntosh. Seven hundred troops from Kentucky rode on a large village near Kithtippecanoe, burning it to the ground, destroying fields of corn, and capturing fifty-eight women and children.[8] After the Kickapoos still refused to surrender, 500 more troops rode up the Wabash and left a trail of torched and pillaged camps and villages. The survivors found refuge with their relatives along the Sangamon or with those who already had escaped across the Mississippi River. Some would even migrate as far south as Mexico, where Hunter would find them years later.

Hunter came to the Kickapoos as their world was crumbling beneath their feet. After the Louisiana Purchase removed the French from the region, the Kickapoos and the other tribes in the Illinois country lost what little leverage they used to have over the Americans. They could not hold back the rising flood of settlers nor refuse the treaty conferences with William Henry Harrison, the up-and-coming governor of Indiana Territory, without handing him a pretext for coercive action. He had the blessing of President Thomas Jefferson to use every means at his disposal to empty the western lands of their Indian inhabitants. His work began in earnest between 1803 and 1807 with several treaties that dispossessed the Kickapoos, Delawares, Shawnees, Potawatomies, Miamis, Weas, Piankashaws, Kaskaskias, Sacs, and Foxes.[9]

Treaty is still the insipid term of choice among historians, even though these were surrender documents. They were obtained by officials who leveraged threats, deception, and bribery to force as many concessions as possible from Native peoples.[10] Harrison was ambitious, devious, and a master of this bureaucratic game. A favorite tactic of his was to divide tribal members and set them against one another by refusing to meet with their accepted leaders or anyone who opposed his demands. He handpicked other men who could be pressured and bribed into giving him what he needed. First and foremost, what he needed was their ink marks on a treaty that would ensure it being received in Washington as an honorable agreement befitting the values of the Republic. He did not seem concerned that the tribes protested that his "annuity chiefs" were being bribed with money, gifts, and provisions and lacked the standing to sign away their land without the binding consent of the people. He was skilled in advancing Jefferson's policy of running them into debt at US trading houses, which included Harrison punishing and cajoling them if they refused his measures to reduce their debt burden. He seemed unbothered by making promises of protection and fairness that he had no intention of keeping. He was just as adept at exploiting the crushing power of his linguistic advantage, as the Sacs and Foxes discovered only after agreeing to the notorious treaty of 1804. By virtue of a confusing clause inserted by Harrison, they had unknowingly been redefined as temporary occupants of the land; even more devastating, they would be required to move once enough Americans had settled in Illinois. After surrendering to US forces years later in western Illinois, the Sac chief Black Hawk, in his as-told-to autobiography, pointed to this trick as "the origin of all our difficulties."[11] One of Harrison's tactics was to purchase territory from one tribe that was also claimed by others, which is what happened when a handful of Kaskaskias sold away 8 million acres in southern Illinois, parts of which the Kickapoos, Sacs, and Foxes claimed as their own.

Harrison's treaties sowed chaos and resistance during the period of Hunter's childhood. Indian tribes in the region often rejected the treaties made in their name and denounced the turncoats among them, the "government chiefs," for the "selling away of their birthright."[12] Groups from different tribes banded together in defense of their land and way of life. Often acting in retaliation against similar acts by whites, they stole whites' horses and cattle, raided their hunting and sugar camps, and burned their homes and barns to the ground. Sometimes they killed and mutilated settlers and captured their children. The government records of "Indian depredations" from these years paint a grim picture of a region drowning in bloodshed and hostilities.[13] Militant factions among the Kickapoos were particularly troubling for Harrison. On several occasions, he summoned the headmen who he believed could bring the militants to heel and unite their people behind the munificent power of the United States. In one address, he scolded them for their insolence and warned them they had no future if they refused to change. They must "bury the tomahawk," give up their seasonal hunting and roaming, and farm small plots of land. They must follow the path of their Cherokee and Creek brothers, who had improved themselves and now were thriving alongside their American neighbors. It was the wise move, both because their Father in Washington thought it best for them and because their people would soon be starving: Game, Harrison told them, "is yearly becoming more scarce, and in short time you will be left without resources, and your wives and children will in vain ask you for food."[14] Harrison had placed too much faith in the power of his words. Not only did he fail to pacify the Kickapoos, but he ultimately galvanized an intertribal insurgency in Illinois. They would soon join Tecumseh's confederacy and go to war against the United States in 1812.[15]

When Governor Lewis Cass of Michigan Territory accused Hunter of fabricating the story of his childhood, he carefully avoided any mention of this history. His accusation against Hunter was disingenuous for many reasons, one of them being his image of a peaceful Illinois country. Rather than ground zero for anti-American resistance, Cass's Illinois was safe, quiet, settled, and under the protection of the United States. His Illinois was a model of the new expansionism that officials like himself and Harrison believed they had achieved through diplomatic triumphs and enlightened rule. Governor Cass tried to defend his accusation against Hunter by exercising the authority of his office. He claimed that he had done an exhaustive review of the records in the War Department and had not turned up any evidence of a white child being taken by Kickapoo raiders in 1801 or 1802 or thereabouts. He did not refresh the memories of those readers who might have forgotten why the Kickapoos had become one of the most reviled peoples on the continent. He omitted any mention of their opposition before the war or the escalating revenge attacks that had hardened the stereotype of the Kickapoos as savage nomads who had no attachment to place, lived in a constant state of war, and brutalized their white neighbors. Leveling his accusation against Hunter in 1823, Cass could count on the passage of two decades causing the public to forget about the furious resistance of the Kickapoos. By then, they already had been forced across the Mississippi.

Cass's self-serving account stands at odds with Hunter's portrayal of the downfall of the Kickapoos. In an exceptional feat of historical witnessing for its day, Hunter stuck to what he had seen and experienced with the Kickapoos. In his telling, they certainly lived up to the Algonquian origins of their name, Kiikaapoa, meaning "people who move about," but that was not because they were nomads with no sense of home or place; in Hunter's view, it was the American land grab that had caused their troubles and made them "much addicted to roving."[16] They were trapped in a vicious cycle of dispossession and displacement. No matter where they managed to find refuge, they were always encroaching on someone else's territory, "much to the annoyance of their neighbors," he noted understatedly. He recalled a tragic moment when the sap was running in the maple trees and they set up their sugar camp on what they thought was an isolated bend of the Kaskaskia River, hoping to find a quiet refuge. It was only when Potawatomi raiders sent them running for their lives that they realized they had been trespassing again.[17]

Hunter was the rare public voice who expressed compassion and respect for the Kickapoos. His unusual stance was rooted in his belief in the universal equality of all human beings, which entitled Native peoples to justice in the present, not in some distant future when they had bettered themselves in the ways demanded by the Americans. Because he recognized the humanity of the Kickapoos and other Native peoples, he placed their fight for their sovereignty and their land in the context of anticolonial struggles and democratic revolutions across the globe: "Every encroachment made upon their territory is, sooner or later, regarded as an infringement of their natural rights, and has frequently given rise to long, cruel, and exterminating wars, not only between different tribes, but between the Indians and the whites."[18] According to Hunter, they were no different from white people in grasping the principles of self-determination and liberty for which the American Republic stood. They, too, perceived their inalienable rights as based in their freedom to move across the vast American landscape and claim a portion of it as their own.[19] He wondered how the killings committed by warriors in defense of their homes, families, and natural rights were any different "from the *legitimized* murders of more refined governments." He wanted his readers to understand that Native peoples were not animals—they "most sensibly fe[lt]" and comprehended exactly what was happening to them. They fully comprehended that each violation of their rights, each encroachment on their land, would "only terminate with their final expulsion, extermination, or incorporation with those they esteem their natural and most bitter enemies." These enemies, the foot soldiers of expansion, were "generally men of indolent, and frequently dissolute habits."[20] These white men were not the pioneers of progress and democracy being celebrated in culture and literature.

Hunter had witnessed them lie, cheat, and murder with impunity; in his view, they were chiefly responsible for provoking all "the scenes of Indian cruelty that are practiced on the frontier settlers." As will become clear later, his interjection into the historical record of the Indigenous struggle against settler colonialism resulted in a storm of backlash against him.[21]

After this pointed aside, Hunter returned to the narrative of his early years, describing the harrowing escape of the Kickapoos from southern Illinois. They finally managed to leave their Potawatomi pursuers behind after crossing the Mississippi, probably somewhere between St. Louis and Cape Girardeau. Hunter recalled their relatively good fortune, since they had escaped "without sustaining much loss," but the arrow assaults from the tree line had still taken a toll. Some of them were wounded, all of them were hungry and exhausted, and they trudged along the bottomland toward the Meramec for several days until they found the river and continued along its banks to a large village of Shawnees called Rogerstown. He correctly believed it was named after its chief, Jimmy Rogers, who had led his people out of the Ohio Valley in 1780.[22] As a boy, Rogers had been taken captive by the Shawnees and adopted into the family of the famed Chief Blackfish, the same man who later captured Daniel Boone and brought him into his family at Chillicothe. Blackfish's adopted sons were familiar with each other. They knew each other from Ohio, became neighbors in Missouri, and occasionally hunted together.[23] Committed to peace and reconciliation, Boone and Rogers moved past the horrible violence their people had done to each other in the Ohio Valley. Boone himself had raided many Indian towns and had been part of General George Rogers Clark's invasion of the Ohio Valley in 1780, resulting in brutal atrocities on both sides. Many years later, a grandson of Boone's recalled his grandfather sitting around the fire with his Shawnee friends and reminiscing about the time he had lived among them as the adopted son of Blackfish.[24] It was quite possible that Boone shared this story when Hunter visited him in his cabin in Missouri, but that story is still to come.

Rogerstown was a refuge for the fleeing Kickapoos. Their hosts fed them, treated their wounds, and instructed them about the trails westward. According to Hunter, they passed around a feathered pipe and smoked in "confirmation of their mutual friendship."[25] They had entered a foreign land, with Spanish, French, and American inhabitants living among dozens of Native tribes. In these years before the invasion of settlers from the East, the survival and prosperity of everyone required stability, cooperation, and accommodation, much like in Illinois a generation earlier. Historian Stephen Aron notes that "the convergence of cultures reached a new level" in the border region.[26] While the French, Spanish, and Americans adopted Indigenous modes of dress (animal skins and moccasins), crops (corn, squash, and beans), and hunting practices, Native peoples adopted their neighbors' modes of agriculture, stock-raising (hogs and cattle), and material culture (cabin architecture). Reports from the time noted the dozens of relatively prosperous Native communities along the Meremac and around Apple Creek, with their log cabins, fenced fields, and pastures with cattle and horses. Perhaps if the Kickapoos had had different aspirations, they might have settled in the area and followed the path of the Shawnees and their neighbors, but the Kickapoos were determined to move farther west as soon as possible.

Rogerstown was also where Hunter inexplicably lost his adopted mother. For reasons the distraught boy never learned, she stayed behind after the Kickapoos had recovered their strength and continued upriver in their quest for a new home. "The separation filled me with the most painful sensations," he wrote, and the trauma of losing her never left him. When he returned to the area as a young man, he inquired in vain about her whereabouts.

After leaving Rogerstown, the Kickapoos traveled through a "delightful country" teeming with herds of buffalo, elk, and deer, but their scouts reported the enemy ahead. A contingent of warriors from an unknown tribe had been shadowing them along the ridge, but their intentions did not seem hostile as much as a warning to the intruders to keep moving. As more days passed into night and the signs of their pursuers became fewer and fewer until there were none, the exhausted refugees finally made camp. The women cut branches for shelter and sent the children for grass and firewood. A few of their best hunters went in search of game. Later that evening, much to their astonishment, they were summoned in their language from a tree line above the muddy bank, and suddenly one of their own was sliding down toward them and screaming for them to follow him. He led them along the ridge to an encampment of emaciated men, women, and children. Raids, hunger, and disease had taken a severe toll on their relatives from Illinois; they had been over ninety warriors strong, but now only a dozen or so survived.

They joined together and headed deeper into the country. Perhaps if they moved away from the large river and its bountiful valleys and forests, they would find fewer buffalo and less fertile land but finally be left in peace. Although there is not enough information to pin down their location, they moved farther west until they came upon a stretch of country that did not seem cursed by bounty. This land, perfectly adequate, promised to "supply all their wants."[27] Their scouts returned without seeing any signs of inhabitants, suggesting this was an ideal place to rebuild their community, and "they again fixed their camps with the hope of enjoying uninterrupted peace, till more of their nation should join them." Unfortunately, their route had taken them along the fringes of Pawnee country, much too close to the Pawnee earthen-lodge villages on the bluffs of the Loup, Platte, and Republican Rivers. The hopes of the Kickapoos were immediately dashed by a group of Pawnees who ambushed them and carried Hunter away as a prize.

His time with the Pawnees was short. All he disclosed—somewhat in disbelief, because he had been raised to despise them—was that he was treated civilly. It was not long after that his life took another drastic turn. A Kansa party raided the camp, swept him up, and took him back to their village on the banks of the Kansas River. His life had been spared for a third time.

CHAPTER TWO

Growing Up Among the Osages and Kansas

WHEN HUNTER CAME TO THE KANSA, they were twenty years away from spiraling into the destruction ravaging so many tribes to the east of them.[1] Their move further up the Kansas River a half century earlier had buffered the Kansa from the diseases and chaos decimating those tribes whose only misfortune was to live too close to St. Louis and the white settlements along the Mississippi and seeping up its tributaries. Make no mistake, the Kansa had weathered their fair share of cholera and smallpox outbreaks, such as the pestilence that had spread from the military outposts around the Great Lakes during the Seven Years' War, but they were intact and surviving. Estimates from French and American officials put their population at around 1,500 from the 1700s to the 1800s.[2] By moving further upriver, they had not discovered some utopia free from the spread of settler colonialism, but they had escaped the fate of tribes to the east of them, such as the Missouria. Around 100 survivors of the once mighty guardians of the lower Missouri recently had abandoned their homes to live with the Iowas and Otoes.[3]

Hunter's new life was far different from the one he had known with the Kickapoos. Kansa country ran along the Kansas River for about 100 miles, roughly from the confluence of the Missouri to the main village, Blue Earth, located near present-day Manhattan, Kansas. They lived much as their ancestors did. There were stalks of grain in the fields and plenty of game in the valleys and forests. He remembered his village being "well provided with venison, buffalo meat, corn, nuts, [etc.]," which seemed like paradise to the boy who had chewed tree bark to suppress his hunger on the escape from Illinois with the Kickapoos.[4] Hunter came to the Kansa before the settler invasion, before the establishment of Fort Leavenworth and the influx of regiments of soldiers, before scores of wagon trains cut across their lands over the Oregon Trail, before the fur trade drove away the buffalo and engulfed the region in war and famine, before they surrendered nearly all of their land to the United States, and before a smallpox epidemic nearly wiped them out in 1827.

Hunter found a new home with a family who had recently lost their boy. The father, Keeneestah, did not pay him any attention, but his wife, whom Hunter did not name, treated him as her son. Like with the Kickapoos, he had the good fortune of growing up just like any other boy in his village. They learned how to hunt by tracking deer, foxes, rabbits, wolves, and elk and observing the animals' habits and idiosyncrasies. The boys challenged each other to shooting contests and sharpened their accuracy and speed with their bows. At first the other boys teased him for being an outsider and goaded him for his lighter skin, but his experience with the Kickapoos had steeled him against every taunt and challenge.

The boys were also learning to be warriors and protectors of their people. Hunter fondly described the beloved elder who had been entrusted with their education: "I was accustomed, in company with Indian boys, to listen with indescribable satisfaction to the sage councils, inspiring narratives, and traditionary tales of Tshutchenau. This venerable worn-out warrior would often admonish us for our faults, and exhort us never to tell a lie." Tschutchenau, whose name meant "Defender of the People" according to Hunter, instructed them by telling stories laced with lessons about being a man and a warrior: Always provide for your wife and children; never steal (unless from an enemy, who always deserves it); defend your territory at all costs; never, ever betray your friends; do not fear death; respect your elders; never drink the trader's brown poison; above all, love the Great Spirit.[5]

A patchwork of scars seemed to hold the old warrior together, each one telling a story about his courage and devotion to his people. He had marched great distances over frozen ground, across scorched prairies, and through snake-infested swamps in pursuit of their enemies. Getting to his feet with some effort, he looked down on the boys with such intense intimacy that Hunter the author confessed that he could not find the words to adequately explain the feeling. The old warrior then waved his hand over the green fields of corn, gestured toward the stores of dried buffalo meat, and gave thanks for their good fortune. He told the boys about the enormous debt they had incurred for their "peaceful enjoyment" of such abundance. His boyhood companions, their ancestors who now spoke through him, had made it all possible through their sacrifice and their courage. Tschutchenau solemnly told them that he was the last of his generation: "Like a decayed prairie tree, I stand alone."[6] With his hand still aloft, he thanked the Great Spirit for sparing him just long enough to share his story with these future warriors. If they honored their ancestors, they would bring glory to their people.

The boys also learned that a man should control his feelings and never show signs of weakness. This ideal was hard to live up to after Hunter's adopted mother drowned in a flash flood while out collecting driftwood. He tried to be stoic after the tragedy, but he was barely holding on and worried about falling into a fit of weeping and thereby proving to everyone that he could never live up to the warrior code. So the boy, already devastated by the deaths of his biological mother and his adopted Kickapoo mother, buried yet another trauma deep down inside: "I bore my affliction in silence in order to sustain my claims to their respect and esteem."[7] Hunter wanted to pay tribute to his Kansa mother, but he worried that readers would not see past the demeaning stereotype of the Indian squaw—a workhorse, stupid and mute, totally lacking the capacity for love and affection.[8] He was in a quandary. If he portrayed his mother as he knew her, then it would suggest that he did not truly understand what he was writing about. He might even be accused, as he inevitably was, of inventing her.[9]

His solution was to place his faith in his readers and ask them for empathy: Imagine if they were children brutally snatched from their parents and taken away to a foreign country. Imagine if they were abandoned there, terrified, hungry, and helpless, until a stranger, a kind and selfless woman, took them in. No more heartfelt words were written about a Native woman at that time:

> I sincerely and deeply felt the bereavement; and cannot, even at this late day, reflect on her maternal conduct to me, from the time I was taken prisoner by the Kansas, to her death, without the association of feelings to which, in other respects, I am a stranger. She was indeed a mother to me; and I feel my bosom dilate with gratitude at the recollection of her goodness, and care of me during this helpless period of my life. This, to those who have been bred in refinement and ease, under the fond and watchful guardianship of parents, may appear gross and incongruous. If, however, the imagination be allowed scope, and a lad ten or twelve years of age, without kindred or name, or any knowledge by which he could arrive at an acquaintance with any of the circumstances connected with his being, be

> supposed in the central wilds of North America, nearly a thousand miles from any white settlement, a prisoner or sojourner among a people on whom he had not the slightest claims, and with whose language, habits, and character he was wholly unacquainted; but who, nevertheless, treated him kindly; it will appear not only natural but rational, that he should return such kindness with gratitude and affection.[10]

His main point, which had to be made explicit in 1823, was powerful in its very plainness. She was not a beast. She was a good woman and loving mother. She had taken pity on him, given him a family, and cared for him. He conceded that his relationship with her probably sounded unbelievable to his readers "bred in refinement and ease" a thousand miles away. But that did not make it any less true.

Hunter was never more Kansa than when he paid loving tribute to his mother, except perhaps when he revealed his aversion for the Pawnees. He blamed their bitter rivals, the "wandering Pawnees," for constantly invading their land and harassing them. He told the story of the bloody summer when Pawnee attacks had caused his people to question whether it might be wise to search for hunting grounds even farther up the Arkansas. There were defeatist murmurs on the council, until a regal young chief named Kiskemas put an end to any talk of submission.[11] His voice rose into a fury as he commanded them to act like men, "stop the encroachments" on their lands, and live up to their ancestors. He then flew into a war dance and the rest of the warriors leaped to his side. The debate was over.

Like everyone else in the Kansa villages, Hunter would have been very familiar with the war that summer. The war would have taken over every aspect of life. Like other boys his age, he would have patrolled the outskirts of their villages and protected their horses. He would have heard the mourning wails of wives and mothers and the honoring songs about the latest exploits of the fighting men.[12] As he told it, they missed their chance on the upper Kansas to end the war quickly. They had surrounded the Pawnees at the "shoals below Neeshkenah, or the Willow Islands of the traders, where there is a safe ford, which is a thoroughfare for the Indians in their hunting and depredatory excursions."[13] With their enemy trapped at the ford, they screamed in triumph, slowly creeping in and tightening the noose, but then suddenly the tall grass was ablaze and their wily enemies plunged into the smoke and flames, vanishing before their eyes.

The "decisive and bloody battle was fought" later that summer, but the Kansa had paid dearly for their victory over the Pawnees. The "brave and gallant Kiskemas" and fifteen of his men were dead. Hunter remembered mourning and victory dances going on for nights on end. The women wailed, scarred their bodies, and danced until they were delirious with exhaustion and hunger. There were "extravagant rejoicings" as their Pawnee prisoners ran through a gauntlet of firebrands, whips, clubs, and stones in the hopes of reaching a painted post some distance away. Each warrior would have been expected to tell the story of their valor in battle, and while Hunter did not reference these stories, they would not have been sympathetic to their enemies. War narratives in every culture tend to be about the clash between good and evil. Even years later, Hunter could not hide his loathing for the Pawnees, these wicked "wanderers" with no "fixed towns," no moral compass, no respect for their neighbors. The Pawnees took pleasure in stealing everything that was sacred to you—your life, your family, your white horses, your happiness.[14]

Hunter was deeply grateful for being rescued from such savages. In the condensed story of his childhood, Hunter focused on the most formative moments, and even those are described in very few words. One of them was his rite of passage as a hunter, when eleven boys, including Hunter, went on their first seasonal hunt with a party of thirty men. They set up camp on the upper reaches of the Kansas, near a spectacular cave, and the boys were excited to go exploring. They ventured inside by the light of their torches, stepping carefully through columns of what he thought at the time were "huge icicles," but "which I now supposed to be stalactite." Their torches gave the scene an "astonishing and wonderful appearance," and the exhilarating roar of the subterranean river drew them deeper into the cave. They stumbled over some rocks, which, upon closer inspection in the flickering light, were not rocks at all but human bones, and the boys frantically retreated through the stalactite maze.

That evening some Native people from the area came to their camp with gifts of food and tobacco. They huddled around the fire and shared their stories. Their guests told them a story about a sacred cavern "through which the first Indian ascended from the bowels of the earth, and settled on its surface."[15] The boys, whispering among themselves, wondered if they had stumbled on this sacred ground. Their camp lay above an ancient salt lick that attracted herds of buffalo, deer, and elk. The boys hid in the woods for hours on end, riveted by the "playful gambols of the collected herds, and terrible conflicts of the buffalos"; when it was time, they returned to camp and prepared their bows and sang honoring songs to the buffalo soon to be sacrificed for their people.

If he had been writing a modern autobiography, then Hunter might have reenacted the buffalo chase and confessed to his fear of falling off his horse and being stampeded to death, but he chose to say nothing about the experience. It may not even have been a mounted chase—they might have trapped the herd in a ravine down the trail—but a reenactment was not as important to him as his message: They killed only as

Figure 2 "Bulls Fighting." Oil on card mounted on paperboard, by George Catlin, 1836(?). The American artist George Catlin was captivated by the intense spectacle of the buffalo during the rutting season. His "Indian Gallery" featured over 500 portraits of Native peoples, scenes from Native life, and western landscapes. *Source*: Courtesy of the National Gallery of Art. https://www.nga.gov/collection/art-object-page.50488.html

many buffalo as were needed to feed their people. They did not slaughter the sacred ones like the hide hunters out of St. Louis, who killed as many buffalo as possible, stripped the carcasses, and left behind mounds of rotting meat and bones. Still, by the time he was putting words to paper, the memory of his first hunt inspired nostalgia and left him feeling despondent: "I have no hope of seeing happier days than I experienced at this early period of my life, while sojourning with the Kansas nation, on the Kansas River, some hundred miles above its confluence with the Missouri."[16]

He also could not forget the white man who staggered into their camp and begged for mercy. By some miracle, the white man was the only one in his group of "adventuring hunters" to escape a massacre by Sioux warriors. He reported to them that wars over "rich and abundant furs" were erupting everywhere. Ever since the return of the Lewis and Clark expedition, fur companies, private traders, and government officials had been expanding their operations up the Missouri and into the relatively untapped Blackfoot country. In Hunter's memory, the booming trade was a world away from them in their idyllic camp below the cavern. They didn't know the white man who had wandered into their camp was the omen of a catastrophe on the horizon.

Most of the Kansa hunters would never see their homes again. They were stopped on their way back by a friendly group of Osages, who wanted to warn them that some bands in their two tribes were at war with each other. They would surely be killed if they continued up the Missouri. "The sky is overcast with clouds," their Osage messengers reported, "all is hostility and war."[17] The best option for staying alive was also the most humiliating: head to the village of White Hair, the Osage chief and a belligerent in the war, and ask for his protection.

They had not gone very far along the route their protectors had mapped for them when disaster struck. Some Pawnee warriors ambushed them and sent them scrambling into the woods. The Pawnee rifles, new gifts of the fur trade, thundered and flashed as night fell, but the Kansa hunters hung together, dragging their dead and wounded from one hill to the next, and launching enough arrows to slow down their hated enemies. It was Hunter's first experience in battle, the first time he had fired his arrows at another man, and he was not sure if any had found their mark. The Pawnees eventually became discouraged, and their "hideous yells" grew more faint until there was only the eerie silence of the woods. Worried that it could be a trick, a few of them stood guard on the perimeter while the others put their bows down and started digging. "In silent grief," Hunter remarked, they buried four of their fallen comrades, perhaps leaving each of them with some corn and beans for the journey ahead, as was their custom.

They traveled freely for several days without seeing any signs of human activity. Topping a ridge at dawn, they gazed over the valley below and saw the largest herd of buffalo they had ever seen. After their scouts returned having found White Hair's village, Keeneestah dispatched "two peace runners with friendly tokens" and the wampum belt given to them by their Osage messengers. They did not have to wait long for a response. On the following day, six Osage warriors with white peace feathers led White Hair up the trail to their camp. Their tribes were rivals but not blood enemies. They were linguistic relatives who spoke different dialects of the Dhegia Siouan language, and whose origin stories told of their being one people before a dispute over buffalo parts divided them into separate tribes. Both cultures shared many of the same values, rituals, and social customs. They sometimes clashed, but they could also be reliable allies during a crisis.[18]

When Keeneestah saw White Hair approaching the camp, he placed his trust in this special relationship. He explained that war had broken out when he and his men had been far away in their hunting camp. It was not their fight; they wished to stay neutral. He solemnly asked White Hair to extend to them the "the rights of hospitality" and protection, reminding him that the Pawnees, their bitterest of enemies, were waiting to exact revenge on them.[19] White Hair wasted no time in settling the matter. He led them back to the village, where over a thousand people welcomed them in the "most cordial and friendly manner," and he invited his guests to sit around the fire and smoke with him and the other chiefs. As the pipe returned to White Hair, he finally stipulated the single condition of his protection: his guests must agree not to return home to Blue Earth until the war between their people was over.[20]

They readily agreed to this condition, which was their only hope of staying alive, but they probably did not expect the war to drag on for several years. They settled into Osage life and embraced their duties as providers and protectors. They hunted for meat and furs, defended the people from enemies, and participated in celebrations and sacred ceremonies. Several of the men married into families, including Keeneestah, which did not bother Hunter. His adopted father, he wrote, "showed little regard for me," and they were not close. Besides, he was happy to be welcomed into the lodge of Shintwheeh. He found a new mother in Hunkhah. "This good woman," he wrote, "took every opportunity, and used every means which kindness and benevolence could suggest, to engage my affections and esteem. She used to weep over me, tell me how good her son had been, how much she loved him, and how much she mourned his loss. 'You must be good,' she would say, 'and you shall be my son, and I will be your mother.'"[21] Hunkhah and his new sister, Weeskeh, doted on him and instructed him in their way of life. They liked to dress him in the deerskin breeches and buckskin leggings favored by the Osages.

After glossing over these first two years, Hunter, as selective as usual, told the story of his first hunt with the Osages. It was fall, game was scarcer than ever before, and they risked their lives by traveling several hundred miles up the Arkansas and through Pawnee territory before locating the herds of buffalo and elk. He once again chose not to reenact the drama of the chase and focused instead on the aftermath, when they returned downriver late that spring with bundles of furs, buffalo meat, and venison. They pretended not to notice the Pawnee warriors pursuing them but then circled back to surprise them in a barrage of gunfire and arrows. Word of their triumph had preceded them to the trading house, and a festive crowd was there to greet them. Some of their furs were bartered for rifles, which were then awarded to Hunter and the other boys who had proven themselves on the hunt and in battle. He was around fourteen years of age.

Another surprise was in store for him when their successful hunt was celebrated by the people. He was given his Osage name. Even though he is tight-lipped about the ceremony, it was customary for a procession of elders to circle the recipient of the honor as they sang the name of the recipient's Osage father (Shintwheeh, in Hunter's case) and grandfathers and recounted their exploits on behalf of their people. The elders bestowed a name that usually came to one of them in a vision. Hunter was very proud of his name. He translated it as "the Hunter," which conveyed only a faint trace of the meaning intended by the elders. His translation sounds too generic, too literal, and too much like the stereotypical name a pretend Indian might give himself, but proper names and their deeper meanings are notoriously difficult to translate with any accuracy. The elders had chosen a significant name for him at a crisis moment for the Osage. Hunting was more precarious, game was depleted, and their way of life was becoming increasingly difficult to sustain. In this context, it is not a stretch to imagine that the name Hunter embodied their vision of recovering the past and once again enjoying the favor of the Great Spirit and the generosity of the animal spirits.

Hunter came to the Osages when they were rapidly losing the power and influence that they had wielded for over a century. As key allies with the French and the Spanish in the fur trade, they had access to more firearms, more gunpowder, and more metal hatchets than their neighbors. The Osages were also expansionists. They used their military advantage to gain control over a vast territory stretching across southwestern Missouri and into parts of Arkansas and Kansas. As they spread across the land during the 1700s, they broke off into more groups and villages, increased their size by incorporating outsiders, and chased the buffalo across greater distances, as far south as the Red River and as far west as the Rocky Mountains. By 1806, the American soldier-explorer Zebulon Pike reported from a village on the Republican River that they had separated into three major branches: the Little Osages, the Big Osages, and the Arkansas Osages.[22]

The Louisiana Purchase proved to be a catastrophe for the Osages. Shortly after, twelve chiefs made what they believed was a mutually beneficial deal. In exchange for gaining the United States as an ally, they agreed to provide safe passage to the exploring expeditions that soon would be moving through their territory. However, they had not been told that President Jefferson envisioned the new acquisition as the solution to the "Indian problem": a remote enclave where eastern tribes could be relocated beyond the expanding white settlements. The Osages did not realize that a section of the purchased land, which they claimed as their own, already was being parceled out in treaties with eastern Indians that were being ratified in Washington. They were soon forced to make room for incoming groups of Cherokees, Sacs, Foxes, Kickapoos, Delawares, Shawnees, Miamis, Choctaws, Chickasaws, Creeks, and Wyandots, which triggered cycles of conflict over territory, boundaries, and hunting grounds. A handful of Osage chiefs ceded nearly all of present-day Missouri and the northeast corner of Arkansas in 1808. Meriwether Lewis, who negotiated the treaty, informed Jefferson that the size of the territory was "almost equal to the state of Virginia, and much more fertile." He boasted how satisfied the Osages were with deal he had given them. Ten years later, in a second treaty, the Osages suffered another severe blow. They lost their land between the White and Arkansas Rivers, which had been earmarked for the Cherokees.

One of the reasons why Hunter's writing was so provocative was that his readers learned of the destructive effects of US Indian policy on the lives of the peoples whom the Americans professed to be helping. Readers learned that the Osage elders who had named him "the Hunter" did not simply accept defeat and resign themselves to the American way of life. They had a plan for saving their people. They tried to inspire an awakening to traditional ways and sacred teachings. They chastised their people for their white ways, their greed, and their dependence on traders, condemning them for desecrating their ancestors and turning the Great Spirit against them. They had been entrusted to watch over all the animals, particularly the blessed ones, the buffalo, deer, and elk, but they had led the white man to them and joined in the slaughter. How could their ancestors possibly recognize them as Osage, as they butchered the blessed ones for trinkets and left their remains to rot on the prairies, then strutted like peacocks to the trading house to barter their souls away for gunpowder, a bit of cloth, and some whiskey?[23] In a sound critique of consumer capitalism, the elders railed against the fur industry for producing, in Hunter's translation, "too great a superabundance, which created factitious wants."[24] No wonder the animal spirits had abandoned them to hunger.

Like all Osages, Hunter's group respected the leadership of their elders, "whose opinions operate with nearly as much force as their acknowledged laws." They urged their people to sever their relationships with white traders and move far up the Arkansas. And that's just what Hunter's group did. In their new home, they returned to the old ways and teachings. They hunted like their ancestors, only to "procure provisions," and they never failed to sing their honoring songs and give thanks to the sacred ones. They also ridded themselves of the evil influence of the alcohol that shattered body and soul. Hunter was nostalgic about their revival of the old ways, but the healing effects proved to be temporary. They returned downriver after one season and were inevitably pulled back into the orbit of the fur trade. Their once happy village had become a pit of despair and abuse. He mourned for those brave men who used to pursue the buffalo across the plains but now huddled around the trader's whiskey barrel and transformed into "demons."

With the Osages, Hunter came into frequent contact with white people for the first time in his memory. The demeaning scenes at the trading houses confirmed the many stories he had heard about them over the years. These stories were in "no ways flattering to my color; they [white people] were represented as an inferior order of beings, wicked, treacherous, cowardly, and only fit to transact the common drudgeries of life."[25] He felt ashamed of his ancestry and confused by it. He recalled an afternoon when some white men greeted him with smiles. They gave him a gift (he does not say what), inquired about his parentage, and told him incredible stories about the land of his birth. "My mind filled with wonder and astonishment," he remarked, thinking about the castles floating on great waters and the cities with buildings higher than the trees, and he wanted to go see this magical land for himself. And he might have gone right then if his Osage mother and sister had not frightened him with stories of people crossing the Mississippi and being snatched by kidnappers and sold into the white man's slavery. Hunkhah and Weeskeh pleaded with him to be patient and wait until he was older and had become a chief. Then he would travel "with impunity" to Washington, they told him, and the white people "would dare not to touch me."

Hunter saw another type of white man, a Christian missionary, in his village on the Grand Osage River. When the missionary assembled them for a sermon, they bowed their heads and listened politely because it would have been disrespectful

Figure 3 "Mo-hon-go, an Osage Woman." Portrait of Mohongo and her child, drawn by Charles Bird King. In 1827 Mohongo was among a small group of Osages deceived by a Frenchman into traveling to Europe, where they were forced to perform in a Wild West show and later abandoned when it failed. The Marquis de Lafayette ultimately paid for their return to America in 1830. King specialized in portraits of Native peoples, creating 143 of them during the 1830s and 1840s.
Source: Courtesy of The Miriam and Ira D. Wallach Division of Art, Prints and Photographs: Picture Collection, 1836–1844, The New York Public Library. https://digitalcollections.nypl.org/items/510d47e1-1b45-a3d9-e040-e00a18064a99

to interrupt his preaching.[26] The missionary, pleased by what he took as a pious gathering of savages, mistakenly believed that they had let God into their hearts and converted to Christianity. Hunter described the scene with bemused irony. They had bowed their heads because they were trying to hide their murmurs and questions about what the white man was talking about. Hunter's point was crystal clear. The Osages did not see themselves as inferior in any way to white people, and it was ridiculous to think that they would suddenly renounce their beliefs simply because this white stranger prayed over them and said they worshipped the wrong god.[27]

This deceptively simple scene challenges the dominant discourse about Native peoples. The missionary who mistook Osage civility for submission stands in for all the Indian experts, the traders, soldiers, travelers, and others, who thought they knew what they were witnessing. Missionaries were widely regarded as reliable sources with no ulterior motive other than spreading the grace of God to the savages, but Hunter notes how their zeal to convert Native peoples had "led to many exaggerated accounts of their conversion to Christianity." However, as Hunter tells the story, something far worse than the ignorance of the missionaries was their inability to see their complicity in the worst excesses of the fur trade. His anecdote of the missionary would not be out of place in George Tinker's *Missionary Conquest*, which surveys the damage inflicted on his Osage people by missionaries. Tinker refuses to separate the missionary and the trader in his historical account, arguing that they were complementary instruments of settler colonialism, the missionary committed to the pacification of Native peoples and thereby abetting the trader's exploitation of their labor and knowledge of the land.[28]

CHAPTER THREE

Western Odyssey

THAT FALL THEIR HORSES had been mysteriously disappearing several at a time, and one day, when Pawnee raiders rode up on the Osage women in charge of tending the herd, they finally had their answer.[1] A detachment of sixty warriors, among them Hunter, immediately gathered their weapons and rations of dried buffalo meat and went after them. They raced along the banks of the Grand Neosho River and closed in on the raiders the following day. They slowed to a silent march until their scouts returned with the report their chief, "well experienced in all the cunning and artifice of Indian warfare," had been anticipating: A contingent of Pawnees had broken off earlier in the morning, doubled back around the bluffs, and hunkered down to ambush their pursuers.

The Osage chief, wanting to conceal their discovery of the trap, whispered to them to stay calm and show no alarm as they walked toward the enemy. Carefully keeping their bows, hatchets, lances, and guns lowered at their sides, the warriors walked casually down the path, as if their enemy wasn't waiting ahead behind an outcropping of rocks. When they were within forty or sixty yards of them, the Osage chief suddenly cried out and his men jumped into action against their stunned and more numerous enemies. The rout was swift and decisive, and their triumph was measured by the recovery of their horses and by the eighteen scalps taken from the Pawnees. It was a moment of truth in Hunter's life, and he wasn't going to shy away from it: "I took a scalp, which was my first and last essay of the kind. I name this, with great repugnance to my present feelings; but, as I set out to give a correct history of my life, I cannot, in justice to the subject, omit this circumstance."[2] He rightly knew how his admission of taking a scalp would disgust many of his readers, but he would not ignore this formative moment in his life.

Killing an enemy in battle was a momentous rite of passage for any young man who had reached fighting age, and Hunter was proud of defending his people and achieving the status of a decorated warrior. Preparations for the victory celebration were underway by the time the men rode into the village ahead of the herd of horses. The dancing and singing began that evening and lasted for several days. In an unforgettable moment for him, he was led before the people and all eyes suddenly were on him. The young women "danced around me in the most extravagant and exulting manner" and "ornamented my head, arms, and legs with feathers, stained porcupine quills, [and] deer sinews." While his valor in battle had been recognized on other occasions, he had never been honored with the Dance of Feathers, commonly called the Scalp Dance by later anthropologists. He had taken a Pawnee scalp, but he had done so while avenging the dishonor done to the women who had been tending the herd. This made the O-don bestowed upon him the most prestigious of war honors.

Hunter's two staunchest critics, Lewis Cass and Henry Rowe Schoolcraft, claimed he was ignorant of Osage culture, but his description of the ceremony shows just the opposite. His description is very similar to the one given over a century later by Osage author John Joseph Matthews in *The Osages: Children of the Middle Waters*. The Dance of Feathers was "a girls' dance, the dance of the eldest unmarried girls. They carried feathers in each hand, and there was a scalp pole in the center of the circle which the dancers made; also in the center was the drum and the singers. The girls danced in jerky steps, and they jerked their hands up and down in rhythm as they moved in the circle in pairs."[3]

It took more than an enemy's scalp to earn the coveted O-don. Before the young women started dancing, Hunter would have been expected to recount his feats in combat. Truth was paramount in the story. If he strayed from the facts, exaggerated his actions, or overlooked key details, his comrades would correct him or add to the narrative. It was not the only time a decorated warrior would share his story. Every ceremony and gathering was an occasion for the warrior to tell it again and remind everyone of their courage in defense of their people. Hunter probably told the story of his highest honor many times before ever writing it down for publication.

Not long after the Dance of Feathers, he described the next turning point in his life, a buffalo hunt across the Great Plains. The dwindling herds had forced his group of Osage and Kansa hunters, thirty-seven men in all, to push further up the Platte than they ever had before. They followed the river "nearly to its source among the Rocky Mountains" and ultimately found immense herds of buffalo roaming across the prairies.[4] Hunter describes the land as a lush country teeming with wildlife and vegetation. Wild rice grew in the wetlands. There were dense thickets of cottonwood, ash, sycamore, elm, and walnut trees. Various kinds of grasses, herbs, and vegetables flourished in the rich soil. Strawberries, huckleberries, gooseberries, blackberries, and raspberries were everywhere. Hunter enjoyed them all.

Hunter's critics accused him of inventing reality, but he simply had a different conception of it. His image of the region contradicted the accepted theory of the day about the Great Plains. Nearly everyone who claimed an expertise in physical geography considered the region a wasteland. Thomas

Jefferson called it an "immense and trackless desert" unfit for agriculture and civilization. Zebulon Pike compared it to the "sandy deserts" of Africa, noting on his 1806 map that "not a stick of timber" could be found anywhere. Fellow explorer Stephen Long labeled it the Great American Desert on his 1822 map.[5] This theory discouraged settlement and slowed expansion into the region for decades. Perceptions only began to change before the Civil War, when railroad companies started promoting the Great Plains as fertile lands open for settlement and investment, a change of image that came much too late to silence Hunter's critics. At the time he was writing, his sketch of the natural abundance of the Great Plains, denying the reports and maps of explorers and scientists, undermining the regime of truth about the land, seemed to be the stuff of fiction. His critics pounced on it as proof of his hoax.

Their pursuit of the buffalo had carried the Kansa hunters into their home country after several years of exile among the Osages. When they reached "the usual crossing-place of the Indians between the Arkansas and Kansas rivers," they were only a few days' walk from the main Kansa village, Blue Earth. What stopped them from returning home was their Kansa brothers who had stayed behind with Chief White Hair to ensure that everyone respected the terms of their sanctuary agreement.[6] Hunter, standing at the crossing, realized he did not feel the same pull as the other men to return to Blue Earth. While grateful for finding a home with the Kansa, he confessed to being happy with the Osages. He had grown into a respected warrior in a powerful nation and been embraced by a loving mother and sister: "I had been a long time from the Kansas, and was not particularly attached to any of the tribe; while with the Osages I had left a mother and sister, who were dear to me, and who loved me in return."

After beginning their climb up the eastern face of the Rockies, they were hailed by an Omaha party and traveled with them up the trail. The Omahas were on a somber mission to retrieve the bodies of their men who had been cut down in a Pawnee attack. Around the fire one night, an elder named Neekishlauteeth, the sole survivor of the massacre, told them about what had happened. They had been camped at a favorite spot overlooking the river when the Pawnees skulked out of the woods in the dead of night and slaughtered everyone except him. He flew through the forest all day until the sun dropped and he stopped to rest and listen; the silence nearly convinced him that he had escaped, but suddenly Pawnee cries ricocheted across the river and sent him scrambling up the bank and into the woods again. This time he circled back to the outskirts of the Pawnee camp. He crawled into a thicket of grass and willows, muddied his face, and buried himself in the sand. He hid for two days and nights, but the Pawnees were not easily fooled. They swept the thickets over and over, nearly stepping on him several times, taunting him with threats to skin him alive, but they never found him. After several days of quiet, he inched out of his hole when the sun went down and dashed into the night, borne along by the guardian spirits of the forty men butchered in their sleep.[7] His people now believed Neekishlauteeth was a prophet and blessed by the Great Spirit. "His influence was great," Hunter wrote.

Neekishlauteeth shared another story about his journey across the Rocky Mountains that altered their destiny. Hunter did not repeat the story, but he explained how it inspired the men to undertake the same feat: "The description this old man gave of his excursion to the great hills of the west excited the curiosity and ambition of our whole party, and was the primary cause that led us to the execution of a similar expedition." Neekishlauteeth's story was also a map that would help them find their way across the mountains, and he had an important piece of information about the route they would be taking. When they neared the headwaters of the Platte, they should exercise every caution and be on guard against a "small but barbarous tribe" called the Stahetah. On their expedition a few years earlier, the explorers Lewis and Clark made no mention of them in their journals, but this was not because the tribe did not exist. The region was a mystery to outsiders. Lewis and Clark reported the presence of several tribes in the area "of which little more is known than the names and the population," which in itself is debatable.[8] Based on what they could learn from their informants, they identified the Staitan as the fearsome guardians of the headwaters and bestowed on them a colorful English name: "They have acquired the name of Kites, from their flying; that is, their being always on horseback; and the smallness of their numbers is to be attributed to their extreme ferocity; they are the most warlike of all the western Indians; they never yield in battle; they never spare their enemies; and the retaliation of this barbarity has almost extinguished the nation." Were they referencing the same small but bellicose tribe as Hunter? Did they simply translate the sounds of the tribe's Indigenous name differently? Were Staitan and Stahetah variant corruptions of the same word? All of these are possibilities. In *The Handbook of American Indians*, Frederick Webb Hodge, one of the founders of American anthropology, proposed a theory. Lewis and Clark's Staitan might have been referring to the Sutaio, relatives of the Cheyenne, and Hodge listed Hunter's translation, Stahetah, as one possible spelling of the name.[9]

Hunter's party traveled across the mountains along the route Neekishlauteeth had given them. According to Hunter's critics, the journey was pure fiction, but we have a much better understanding today of the vast distances covered by Indigenous hunters centuries ago. It would be many years before scholars acquired even a limited understanding of the depths of their knowledge of the land and the extent of their travels. Songs and stories, like the one Neekishlauteeth had told them, could often be very practical in mapping the physical world and sharing important information about the land and its inhabitants. Maps were also drawn on animal skins, tree bark, and rock, sketched in the dirt and sand, and sewn into ceremonial robes. These could be as highly functional as Western maps in representing trade routes, sacred sites, historical events, and geographical features.[10] In the view of whites, Natives' spatial practices were crude compared to the European standard. It seemed unthinkable that Indian hunters had equaled the achievements of Western explorers trained to locate themselves in space by the scientific conventions of scale, longitude, and latitude.[11]

Neekishlauteeth had prepared them for a journey rife with hazards. Every tribe they encountered greeted them suspiciously and inquired about where they came from and what they were doing there. They all spoke a branch of the Dhegia Siouan language, so with the words they shared, and also very likely with gifts of tobacco and dried meat, the Osage and Kansa travelers successfully conveyed their peaceful intentions. They were, Hunter remarked, "uniformly received with friendship, and treated with hospitality."[12] As they went deeper into the mountains, the travelers met people whose languages were "altogether unintelligible" to them and they were "obliged to communicate wholly by signs," which they also did successfully. They were provided with food and shelter, information about possible routes, and guides for part of the way.[13] Hunter contradicted the era's stereotypes about the savages who were thought to inhabit the far west. Diplomacy and cooperation were fundamental values and had helped them to maintain stability and keep their people safe. They were not bloodthirsty killers. The Native peoples they met along the way "had frequent intercourse with each other, without exciting the least suspicion or jealousy. These circumstances facilitated our progress very much, for we were always accompanied by some of them, from one group to another. Besides, we frequently had the use of some of their canoes or rafts, to assist us on our way."[14] As they were passed from people to people along their journey, they were told stories about a majestic body of water farther to the west.

Hunter wasted few words in getting to the incredible moment they stepped on the shores of the Pacific. They were awestruck by the limitless horizon and deafening roar of the surf. They were convinced they had entered a sacred realm and began singing in gratitude to the Great Spirit: "We offered up our devotions, or I might rather say, our minds were serious, and our devotions continued, all the time we were in this country."[15] It was his memory of standing in awe of the Pacific that most aggravated officials in the War Department. Cass and Schoolcraft, two of the most respected of the Indian experts in the United States, maintained that what was known about Osage culture proved Hunter to be a fabulist. Cass stated matter-of-factly that there were no oceans or large bodies of water in Osage creation stories: "The Osages occupy a country of boundless plains. They know nothing of the ocean, nor do they believe, that the land of departed spirits is beyond it. The Heaven of the Indians is as sensual as the Mahometan paradise."[16] When reading the words and theories by the Indian experts of nineteenth century, it is often necessary to acknowledge, and then set aside, the rank prejudice that translated foolish speculations into settled facts. For one, the Osages knew something about oceans. An Osage delegation crossed the Atlantic on a diplomatic mission to France in 1725; another delegation traveled to New Orleans and stood on the shores of the Gulf of Mexico in 1794; another, while in Washington in 1803, probably took an excursion to the coast. The delegations returned home with the stories of what they had witnessed on their travels.

Cass and Schoolcraft were just as oblivious to the large bodies of water in Osage creation stories. Different versions related how their ancestors, the Little Ones, descended to earth only to find it submerged in water. They were rescued by Great Elk, who threw himself upon the earth, turning parts of it dry and habitable, and in the process creating the wind and the plains, rivers, and mountains, and leaving behind the earth and its waters for the Little Ones and their descendants.[17] In this light, Hunter's awestruck description of a religious pilgrimage, of the men believing the Pacific was sacred water, was a far more accurate description of Osage beliefs than anything Cass or Schoolcraft ever had to say on the subject. "In truth," Richard Drinnon argued in defense of Hunter, "the Osages knew of the ocean from long ago, from before the white man came, before there were centuries, even before the living creatures had names."[18]

To be fair, skepticism of their journey was to be expected, although for no reason having anything to do with Hunter. The large body of travel and exploratory writing about the American West was chock full of rumors, myths, legends, and tall tales, the Seven Cities of Gold, Prince Madoc's Welsh Indians, the Great American Desert, and a lost tribe of Israel among them. Dating back to the early 1700s, there were reports of Indian hunters who had traversed the continent all the way to the Pacific. For example, a Yazoo Indian by the name of Moncachtapé told his story to the French historian of colonial Louisiana, Antoine-Simon Le Page du Pratz, who then transcribed it in three chapters of his *Histoire de la Lousiane*, published in 1758.[19] The historian was accused of hoaxing the public and doubts about the veracity of the Yazoo's achievement seeped immediately into the historical record, where they have remained ever since, and will remain indefinitely, barring some miraculous discovery in the archives. We do know that Lewis and Clark did not dismiss the story as a hoax. They valued it enough to carry an English edition of the book across the continent, but they did not mention Moncacht-apé or any of his observations in their journals. One scholar suspected they had trouble acknowledging that a Yazoo explorer may have preceded them to the Pacific by a century.

Hunter's journey was not as implausible as his opponents claimed. The fur companies had been racing to establish a trading route over the Rockies to the Pacific ever since the triumphant return of Lewis and Clark in 1806. Five years later, David Thompson of the Northwest Company had mapped a route across Athabasca Pass in the Rocky Mountains to the mouth of the Columbia. The following year, 1812, Wilson Price Hunt and Donald McKenzie of the American Fur Company led an expedition from Saint Louis to Astoria. That same year, Robert Stuart returned overland to St. Louis with six men. Stuart had sailed to Astoria aboard the ill-fated *Tonquin* and is recognized today for discovering the South Pass and mapping the Oregon Trail between the Columbia and Missouri Rivers.[20]

All these expeditions relied heavily on Native peoples with local knowledge about possible routes, the terrain they would cross, and the different peoples they would meet along the way.[21] The expeditions were all taking place around the same time Hunter's group would have traversed the western part of the continent, but his version of the journey was very different from typical exploratory writing. His party of hunters was not consumed with blazing trade routes, staking claims on the land, or asserting the authority of a new nation-state. Hunter's perspective resembled that of the naturalist and philosopher more than it did that of the soldier and explorer. He and the other men relished the discovery of new rivers, fauna, and wildlife. They enjoyed learning about all of it from the many peoples who gave them refuge. They marveled at the prairies, rivers, and mountains.[22] He made it clear that his companions

Figure 4 "View of the Rocky Mountains on the Platte 50 Miles from Their Base." Francis Kearney, engraver, and Samuel Seymour, 1822. Samuel Seymour, the illustrator for Major Stephen Long's exploring expedition, portrayed their approach to the Rockies along the Platte River. It was published in Edwin James's *Account of an Expedition from Pittsburgh to the Rocky Mountains* (1822–23). *Source*: Courtesy of the Library of Congress. https://www.loc.gov/item/2007683611/

were endowed with higher virtues. They enjoyed life. They had a thirst for knowledge. They were curious. They possessed the same desire to explore the unknown world as any white person. Writing in this way about the inner lives and feelings of Native peoples, in 1823, was unexpected and shocking, a radical act in a fledgling democratic society.

After a few months of exploring the northwestern coast, the men had tired of the incessant rains and decided to set out for home. They likely followed an ancient route across the high desert of central Oregon, which the Nez Perces, Yakamas, Umatillas, and other Sahaptian-speaking peoples had been using for thousands of years. The Columbia River would have taken them to the Willamette and then upstream to its headwaters, where their trek across the Cascades would have led them to the Deschutes and dropped them into the hazardous rapids and falls later travelers and explorers called the Dalles. The first snows had started to fall by the time they reached "the neighborhood of the Great Mountains," and they wisely decided to hunker down for the winter.

Near their encampment were hot springs for drinking, cooking, and a soothing soak. In his editorial commentary on the autobiography, Drinnon speculated they might have camped near the thermal waters in what is known today as Yellowstone Park.[23] Since they were running low on gunpowder and shot, they hunted mainly with bows and arrows, but a few men carried rifles to go after buffalo and elk and to guard against the bears, panthers, and wolves that "prowled around our camps." They passed the time by dressing buffalo hides and turning them into moccasins, leggings, and robes. They collected obsidian and chipped it into arrowheads and knives. They played games of chance and told stories. As always, they were mindful of being outsiders in a region far from home. After their peace runners fanned out along the trails, their neighbors began arriving in their camp with gifts of beans, roots, and nuts, and preparations began for a feast of buffalo meat and venison. Some tobacco, another gift from the locals, was put into a pipe and smoked by all. By this ancient custom, they "strengthened the relations of friendship" and the feast commenced.

When the flowers started blooming, it was time to resume their journey, but not before a farewell ritual at the springs. They scattered tobacco over the waters and lifted their voices in gratitude. They gave thanks to the Great Spirit for leading them to the source of life, supplying their wants, and preserving their health and safety during the winter.[24] The first days of their journey were pleasant and nearly distracted them from the great struggle to come. Before long, they were ascending the foothills of the Rockies, laboring over rocks and through the snow crust, cursing the bitter cold and the imposing peaks ahead. The trail snaked around and below sheer precipices and saved them from an even more hazardous climb—they had found the Continental Divide, according to Hunter, "the place where the waters were flowing eastwardly and westwardly from each other." Weeks later, with fortune on their side, they were hiking down the eastern side of the mountains. They shed their buffalo robes as the sun melted the snow under their feet, probably smiling at their good fortune in finding what appears to have been the South Pass, which the history books credit Stuart and the Astorians for having discovered.[25]

Their good fortune soon turned bad, as the southern crossing had taken them off course and cast them adrift in unfamiliar territory. Hunter remembered how peculiar the experience was for all of them: "Our whole party was completely lost, which, in fact, was the first time in my life, that I had ever known of an individual occurrence of the kind, though they sometimes happen."[26] Teams of men took short excursions in every direction, but they could find none of the familiar landmarks to point them toward home. They walked along the banks of a small river—a tributary of the Arkansas, they later learned—with their rifle muzzles lowered to the ground to look as nonthreatening as possible. They caught a break when a group of Indians hailed them from up ahead and understood by the signing of the travelers that they were lost. In exchange for a few rifles and robes, they gave them food and shelter for several weeks. Hunter disclosed very little about their experience with the group he called Teton, also known as Lakota, except to remark they had spent their time building four canoes with willow frames and buffalo hides. The Arkansas was swelling with snowmelt when they finally departed, so they careened downstream for several days before passing through a perilous stretch of rapids that dropped them in an eddy where some imposing Pawnees were waiting for them. Surprisingly, the Pawnees held up their hands in peace and helped them to drag their canoes ashore. After exchanging gifts of tobacco and corn, some of the Pawnees carried over a pile of beaver pelts and suggested a trade for a few more Osage rifles, which was an offer the outnumbered travelers felt they could not refuse.

The Arkansas eventually carried them out of the mountains, through canyons, and across forests and prairies. Hunter did not describe how they might have reacted as the river meandered between the Verdigris and the Neosho, but some of the men probably shouted cheerily because they had made it to Osage country. Hunter's narrative jumped ahead to the moment they saw their village and were greeted by their people crying out in joy and disbelief. They had been gone for sixteen moons, or roughly eighteen months, and everyone had assumed they were dead. At that evening's feast, the returning heroes told their stories of the remarkable journey. In Hunter's words, "The old men and warriors listened with wonder and astonishment at the narration of our adventures, and lavished on us the meeds of praise, and high encomiums, heretofore only bestowed on the most distinguished of their nation."[27] Hunter's mother and sister were not the only ones who embraced him. All the women, young and old, danced around the men and sang the songs typically reserved for warriors who displayed exceptional prowess in battle. The men now "ranked among the bravest of warriors," and some began to find ears of corn, left by the young women who wished to marry them, outside of their lodges. If an ear of corn was left for him, a reticent Hunter did not mention it. But he did admit that they had been dreaming about such a glorious homecoming ever since Neekishlauteeth, the Omaha elder, had inspired them with his story of crossing the mountains.

Word of their journey across the Rockies spread to one of the most influential fur traders of the era. The following spring,

Manuel Lisa recruited Hunter and his Osage and Kansa companions to join his annual expedition up the Missouri. Born in New Orleans in 1772, Lisa arrived in St. Louis around 1790 with a license to trade on the Grand Osage River, which was never going to satisfy someone who dreamed of making the Missouri a gateway to the Pacific.[28] In 1809, he joined the Choteau family, William Clark, and several other well-connected traders and merchants in founding the St. Louis Fur Company. Their success was precarious: Their profit margins continually fell short of their targets, which had not adequately accounted for the falling prices for beaver furs, the rising costs of merchandise, and Blackfoot attacks on trappers and trading posts. When Lisa took over a smaller and less capitalized firm in 1813 and renamed it the Missouri Fur Company, he enjoyed a run of relatively good luck. The war between the United States and England had disrupted the fur trade for seemingly everyone but Lisa. It was his duty as the newly appointed sub-agent of Indian affairs for all tribes above the Kansas River to keep trading with the tribes and make them happy, so that they would not abandon the United States for the British. At the end of the war, Lisa stood by the side of his former business partner, Governor William Clark, at the treaty conference at Portage des Sioux and demanded land cessions and loyalty oaths from their allies.[29]

Hunter regretted the day he ever met Manuel Lisa in the Grand Osage village of Chief Clermont, where Hunter and his companions were visiting. The memory of their encounter pained him: "This Manuel Lisa was an artful, cunning man: he had several private interviews with me, and used every argument in his power to persuade me to accompany him in his intended voyage."[30] Whatever promises or inducements were given, Lisa eventually wore him down, and he agreed to go on one condition: Twenty of his Osage and Kansa companions would also join the expedition, which suited Lisa just perfectly.

Figure 5 "Osage Indians." Oil on card mounted on paperboard, by George Catlin, 1836. George Catlin's 1836 painting depicts a group of Osages gathered around Chief Clermont (armed with his war club), the son of the Chief Clermont described in Hunter's narrative. *Source*: Courtesy of the National Gallery of Art. https://www.nga.gov/collection/art-object-page.50377.html

The yearly expedition to the company trading posts that stretched from the lower Missouri to the Arikara and Mandan villages required an enormous amount of manpower. Big traders like Lisa had adopted Lewis and Clark's military strategy for traveling through the region. Anywhere from 50 to 175 boatmen, the size of an army company, mobile and well-armed, powered the fleet and protected the merchandise. In the spring, their barges went up the Missouri stocked with guns, powder, flints, whiskey, knives, hatchets, blankets, cloth, colored beads, kettles, bridles, mirrors, looking glasses, and more. Merchandise was the lifeblood of the fur trade. A portion was given as tribute to the chiefs who controlled the river and who permitted them to travel through their territory, but most of the merchandise was traded for furs, skins, tallow, and salted tongues. In the fall, if fortune had blessed the men, their hefty barges returned downriver to St. Louis.

Hunter and his companions received a rude awakening on the first days of their voyage. They did not realize the enormous amount of hard labor required in moving a convoy of loaded barges against the current, over sandbars, and through snags. Most of the crew, a motley mix of Native peoples, French *engagés*, Spaniards, and Americans, participated in the grueling work. They seemed to spend more time in the frigid water than on deck, their hands raw and backs aching from pulling the tow line for hours on end, their nerves frayed from the first mates scolding them and pushing them to work harder. It was a foreign and disorienting experience for Hunter and his companions, who never in their lives had been forced to toil like slaves. In those early days on the lower Missouri, Lisa impressed Hunter as a tough but inspiring leader. He varied the harsh cadence of his first mates with timely shouts of praise and encouragement. "He made me forget my sufferings," Hunter recalled, "and excited me to increased efforts and turmoils."[31] It was an impression that would not last for long.

The villages and trading posts they stopped at along the way provided a brief respite from their ordeal. At one village, he was welcomed ashore by some Kickapoos whom he recognized immediately from his time with the tribe in Illinois. They spent the evening smoking and reminiscing, and Hunter, with so many questions about his past, tried to fill in the gaps in his memory. Could they tell him anything about the circumstances surrounding his capture? Who were his white people? Did they know where he came from? What about his Kickapoo mother, whom he had last seen at Rogerstown? They were pained that they could not shed any light on his past. Years later the thought occurred to him that they knew more than they were letting on and had shown him a small mercy by hiding the truth from him.

Several days later they arrived at the confluence of the Kansas and Missouri Rivers. When the Kansa men had been here on their last buffalo hunt, they could not return home without violating their agreement with White Hair, but the war between their peoples had since ended and now there was nothing stopping them from returning to their families. Many of them immediately walked away from the barges and headed down the trail to their villages. Hunter believed this had been part of Lisa's plan all along. He wanted the tribe as trading partners, and there was no better way to earn their trust and goodwill than by escorting the men back to their families. It was not an uncommon bargaining practice in the War Department, as Lisa well knew, so he turned their convoy up the Kansas toward Blue Earth. It was a moving homecoming for Hunter: "I was received here with every mark of the warmest friendship and affection." While happy to rekindle old relations, he would not be staying. His feelings had not changed. He had found a satisfying new life with the Osages and could not bear to abandon his Osage mother and sister, who depended on him. He was a skilled hunter and warrior. He proudly admitted that he had grown into a leader who was "much respected and esteemed by the whole nation."[32] Manuel Lisa used his powers of persuasion to keep Hunter in his employ, but it was hardly necessary. He already had made up his mind to stick with the expedition and return to his Osage village afterward.

He might have decided differently if he knew the catastrophe awaiting them upriver. The intense competition for furs and skins had created killing fields of slaughtered beaver, elk, and buffalo. Far up the Missouri, the carnage shocked him and left him despondent about his involvement in the trade:

> I witnessed, for the first time in my life, with painful sensations, the wide and wanton destruction of game, merely to procure skins; so much disgusted was I, on seeing the buffalo carcasses strewed over the ground in a half-putrefied state, that my reluctance to fulfill my engagements was so much increased, as to occasion me to reflect seriously on absconding from the party.[33]

The convoy had traveled too far upriver for him and his comrades to turn back. They would never make it back safely through enemy territory. He was distraught, but they were trapped. They reluctantly fulfilled their duties, trapping and hunting along the way and moving the barges up the Missouri. "I gradually became more reconciled to this barbarous practice," he confessed, his shameful complicity still burning years later.[34] One day, as they neared the Platte, the clouds that had been churning and darkening suddenly burst into a torrential downpour, followed by terrifying thunderclaps and lightning bolts. Even a decade later, he shook with fear at the memory of how the waters "swelled into a devasting flood, covered the islands and alluvial grounds, and bore off whole herds of buffalo and forests of trees on its surface; the sight was so distressing and awful as to surpass my powers of description."

Hunter apologized for being unable to find the English words to describe the pain of seeing herds of buffalo being swept downriver, but he could not have chosen a more fitting metaphor than the flood. He had experienced the massive floods caused by the New Madrid earthquakes of 1811–12, but he also remembered Tecumseh saying, in his speech to the Osages, that the Great Spirit "speaks in thunder and the earth swallows up villages and drinks up the Mississippi" as punishment for the slaughter of the buffalos. That day at the mouth of the Platte, the Great Spirit was also speaking in thunder and delivering his wrath upon the earth. He had raised the rivers to carry the sacred buffalo to safety and away from these barbaric humans.

The flood was a bad omen for the men. After putting the Platte River behind them, which was considered the border between the lower and the upper Missouri, Manuel Lisa "threw off his disguise" as a strong and capable commander and turned into a monster. He was no longer praising and cajoling the men on the cordelle line as they pulled the keelboats upriver; after crossing the Platte, he abused them in fits of pique and berated them for the slowness of the journey. Hunter's account matches what later historical evidence revealed about Lisa's temperament and the hardships of a Lisa expedition. He was usually in a hurry to get upriver and rarely satisfied by the pace of the convoy. "Lisa drove his men unmercifully in order to make up time," wrote his sympathetic biographer, Richard Ogelsby, who had pored over the records of the Missouri Fur Company. Lisa scolded them for their supposed laziness and weakness, forced them to work from sunup to sundown (and longer under the light of a full moon), cut their rations to motivate them, and threatened to abandon them in enemy territory.[35] Desertions and defiance were commonplace on Lisa's expeditions, which is exactly what Hunter reported. The men quickly grew unhappy with the abuse and began whispering of resistance. As the leader of his group, Hunter approached Lisa for a conversation, but they had "harsh words" and Lisa grew even more enraged at his Indian crew. Hunter and his men decided they had had enough. The next morning, just below the Arikara and Mandan villages, they walked away from the expedition as Lisa cursed their backs. (He probably did not let the matter rest. He was aggressive in using the government to pursue deserters and force them to pay their debts to the company.)

Hunter's account seems credible in every detail, which might be why Lewis Cass dismissed it as irrelevant and lacking in proof: It contradicted his case against Hunter. If his account of the Lisa expedition was accepted as truthful, then it would be even more difficult for Cass to discredit Hunter, but he was not to be deterred. He was able to use the lack of corroborating evidence about the Lisa expedition to insinuate that Hunter had made it up, as if corroborating witnesses or documents were plentiful and easy enough to find. They decidedly were not. What Cass did not say, and may not even have been aware of, was that Lisa had fallen off the map, disappeared, around the same time Hunter said they were traveling up the Missouri. Incredibly enough, the activities and whereabouts of one of the most well-known and well-connected persons in the American West are largely *unknown* for two years after the War of 1812.[36] There is no trace of his movements in his personal papers, in the records of the Missouri Fur Company, in the correspondence of William Clark, Pierre Choteau, Ramsey Crooks, Charles Gratiot, Thomas Hempstead, Pierre Menard, and other Missouri merchants and traders, in the archives of the War Department, in the reports of explorers and travelers, or in the *Missouri Gazette* and *St. Louis Enquirer*. This was still a world where someone as important and widely known as Manuel Lisa could vanish with hardly a trace.

But there was one witness, John Dunn Hunter, who saw Lisa, and who knew where he was and what he was doing in 1816. This proved to be a dilemma for Oglesby in his otherwise scrupulous biography of Manuel Lisa. It was only after Lisa's paper trail vanished in 1816 that Oglesby grudgingly turned to Hunter, whom he assumed to be the notorious hoaxer: "What his activities were that spring remains unknown, although there may be some indication in the writings of John Dunn Hunter, who claimed to have been recruited with a band of Osages to trap the upper Missouri for Lisa and Company."[37] Oglesby twisted himself into knots trying to justify cherry-picking evidence from Hunter's personal narrative, claiming that some parts of the "fanciful tale" were faithful to the facts of the fur trade and therefore were essential to filling in Lisa's missing years. Here is a dubious landmark of sorts in historical scholarship. Oglesby was the first modern historian to use Hunter's book as a resource for researching and understanding the American West. After drawing on Hunter's recollection of the expedition, he tried to get back to his history of Lisa and the fur trade, but Hunter's presence kept nagging and confusing him. His writing clearly demonstrated his experience and knowledge of working as a boatman under Lisa. How had he acquired such rich and detailed information? Oglesby wanted to avoid digressing down this rabbit hole, but his academic training required him to justify his use of a supposedly tainted witness, so he buried Hunter in a footnote with a bogus theory. He insinuated Hunter had lifted the details about Manuel Lisa from *Three Years Among the Indians and Mexicans*, written by Thomas James, who had been on Lisa's expedition in 1809. In Oglesby's judgment, Hunter's "description of Lisa tallies very closely with that of Thomas James, and he may have gotten his information from that source," which turned out to be wishful thinking: *Three Years Among the Indians and Mexicans* was not published until 1846, twenty-three years after Hunter's book.[38]

CHAPTER FOUR

Sugar Moon

THE FLOOD WAS NOT THE ONLY OMEN of the perils awaiting them on the journey home. A day or so after they walked away from Lisa's expedition, a rattlesnake struck their most decorated warrior, Wengashee, in the calf. After one of the men cut away the flesh and cauterized the wound with a heated stone, they marched on as the venom spread through his bloodstream, slowly inflating his leg into a putrid black mass. When he finally collapsed in a heap, they carried him to shelter in the forest, wafted tobacco smoke over him, and asked the Great Spirit to spare his life. They fretted for several weeks until the fever broke, and when he no longer seemed in danger, they hit the trail again, though at a slower pace, taking turns dragging Wengashee by a travois.

They were no longer under the protection of Manuel Lisa and the expedition, and each day down the banks of the Missouri brought them closer and closer to the lookouts of the Sioux. Dragging Wengashee over the trail gave them too much time to worry about the hornet's nest they were walking into, but they were rescued one morning by a timely encounter with a group of white trappers. "By signs," Hunter wrote, "we made them understand our apprehensions of the hostile Sioux, which were settled lower down, on the Missouri."[1] The trappers nodded vehemently and told them of a safer route, avoiding the Sioux. This was familiar territory for white men whose traplines had been steadily extending into the region for years. They instructed Hunter's party to cut across the serpentine course of the river and head overland along one of the trails toward the Mandan villages, which were located farther down the river. After reaching the villages of Matootonha and Rooptahee, the longtime hub of the fur trade, they could choose to return home by way of the Missouri or continue east "till we struck on the waters of the Mississippi, and then, to descend that river."[2] The mental map of the white men was based on their experience hunting and trapping in the region, but perhaps they also carried a copy of one of the most popular books west of the Mississippi: Zebulon Pike's recent account of his exploring expedition, in which he described in detail his canoe voyage from the headwaters of the Mississippi to St. Louis in what was then an incredible thirteen days. The book and its maps were prized as a travel guide for the West.[3]

After trading some furs to the white men for gunpowder and shot, Hunter and his comrades set out across the plains of present-day North Dakota. They were in a race against winter. Sometime later, maybe a few weeks, they arrived at one of the Mandan villages, Hunter did not say which one, and wasted little time in bartering for more supplies and gathering information about the next leg of their route.[4] Hunter did not explain why but they decided to head for the Mississippi along an ancient network of trails connecting the great plains of the upper Missouri with Leech Lake in the upper Mississippi watershed, about 400 miles away. Days after leaving the Mandans, they were stumbling through thick clouds of smoke and could not see the horizon. The prairies were on fire, and the men lost sight of the sun and stars for days.[5] At last the smoke cleared and, taking their bearing on the horizon, they now could find their way. Over the next few days the temperature plunged, and they wrapped their robes about them; eventually they arrived at what they guessed was a branch of the Mississippi.

They were overjoyed, for one pleasant evening, by the apparent success of what Hunter called their "blindfold excursion."[6] However, they awoke confused, then crestfallen, as the sun rose too far to the right of them. Their vector from the Mandan village had taken them far off course.[7]

If they had heeded the twin omens of the flood and rattlesnake, then they might have turned back and spent the winter with the Mandans. But they pressed on through the bitter cold, confident they could find their way, encouraged by the animal tracks in the snow. At least there was food. A while later, as they trudged along the frozen shores of a "considerable lake," perhaps Leech Lake, a party of Ojibwe hunters called to them. An Anishinaabe people, the Ojibwes (also known as the Chippewas) lived in small bands, moving seasonally between beds of wild rice, fishing grounds, and sugar bush.[8] For many generations they had been the important middlemen in the fur trade and were accustomed to guiding travelers through their densely forested country with its warren of lakes and rivers. "They treated us kindly," Hunter said of them, "and informed us where we were, and of the route we ought to pursue."[9] The Ojibwes put them on a southward course that led them directly to the Mississippi River.

They barely survived their journey to the Mississippi. A storm had encased the forest in ice, and every step shattered the snow crust and sank the men to their knees. Hunter estimated they plowed through the icy snow for ten to twenty grueling miles per day. The animal tracks, once so encouraging, vanished. They grew weaker every day from hunger, hypothermia, and frostbite. They lost the feeling in their extremities. "Our moccasins and leggings soon gave out," Hunter recalled, "and our feet and legs became nearly frozen, and very much lacerated."[10] They could not stop shivering. Their feet were a major problem, shredded from the path and ice. They cut patches out of spare buckskin, even out of their buffalo robes, but they could not keep their feet warm and dry. Two of the men had feet so badly frozen that gangrene set in, and they had to be carried over the trail.

By the time they reached the river that was supposed to carry them home, the storm had turned into a deepening blizzard and the men were thrown across the ice. With only scraps of dried buffalo meat left in their pouches, the exhausted and famished men wisely decided to build an emergency shelter until the blizzard passed: "We . . . cleared a spot in a small growth of woods, fixed poles, thatched them with brush, and finally covered the whole with a thick stratum of snow; which, with the fire we kept, and the few skins we had, formed, as to temperature, a comfortable lodge."[11] Since the snow was too deep for them to hunt, they dug and foraged for roots. When the weather finally broke, they at least had enough energy to venture out "in hopes of finding some Indian lodge, or falling in with game."[12] Then, days later, a blizzard more powerful than any the cursed men had ever experienced swept them up and pinned them to the frozen ground. As the winds battered them, they huddled together with their robes pulled over them. They screamed their prayers into the howling winds, perhaps begging forgiveness for what they had done to the buffalo, and fully expecting to be buried alive. In Hunter's words, "We devoutly resigned ourselves to the disposition of the Great Spirit."[13]

What he remembered next were the muffled howls of a wolf rousing them from a deep slumber. The blizzard had blown by, and somehow they were still alive. They dared not sit up lest they collapse the ceiling of their snow cave and expose themselves to the wolf outside. The wolf would not attack on its own, which Wengashee, lying with his rifle under the rays of a "brilliant moonlight night," was counting on. When the pack eventually appeared and the alpha crept atop the snowdrift, Wengashee took aim and shot it dead, and the other wolves dispersed into the forests. After a few men retrieved the body, the men huddled in the cave and sang in gratitude to the wolf for giving its life to them. Since they were starving and had no fire, they devoured the wolf "while it was yet warm in its blood."[14]

The wolves soon returned and patrolled the perimeter of their cave. Some of the men roared like bears to keep them at bay, while the others dug out a floor so they could stretch their legs and prop themselves up by their elbows. "We lighted our pipes," Hunter remembered about those dreadful days, "and smoked the day away in gloomy silence."[15] The bravest wolves took turns sniping at the walls of their cave. When they shot one dead, the furious pack would retreat into the darkness, and as their howls grew fainter in the distance, several men would edge outside and go to work on their cave. They cut down several pine trees and used the trunks to fortify the walls and pitch a roof over it. They "thatched it with branches and leaves, and finally made it tight with the snow which we broke away from the arch and walls of our snow cell below."[16] When it was completed and pine boughs were spread on the ground, they built a fire over which they roasted the meat.

However, they had unwittingly made the situation worse by driving off the pack, their only source of food. They could not find "a trace of any living creature" on the fresh snow other than the tracks of the departing wolves.[17] As they grew famished, they resorted to eating moss and gnawing on bark; "our situation became extremely alarming, from the prospect of starvation."[18] Stationed on the tree line at the bleakest moment, Hunter was delirious with hunger when he suddenly experienced a vision of an "extraordinary large elk" strolling toward him "in a careless and easy gait."[19] The vision seemed so real to him that he braced the rifle against his shoulder and fired a single shot; as he crawled forward and saw the magnificent creature jump up and dart into the trees, he realized his vision was real. The other men, roused out of their stupor, chased the wounded elk into a ravine, but a panther had beaten them there. It turned from its prey and sprang toward them just as one of the men was firing, and the big cat fell dead at their feet.

The elk gave the men new life. After butchering the animal, they roasted the meat over the fires, and ate as much as was necessary to satisfy men who had been surviving for days on moss and bark. When they next lit their pipes, it was done not in gloomy silence but in joyous communion. They could be excused for thinking the bad omens had gone away. In his memoirs Hunter, focused on the literal incident of the elk saving their lives, did not explore the deeper meaning of the scene for his readers, as we might expect from a modern autobiography. What I find remarkable is how the episode echoes one of the Osage creation stories: The ancient ancestors of the Osages assumed the form of eagles, sailed down to earth, and alighted in the branches of seven trees over an immense sea, where they were doomed to spend eternity because a great flood had made the earth uninhabitable; however, their pleas for deliverance reached the ears of Great Elk, who threw himself on the earth and created the prairies, lakes, and rivers and blew winds in the four cardinal directions. It was then safe for the Osages to come down from the branches and commence their life on earth.[20] When Hunter settled on the word *extraordinary* to describe the elk that appeared on that miraculous morning, I believe he had something more in mind, perhaps unconsciously, than the physical size of a giant bull elk. This extraordinary elk that had come to rescue them was their guardian spirit. Like their ancient ancestors, the men were stranded with little chance of survival until their pleas moved the elk to help them: "We were in a nearly helpless situation, and despondency had seized on us, but in the midst of our distress, the Great Spirit forsook us not."[21] The elk would guide them home.

They continued south through the territory of the Ojibwes and were "kindly treated" by them. A few days farther down the trail, they ran into some trouble outside of a Sioux village. Hunter and the men waved and smiled, but their diplomacy did not work: "The friendly salutations we made were returned with threatening and hostile gestures and expressions."[22] Then, for emphasis, the guard dogs were set on them, and the men ran for their lives into the woods. They broke their route to the southwest, angling away from the Mississippi, and eventually hit the banks of the Grand River somewhere near the current Iowa-Missouri border. Following the river south, it was their good fortune to reach a friendly Sac village on the day of a wedding feast.[23]

Afterward, their hosts gave them some gifts to deliver to some of their people who lived several days downriver. Judging by Hunter's word choice, they were no longer walking and must have received some canoes, since their journey home was swift: "We passed over the country, crossed the Missouri near the mouth of the Kansas River, struck the Osage, and coursing along its banks, arrived at the villages of the Osages, who received and treated us as relations and friends." Sugar season was just coming to an end, and the men recuperated and enjoyed the festivities with their northern relatives. On their final leg, they headed southwest on a network of trails crisscrossing Missouri and Arkansas, long used by the Osages; a few weeks later, they arrived at their village on the Arkansas River, "where we were received in the same manner as we had formerly been, on our return from the Pacific Ocean."[24]

Osage homes along the Arkansas and its tributaries were located far away from the white settlements growing up around St. Louis and New Orleans. The southern bands of the Osages could more easily maintain their way of life than their northern relatives. They could more easily procure their own food, make their own clothing, cultivate their own fields, make their own tools, follow their own customs, and practice their own ceremonies. Fewer white people were in the Arkansas River Valley, which meant fewer trappers and hunters draining their hunting grounds, fewer traders peddling whiskey and merchandise, fewer farmers encroaching on their lands, fewer missionaries trying to save their souls, fewer officials trying to move them to the north. The southern bands could still chase the buffalo across the plains, just as their ancestors had done, and pretend as if the scattering of white people would never threaten their existence, but they still had a major crisis on their hands.

Their home in the valley became less and less remote in the years following the Louisiana Purchase. At the time of the deal, in 1803, the scattering of whites in Arkansas amounted to around 400 people, but their population topped 14,000 by 1820.[25] The Osages were under enormous pressure to cede their lands to the United States, which would then be used to resettle eastern tribes, but the leaders of the southern Osages had refused to take part in a treaty conference at Fire Prairie on the Missouri. As a result, they could not avert an all-too-familiar scheme of treaty-making: In the absence of the southern Osages, federal officials designated a handful of chiefs from the northern bands as the decision-making body of all Osage bands, and these chiefs ceded much of Osage territory to the United States, including the land of their relatives on the Arkansas.[26] The southern Osages had no intention of leaving their homes and moving north to make way for groups from the East—Cherokees, Choctaws, Sacs, Foxes, Kickapoos, Delawares, Shawnees, Miamis, Ojibwes, Ottawas, Illinois, Chickasaws, and Creeks, all of whom had been promised a new start in the soon-to-be-vacated lands of the Osages.

The newcomers received a hostile reception in the valley, where the Osages were fighting for their very survival. Osage warriors razed the new arrivals' homes and farms to the ground.

They shot their cattle and destroyed their crops. They raided their hunting camps and stole their horses. As they resisted the intrusions into their valley, the southern Osages developed a reputation for being particularly savage and hostile to the government's hopes and plans for them. The explorer and scientist William Dunbar disparaged this formerly dominant and respected people as "a lawless gang of robbers, making war on the whole world." On his expedition up the Arkansas, Zebulon Pike reported on a troubling development for future settlement: Warriors from the north were flocking there, and the main Osage village had become a "place of refuge for all the young and daring, and discontented."[27] They were determined to maintain their autonomy and way of life.

An Osage version of this history had never been seen in print until Hunter's book appeared in 1823. He provided heartbreaking insight into their struggles for survival in the valley, which was a story dovetailing with his personal battle for his sense of self. The sugar moon marked the opening of the fur season in the valley. The coming of large groups of white men was an especially strange time for Hunter. They were surprised by the sight of one of their own who looked and walked and talked like an Indian. They inquired after his parents and how he came to be with the Osages. They showed him confusing kindnesses, which concealed a single motive: "They gave me some small presents, acquired my confidence, and, in the most pressing and persuasive manner, invited me to accompany them back to the white settlements." He was insulted by their scheming and rejected all their offers. It seemed preposterous to him that he would turn his back on his people, to whom he was a protector and a provider: "I was strongly attached to the habits and manner of life I had acquired and regarded my relationship and connection with the Indians of too sacred a character to be thus violated."[28]

He didn't know it yet, but his life was about to change forever. Ever since the end of the war, the camps and trading posts of fur companies had been seeping up the Arkansas and its tributaries. The intensifying competition for furs and hides was depleting the Osage hunting grounds and driving the buffalo farther and farther away. After several years of scarcity, many Osages were dismayed by the large parties of traders and trappers who were overrunning their homeland, squatting in their best camps, and stoking conflicts and violence. Tensions boiled over that season when the sight of a "great quantity of furs," bundled for transport in the camp of an American trader named Colonel Watkins, enraged a group of Osage men. Watkins, who would come to play a very important role in Hunter's life, placated them for a little while with drams of whiskey. But after the men became drunk, they stole his horses, bolted across the prairie, and eventually rode up on the camp of a trapper everyone knew named LaFouche. In past years the Frenchman had kept to himself and worked his own traplines, but that season he had camped near the Americans for protection and appeared friendly with them. As far as the Osage men were concerned, this made LaFouche their enemy, and they clubbed him to death and took his scalp and his whiskey.

Hunter could still see in his mind the crazed and drunken men riding into the village on their stolen horses. Passing triumphantly before the lodges, holding aloft the trader's scalp and skins of whiskey, they called for "similar vengeance" on all the whites "who had trespassed on their rights, and robbed them of their game."[29] They must act quickly: Once the great pile of furs was ferried downriver, even more whites would flood into their hunting grounds in the pursuit of riches. As the skins of whiskey made the rounds, the people grew more furious and raged against the invaders. At last, a proposal was made: The only way to prevent the surge was to kill every member of the Watkins party before they headed downriver with their cargo.

Hunter's life unraveled after the killing of LaFouche. Hunter, like the other men, had shouted in support of the proposal, but he secretly believed they were about to make a terrible mistake. From that day forward, he wore his consent as a badge of shame. A true warrior was supposed to be a leader, to speak the truth in trying times, but he had been too scared to defy the will of the people. He often daydreamed about what he might have said, about his eloquent and convincing dissent, if he had not remained silent in the heat of the moment. If he could do it over again, he would have praised his brothers for their bravery in protecting their people, but he would have condemned them for sullying the honor of their brother warriors. They had lost their minds "in a drunken frolic" and butchered an innocent man who had done them no harm. His speech would have been clear on the principle that their drunken rage did not justify an honorable war measure; for good measure, he would have rebuked them for jeopardizing the safety of everyone by killing the white man, which often resulted in reprisal attacks. If only he had been brave enough to speak his mind.

Later that evening, as the men slumbered under the "stupefactive influence" of the whiskey, Hunter realized what he must do. He crept through camp and removed the flintlocks from their guns, emptied the primers, and eased himself on top of one of the stolen horses. He pressed his cheek to the horse's neck, quietly coaxing the animal into a walk until they were safely away, then grabbed fistfuls of the horse's mane and kicked his heels into its side; instantly they were careening through the thickets of brambles and undergrowth. He had company, a baying hound, "a constant source of annoyance," who refused to return home and threatened to give him away. Reaching the fork in the river at daybreak, he goaded the weary horse to the top of a steep ridge to look for Well's Trace; after he spotted it a few ravines over, they scrambled and slid downhill and picked up the trace for several miles. He was convinced that his brother warriors were in pursuit. He pleaded and pleaded with the baying hound until finally he had to kill it. They came upon a stream, riding up it to hide their tracks, found a break in the willows, and bolted across the prairie to the Watkins camp. He was quite a sight after the perilous ride, lacerated from head to toe by brambles and branches, caked in blood and dirt. Even if there was someone who could understand Osage, the meaning of the distressed rider was clear enough: A storm of trouble was blowing their way.

Hunter had not thought through what might happen next. He assumed the white men would quickly break down their camp, load their barges with the bundles of furs and pelts, and push off downriver, but he heard Watkins screaming, saw him madly gesturing, saw the men running for their rifles and hatchets. They began burrowing shallow trenches and putting up barricades of trunks and branches. It did not make any sense to Hunter that they would stay and fight rather than leave with their cargo. He heard Watkins shouting at him to join the men in securing the camp, but he could not quite believe it. He declared that he would never betray his people, his Osage "countrymen," by taking up arms against them, but Watkins admonished him, shouting that they "were not my countrymen; that I was a white man." It had been his duty, as a fellow white man, to warn them of the ambush, just as it was his duty now to defend their camp. The scolding shocked him to the core. "I now despised myself for the treachery" of betraying his Osage people, he recalled thinking at the time, and he suddenly "hated the very looks" of Watkins. Finding the courage that had eluded him the night before, he stood his ground and insisted that Watkins respect the sacrifice he had made to save them. Bloodshed must be avoided at all costs.

Watkins, perhaps grasping that retreat was the more sensible option, surprised him by conceding to his wishes. They were nearly finished packing the last of the bundles of furs and pelts for the return to Arkansas Post. Why risk it all in a skirmish?

In his mind, Hunter had atoned for his shameful silence by averting bloodshed and thus protecting his people from the payback of the whites. Standing in the middle of the bustling camp, the adrenaline from the ride draining from his body, it suddenly dawned on him the trouble he was in. He had betrayed his people to the whites, and no amount of explaining would save his life. His actions, as he put it, "produced a highly important revolution in my life" by destroying the sacred and inviolable bond he felt with the Osages. He could not stay there, so he did not object as Watkins rushed him to the landing to board the flatboats and they pushed off downriver.

Watkins turned out to be quite a raconteur, entertaining the camps downriver with the tale of Hunter's midnight ride. Afterward, some of the white men would sidle up to him with smiles and outstretched whiskey skins, doing their best to recruit him to their traplines and scouting parties. It was Manuel Lisa all over again. All their talk about their "gilded prospects" disgusted him and brought back the painful memories of the slaughter on the upper Missouri. He could not imagine a life among the whites in the settlements, but where else was he supposed to go? The hub of Arkansas Post, where they would land soon, was out of the question. At a bend along a bank in the river, near the Quapaws to whom he would tie his fate years later, he called out for Watkins to cut close to shore. Hunter then stepped into the shallow water and bid farewell to the trader. He turned up the hill and made his way toward the White River. Finding refuge with "even the most degraded tribe," he reassured himself, would be "infinitely more tolerable" than living among the whites.

CHAPTER FIVE

Sanctuary

HUNTER CROSSED A STEEP PLATEAU divided by creeks running south and north, turned up one of them, and eventually hit the White River. He rambled along the curling banks, and the river narrowed with each passing day and night, its bends sharpening, its gorges deepening, until it slowed to a trickle in the Ozark Mountains. He was alone for the first time in his life and experiencing a personal crisis. He had lost everyone who was dear to him because of his decision to warn the Americans. He told himself he had done the right thing by heading off the attack, but he also had not considered the awful consequences. He looked like a traitor to his people. Each morning he opened his eyes to the painful truth that he was now "hated and despised by those I sincerely loved and esteemed." He had escaped into the mountains only to fall into a pit of despair and loneliness.

He described this period as a vision quest that ultimately put him on a new path in life. Like all the Kickapoo, Osage, and Kansa boys he had grown up with, he would have gone on his first vision quest when he was on the brink of manhood. They went alone to an isolated place in the hopes of receiving a vision about their destiny; they fasted from food and water for several days, sang and chanted to the spirit world, and immersed themselves in nature and its cosmic truths. Vision quests were not reserved for boys but were taken by anyone who needed healing and guidance in their lives. Warriors went to their sacred place before battle, hunters before the chase, mothers and fathers after losing a child, women during the growing season, and chiefs during a crisis. The visions they experienced helped them to grow, find meaning in their lives, and weather hard times.

The vision quest ceremony helped Hunter to make sense of his experience in the mountains. He was trying to cope with the pain of being separated from his people and being alone for the first time in his life. As he tells it, his suffering began to ease as the weeks passed in his sanctuary. He became absorbed in watching the animals around him: the clever beavers hard at work on their lodges, the buffalo bulls bluffing and fighting for hours on end, the panther leaping after its prey, the black snake strangling its enemy the rattlesnake, the deer crushing the rattlesnake to death with its hooves. Like a future Henry David Thoreau lost in a reverie of nature, Hunter was fascinated by even the smallest creatures: "Indeed, I have lain for half a day at a time in the shade to witness the management and policy observed by the ants in storing up their food, the maneuvers of the spider in taking its prey, the artifice of the mason-fly (*Sphex*) in constructing and storing its clayey cells, and the voraciousness and industry of the dragon-fly (*Libellula*) to satisfy its appetite." The animals filled him with wonder and took his mind off his troubles.

He sensed that he had been transported back to a primordial time when nature was in its infancy. He felt the presence of the Great Spirit. He emulated the behavior of the animals, hunting only to satisfy his appetite, never taking more than his subsistence required. Rejuvenated by the simple act of bathing in the river, he bellowed joyously to Great Elk for having thrashed about in the ancient waters and making the earth habitable. After a while, he found some peace of mind in his solitude: "The tumultuous agitations of my mind gradually subsided into a calm; I became satisfied with the loneliness of my situation, could lie down to sleep among the rocks, ravines, and ferns, in careless quietude."[1] He now slept so soundly that not even the wolves prowling around his camp or the rattlesnakes coiling up alongside him for warmth could disturb his slumber. He had become one with nature, which was a principal aim of the vision quest.

His sanctuary seemed a world away from the wreckage of civilization in the valley. There were no cabins, cattle, fences, or any other signs of settlers. There were no forts or trading posts. There were no company boats with gangs of traders, hunters, and trappers coming up the river. There were no carcasses littered across and rotting on the ground. In fact, buffalo were still plentiful in the valley below him. On one unforgettable afternoon, he slept away the heat in the nook of a tree until "a thousand buffaloes running at full speed directly towards me" startled him awake.[2] As the herd rumbled around and past his quavering tree, the lone hunter in pursuit was their ancient enemy the panther; just as quickly, the herd vanished over the horizon and he was enveloped in quiet again. He might have thought he had been dreaming if not for the broad trace pounded into the prairie below him.

Hunter's celebration of the healing powers of nature expressed the Zeitgeist of the period. In the cultural movement known as Romanticism, a remote and rugged environment was imagined as a retreat from the corruptions of the modern world, and the solitary seeker, communing with flora and fauna and embracing the cosmos, was the bright-eyed hero of the age. When Hunter arrived to great fanfare in London, it was in part due to his resemblance to this Romantic hero, which is a story still to come.[3]

Hunter did not need reminding that his sanctuary was temporary and too close to the settlements. A striking image marked the end of his vision quest and the transition into the next phase of his life: five white hunters along the ridge line, walking through the morning mist toward his camp. Slipping away into the woods to stay hidden, he fumed that the white men had "interrupted" his solitude, but then he could not believe his ears—friendly shouts in Osage! "My conduct and feelings underwent a total and instant revolution," he recalled, "and I actually danced for joy."[4] They were not Americans, as he initially feared, but Frenchmen "on an exploring excursion to search out the most favorable places for taking furs, as soon as the hunting season should arrive." They broke bread together and shared their stories, and the sounds and rhythms of their Osage speech made him emotional. His eyes fell on the embroidery, bead work, and feathers adorning their cotton shirts, deerskin leggings, and buckskin moccasins. They had even adopted the style of the Osages. At the end of a delightful morning, they surprised him by inviting him back to their hamlet near the falls. Before long, teams of trappers from the fur companies would be swarming the river and creeks. He decided to take his chances with these Frenchmen.

They traveled downriver to a place called Flee's Settlement, which Zebulon Pike had marked as "white colony" on his map of lower Louisiana with no commentary about its inhabitants. Hunter provided what little evidence there is of life in the settlement. He received a warm welcome from the mix of French and American inhabitants, who made their living farming, hunting, and trapping. According to Hunter, these frontier people followed the example of the "Indians in their modes of life," from hunting, planting crops, and dressing skins to making moccasins and leggings, foraging for roots and herbs, and constructing their dwellings.[5] They were so at home in the wilderness that Hunter thought they resembled Native people more than they did their own countrymen. They spoke their native languages, but they also communicated in a lingua franca that combined all of them, including Osage and other

Indigenous tongues. Hunter began picking up some more English from the Americans. At the behest of some of the women, he even started wearing an American-style waistcoat.

European empire-building and the global fur trade had made an already polyglot region even more so. Among Europeans and Native peoples, an openness to mixing through marriage, business alliances, and political partnerships was the key to sustaining the lucrative trade in furs and pelts for over two centuries. An estimated 80% of the population in the hubs of St. Louis, Michilimackinac, Green Bay, Cape Girardeau, Santa Fe, Nacogdoches, and Prairie du Chien were of multiple and mixed ancestries.[6] Their world disintegrated after the Louisiana Purchase subjected them to American rule. They were now part of a nation-state with a growing sense of its supposed racial superiority and thus a total aversion to the intermingling common on the western borders. An emerging belief in this Herrenvolk democracy was that people with mixed ancestries, those despised "half-breeds," were degraded and incapable of improvement, which ran counter to the Enlightenment philosophy of Jefferson, Madison, Franklin, and their generation.

Reports from the western frontier provided plenty of evidence that supposedly validated this belief. Explorers, travelers, missionaries, bureaucrats, travelers, and settlers sent back accounts of their encounters with the amalgamated populations of the border region. From his post in Detroit, Governor Lewis Cass, Hunter's nemesis, guessed that "four-fifths of Michigan's white population were of that class of people."[7] He complained to his superiors that it was impossible for him to assimilate such damaged people into a republican society. They were too far gone and could not be saved. His contemporary Timothy Flint, also regarded as an authority on western life, gave a similarly distressing account of the miscegenation along the entire length of the Mississippi River. His journey from Cairo to New Orleans was spoiled by the sight of mixed villages dotting its banks. As racial attitudes hardened during the 1820s, even minimal interactions with Native peoples were thought to be hazardous for white people. Proximity could possibly blunt the intellect of whites, sap their vigor, darken their skin.[8]

Flee's Settlement was good for Hunter for all the reasons that places like it disturbed so many of his contemporaries. It was a community without a fixed standard of cultural or racial purity, where people of multiple and mixed ancestries and nationalities lived peacefully together and unabashedly looked to their Indigenous neighbors for guidance in surviving in an environment they knew very well. Watkins, the fur trader whose life Hunter had saved, had been appalled by his loyalty to the Osages: Hunter was white by birth, and Watkins assumed his true friends and countrymen must be other white people. However, during his time at Flee's Settlement, he was not forced to choose between the two sides of his identity. It was an epiphany that changed his life: There was a place for someone like him in America.

The inhabitants of Flee's Settlement respected him and valued his upbringing. They "entertained a high opinion" of what was popularly called Indian medicine, but no one knew how to practice it with any success. Since doctors were scarce in the West, people often had to be resourceful and care for themselves. They picked his brain about the remedies used by Native peoples to treat various maladies. When a virus swept through the community, they came to him and asked if he would accept the responsibility of treating the sick. They brushed off his protestations that he lacked the competence to heal those who were suffering. He had come from the Osages, whom the *Western Gazetteer* had recently called the "most skilled in medicine," and the settlers desperately hoped Hunter had learned some of those skills during his years with them.[9] Putting on a brave face, he headed into the forest to search for medicinal flora and was pleasantly surprised to recognize a few plants and roots that the Osages commonly mixed into a remedy for the alleviation of fevers. As he stuffed his pouch, it suddenly dawned on him that he possessed some expertise compared to the settlers. He came from a place where everyone was schooled in the treatment of illnesses, where, in his words, "we seldom meet with an Indian who has not a sufficient knowledge of their medicine to prescribe on all ordinary occasions."[10] Nobody was more surprised than he was when his remedy relieved their illness. "I treated their cases with the happiest success," he proudly remarked.

Here was a glimpse of his first passion for medicine and botany, which before long he would be studying in Philadelphia, New York, and London. There were so many myths and falsehoods about Native healing practices that he felt if he did not dispel them, he would be misunderstood, dismissed, or typecast as a sorcerer. He conceded there were primitive tribes whose medicine was more like magic and lacked a rational basis. In these tribes, the medicine man was like the sorcerer in white legends, wearing a crown of buffalo horns and dressed in the "most grotesque habiliments" of skins. After ingesting hallucinogens to make him feel more powerful than the evil spirit said to be "the cause of their patient's disease," the sorcerer turned into a whirling dervish and stalked the evil spirit with "juggling, charms, and conjurations." If the sick person recovered, then the medicine man reveled in his healing powers, but if the suffering persisted, he began asking what grave offense the sick person had committed against the evil spirits.

Indian medicine was infinitely more complex than this primitive picture, but Hunter sensed the futility of getting past myths and fantasies. The historian Virgil Vogel, whose seminal *American Indian Medicine* (1970) drew extensively on Hunter's work, faced the very same dilemma, and he responded in the very same way. He lamented how the obsession with incantations, prayers, dances, rattles, drums and other "irrational features of Indian medicine" had produced a lopsided field of research and "obscured much that is potentially useful in aboriginal medicine."[11] Like Hunter, Vogel worried that deeply held prejudices about Native peoples and their fabled medicine would defeat his effort to explain the complexity and usefulness of their healing practices. His best idea for overcoming this bias also echoed Hunter in its elegant universality: Always emphasize that Native peoples are the same as other human beings across history who see a supernatural hand in suffering, misfortune, and death. The soul leaves a body in a terrible dream and the individual never wakes again. Evil spirits spread deadly diseases. Providential spirits inflict injury and death as punishment for witchcraft and other sacrilegious ways. Animal spirits bring famine as retaliation for dishonoring them. Ancestor spirits protect families from harm.

Hunter described the traditions and practices of Native healers in the ethnographic section of his book. He catalogued botanical and herbal remedies, including wild gentian for stomach ailments, anise for flatulence, milkweed for dysentery, hazel bark for ulcers, mayapple as a cathartic, and Indian turnip for asthma, along with myriad combinations of charcoal, black locust bark, beaver root, oak bark, prickly ash, sassafras, Seneca snakeroot, dogwood bark, and yellow root.[12] Like an ethnologist or anthropologist, he also provided insight into the cultural complexity of Native healing practices. Not all Indian tribes were the same. There were various kinds of healers in any tribe, including the priest, shaman, seer, midwife, and herbalist, each with their own specialty and training. On top of that, every tribe had developed their own variations of healing rites and practices, and each of those variations was bound up with distinct religious, cultural, and political traditions.

Not simply documenting healing practices, Hunter cleverly used his expertise as a healer to diagnose an ailing American nation. Too many people were suffering and dying because their physicians did not understand ailments and symptoms long known to Indian healers and arrogantly refused to learn from them. It was a "matter of great astonishment" to him the way physicians "had uniformly inculcated their own superior skill and excellence over those of the Indians in every moral and physical department." Their sense of superiority in relation to Native peoples was ruining the nation's health. By leveling this criticism, Hunter shrewdly interjected himself into a scholarly debate older than the nation itself, including distinguished intellects like Benjamin Franklin, John Bartram, Thomas Jefferson, Benjamin Rush, David Hosack, and many others. They agreed that America must free itself from its dependency on European ideas by developing its own branches of knowledge, and they knew that the astonishing biological diversity west of the Mississippi, which they were only beginning to understand, would be a rich source of new medicines and treatments.

But Hunter was calling attention to how the prevailing disregard and ignorance of Indigenous knowledge of the physical environment had set the nation back in its pursuit of true independence, politically and culturally, from Europe. Americans were harming themselves by being reluctant to learn from a people they viewed as primitive and on their way to extinction. A generation before, the radical idea that "all men are created equal" had rested on the premise that that even lowly Indians and African slaves were blessed with natural intelligence and therefore capable of improvement and intellectual achievements. In the thinking of the American revolutionaries, environment, not biology, explained the achievement gap between advanced and primitive peoples.[13] Once they changed the environment of Native peoples by restricting their hunting practices and moving them to an agricultural way of life, then Indians too could trudge up the ladder of progress and be assimilated into the nation.

This optimistic theory of human development did not last a generation. Native peoples everywhere naturally resisted the government's attempts to instruct them in "civilized life," which usually began with the demand they relinquish their lands and move out of the path of American settlers. The nation's growing impatience with the slowness of the pace of change grew into indignation during the War of 1812, when many Indian tribes joined the British. Many Americans believed that all their good faith and generous policies apparently had been for naught: The tribes seemed fixed in a state of savagery and incapable of improvement, let alone gratitude. After the war, dozens of treaties still expressed the "official hope," as the historian Reginald Horsman notes, that Native peoples finally would adopt white ways of living; for the purposes of governance, though, the hope in assimilation and universal human progress had withered away by the time Andrew Jackson assumed the presidency in 1829. The United States had concluded that Indian tribes were standing in the way of its destiny and must be removed west of the Mississippi.

Hunter's account of the complexity of Native healing practices was one of the ways he gave voice to the unfulfilled promise of the revolutionary movement. He was shockingly insistent on the equality of Native peoples and whites. He had been raised in Indian lodges and villages, and that environment had neither degraded him nor stunted his development. His Kansa and Osage families had cared for him, mentored him, and taught him the cardinal virtues. He liked to think that he had adopted many of their best qualities. He had demonstrated his physical and moral courage on many occasions. After entering American society, he learned how to read and write, thrived as a trapper and trader, developed into a scholar, and wrote an acclaimed book that was translated into three languages. In the polarizing climate of his day, there were bound to be questions and doubts about Hunter. Was he a real Indian captive? How did he improve himself so quickly, only a few years removed from his life with the Indian tribes? Was his book a hoax? To accept his story as authentic was to risk conceding that the popular belief in the inferiority of Native peoples was itself a hoax.

Hunter wrote under the burden of having to prove why living among the tribes and chasing the buffalo across the plains had not debased him and made him unfit for white civilization. In this effort, Hunter sounded truly Jeffersonian by suggesting that the fur trade, if properly regulated by a wise government, was the first step toward ushering the Indian tribes into the modern age.[14] An ethical trade theoretically offered fair prices, honest brokers, generous credit terms, and plenty of merchandise; as Indian tribes accumulated more debt with each passing season, they would become increasingly dependent on their American partners and guardians. Compounded debt was not a bug but a feature of the trade for Jeffersonians, producing a *beneficial* state of dependency that supposedly would propel Indian tribes to a higher stage of civilization. An ethical trade, encumbered by swelling debts, would inevitably force the tribes to sell their land and shift to settled farming. An ethical trade would create new desires that only the market economy could satisfy; breed respect for private property and the laws necessary to protect it; and provide opportunities for learning and religious uplift. Above all, an ethical trade promised to inculcate the principles of self-government and democracy among Indian tribes.

Hunter provided contrasting examples of the power of the fur trade to accomplish these goals. He had received an appalling education in tyranny under Manuel Lisa of the Missouri Fur Company. The keelboat was as brutal and oppressive as the factory floor or plantation field. Hunter and his Osage comrades labored on the lowest rung of the hierarchy, below the French Canadian and American hunters on three-year contracts, below even the greenhorns who had never stepped foot west of the Mississippi. A massive amount of manpower was required to move a fleet of keelboats, each on average sixty to seventy-five feet long and eighteen feet across the beam, up the Missouri.[15] Stories and rumors abounded of captains who were no better than overseers, driving and flogging the boatmen like slaves as they lumbered along the shore with the cordelle line, pulling the hulking vessels upriver for fifteen or twenty miles per day. When the cordelle could not be used, they sank their poles into the silty bottom and drove the boat against the current by walking single file from bow to stern. Deep water was a blessing, as then oars could be used, and occasionally a sail, billowing and magnificent. Moods quickly became sullen, and desertions were frequent, like the moment Hunter and his comrades, fed up with Lisa berating them to increase the pace of the voyage, walked away. As Hunter saw it, the company expedition, cursed by greed and ambition, could never instill in the men the virtues of a democratic civilization.

The next time he participated in the fur trade was at Flee's Settlement. This time he was not bound to an abusive captain of a St. Louis company. He was a private trader, known as a freeman, working in solidarity with other freemen from the settlement. The men made their own decisions, governed their own lives, and balanced their personal needs and desires with those of the group. Hunter was looked upon as an equal by the other men, who respected him and valued his experience. Here was the ideal training ground for a frontier democracy. The men followed Hunter back to his favorite hunting spot near his old camp, laying down their traplines along the river, and ultimately obtaining an "extraordinary quantity of valuable furs."[16] His pride in their success almost seems hypocritical for someone who condemned the slaughter of buffalo on the upper Missouri. However, it's important to note that they were a small outfit and their haul of furs was minuscule compared to the commercial expeditions, which his readers certainly understood. He did not oppose the fur trade in principle—it had dominated the region for over two centuries—but he condemned the scorched-earth tactics of the fur companies. In his experience, they pursued profit above everything else. They cheated the Indian tribes, pitted them against each other, and trapped them in debt. They poisoned them with liquor, desecrated their lands, and attacked their beliefs. In this earlier stage of capitalism, fur was what today is called a conflict resource, such as uranium, ivory, and blood diamonds, in which the extraction brings violence and death and tramples on the rights of the people. In Hunter's telling, democracy cannot take root in such a polluted environment.

In contrast, Hunter thrived with his collective of freemen and enjoyed the new life he was making for himself in America. He very nearly achieved Jefferson's vision of an ethical fur trade, but the next part of his story exposed the major flaw in that vision. Things began to unravel after the milestone of his first transaction as a freeman. After selling his share of the furs, he was approached by an elderly gentleman named Wyatt who wanted to offer some practical advice about managing his money. He advised Hunter to purchase a plot of land and give up hunting for a farming life. An investment in agriculture, Wyatt counseled him, was the "most certain, independent, and elevating in its results." Such advice might have come from Jefferson himself. Hunter might have ended his life story there, on the verge of becoming a farmer, if only he hadn't been fleeced at the trading house. He did not realize that he had been paid in counterfeit bills until after handing Wyatt $650 to make the purchase and then seeing the old man count out $28 in genuine currency on the table. He had been cheated out of six months of earnings. While skilled with his rifle and traplines, Hunter had no experience in spotting the counterfeit bills and banknotes that were a plague on the frontier.

Hunter's scene at the trading house boldly critiques Jefferson's misguided vision. At its root, the fur trade was corrupt and preyed on innocent people. Getting cheated infuriated Hunter and, in his words, "disgusted me more than ever with white people."[17] He should have known better. His Osage and Kansa families had "constantly inculcated on my mind . . . that fraud, cupidity, and perfidiousness, were indiscriminate traits in their character." He had learned from experience not to trust or believe white people, who were, with very few exceptions, devious and dishonorable. He expressed these feelings to Wyatt, one of those exceptions, who tried to calm him down by saying that his prejudice toward whites was unwarranted. Indians and whites were part of the same human family, and thus equally capable of doing good and evil. Wyatt said that the problem was that they were living on the edge of civilization, far away from republican society and government, where even white men hunted for their food and lived in the wild. Wyatt assured him that these white people were not the norm. As one traveled toward the east, the ratio between immoral and moral white people gradually flipped: "As you advance into the settlements the proportional number of such wicked people becomes very much diminished." Hunter remained unconvinced. He made up his mind to get away from them, and from America, as quickly as possible.

He set out the next morning for his boyhood village on the Kansas River. His route took him back along the Arkansas and up the White River to Flee's Settlement; he expected a happy reunion, but everyone was unnerved by the news of a Delaware massacre at a nearby settlement. According to Hunter, these Delawares had been relocated years earlier from Indiana and had been righteously defending what they saw as encroachments on their treaty land. When Hunter was asked why he was returning to the Kansas, the sordid story of getting swindled at the trading house spilled out of him, and he realized too late he had spoken too freely by airing his acrimony. As the settlers "became acquainted with my disposition towards the whites," they tightened their circle around him and admonished him that he would not be continuing his journey upriver. He was stunned. They questioned his loyalty and wondered openly why he had reappeared just as the Delawares were attacking their neighbors. Was his plan to return to the Kansas just a ruse for him to sneak over to the Delawares? They did not wait for an answer before rendering their judgment: "I was told, that my intended movement was of an unfriendly and hostile character; that I had now become an enemy to the white people, and was going to join their Indian foes." Suspecting of being a traitor to them, he must stay with them until the conflict was over.

Hunter was offended by the accusation of betrayal from the people who had given him a new start in life and made him believe that there was a place in America for someone like him. Why would he ever betray them? "Such an idea had never entered my mind," he wrote, "[and] this charge wrought my feelings up to a degree of excitement bordering on frenzy."[18] As if he needed more encouragement to get away from America, there was no way he was turning back now, but neither could he continue upriver. He was effectively their prisoner. He quickly regained his composure, telling them he was no traitor, that he had never stopped being a devoted friend to them, and thanking them for providing a refuge for him once again. He hoped his charade was convincing and would buy some time until he could safely escape.

CHAPTER SIX

Freeman

WHEN TWO TRAPPERS FROM MISSOURI ARRIVED in the settlement a short time later, Hunter saw his chance to get away without arousing suspicion. Their names were Tibbs and Warren, and they were looking for a local like him, someone who could lead them to the best locations for beaver and deer and steer them away from the Delawares and Cherokees. They passed the sweltering summer in a French hamlet on the St. Francis River, scouting the area in the mornings and sleeping away the afternoons. They hunted small game, began building a raft, and stacked firewood for the villagers. Hunter learned the alphabet from a rosary book, under the exacting eye of a matron who tried to convert him to Catholicism. As fall came, they set their traplines near several beaver lodges along the west fork of the river and finished building their raft.

Hunter's narrative skipped over the details of their fall hunt and instead focused on their success at the trading house in Natchez. His share came to $1,100, nearly double his earnings from the season before, which spoke not only to the fairness of Tibbs and Warren but also to his continuing education. He wasn't going to be cheated again. He studied the script and symbols on the notes, compared them against those of his partners, and counted and recounted the sum. When he was finally confident in the transaction, he deposited the money "for safekeeping in the hands of Doctor Sanderson, a very respectable physician of that place," which was a common practice before there were banks on every corner.[1] In these final pages of his life story, Hunter presents himself as a success story of a frontier democracy. He had fused the best qualities of his Indian upbringing with the virtues of American civilization. He had bettered himself and the lives of those around him. He had invested in his education and learned how to read, count, and handle his own money. He was principled, enterprising, and a productive citizen.[2]

He had entered a new world of freemen, boatmen, and other laborers who were also trying to pull themselves up by their bootstraps. He found work with Tibbs and Warren on a keelboat bound for New Orleans. When they landed there at the docks, Hunter walked along the levee and marveled at the hundreds of tall ships, keelboats, flatboats, barges, and rafts. He saw, for the first time in his life, a steamboat churning against the current; he looked up and down the levee in astonishment, but there were no gangs of men heaving against the cordelle lines, and he wondered if "invisible spirits" were moving the vessel upriver. As he followed a stream of people into the city, street hawkers stepped out from their stalls and greeted him as if they were old friends. He passed through a square and was knocked about by a crowd "in all the intermediate shades" of color between black and white, an observation that was already a hallmark of writing about New Orleans. Benjamin Latrobe, architect of the US Capitol, who was in town at the same time building the waterworks, recorded a similar impression of the city: "White men and women, & all hues of brown, & all classes of faces, from round Yankees, to drisly & lean Spaniards, black negroes & negresses, filthy Indians half naked, mulattoes, curly & straight-haired, quarteroons of all shades, long-haired & frizzled, the women dressed in the most flaring yellow & scarlet gowns, men capped & hatted."[3] Visitors commented frequently on the "astonishing diversity" of

New Orleans. Twenty years after becoming an American possession, the city was still largely French and Catholic, and too many of its 27,000 inhabitants did not seem quite white in the eyes of American visitors from the East.[4]

Like other visitors to New Orleans, Hunter was equally astonished by the vices and temptations that led many young men astray in the port city. He was clear that his morals were intact after sojourning in the city. He complained about the "intemperance and debauchery of the boatmen and sailors," who drank and gambled away their money in the "swamp" of Girod Street.[5] He, on the other hand, had walked a straighter path through the city. He spent his time in the civilized quarter above Canal Street, where his stories of growing up among the Indians won him some admirers among the leisure class and not a few patrons.

Their letters of introduction, which spread his renown through respectable society, secured him places in several schools. The first was in Cape Girardeau, Missouri, about 100 miles south of St. Louis, which was where he headed next. He left no clues about his route from New Orleans, but he traveled on foot with Tibbs and Warren along the Natchez Trace, which was the common trail for boatmen returning north. They walked along the muddy bottomlands of the Mississippi for several days until turning up a jagged trail into Choctaw and Chickasaw country. An agreement between those peoples and the United States had widened the trail into a wagon route between the Yazoo and Tombigbee Rivers, and there was a popular campsite outside a Chickasaw village for travelers to rest and eat before moving on their way. Several days later, northbound travelers reached the ferry crossing at the Tennessee River, operated by Chief George Colbert, or Tootemastubbe, hero of the Creek War and the War of 1812, and then crossed a rugged stretch of knobs and swamps all the way to Nashville. From there, travelers had the choice of several roads to all parts of the region, or they could take the Cumberland River to the Ohio and the ports of Paducah and Cairo.

Hunter broke off somewhere along the way and headed to Cape Girardeau. He appeared at the door of the school's headmaster, presented him with a letter of introduction from a mutual friend in New Orleans, and began the next stage of his education. It was, he said, "a respectable school, conducted by Mr. G. Simpson, a native, I believe, of the state of New York." He worked hard at his studies during the six-week term, "acquiring a rudimental knowledge of the English language," despite having to endure the bullying of the other students. They called him a dirty mongrel. They teased him incessantly. They made fun of his clothes and strange accent. He did not want to be expelled, and he did his very best to stay calm, but they probed for openings and eventually found his weak spot as one of them badgered the orphan with questions about who his parents were. He dropped his mask in a flash of anger and stood ready to fight all of them before they backed away, jeering and laughing at him. Every morning thereafter they called him by a different surname, every one of them a slur on the memories of his people, and he no longer turned the other cheek. "I never suffered them to go unnoticed" was his tactful way of alluding to the fights that ensued.

His teacher grew tired of the fighting and was on the verge of expelling him for always being at the center of the trouble. One student, whether out of kindness or frustration, took him aside to tell him the taunting might stop if he gave himself a proper name; that night, the comment left him awash in sorrow for all he had lost since leaving the Osages. Changing his name would feel like he was erasing his past and the essence of who he was. His name was sacred to him and his people. "While with the Indians," he emphasized again, "they had given me the name of Hunter, because of my expertness and success in the chase." His name literally translated as "hunter," as somebody skilled with the bow and rifle and in tracking game, but, as noted in Chapter 2, its meaning in Osage culture was more personal and complex than that. Whatever name he went by before, he did not say. Recall that he had not earned the adult name of Hunter until after riding off with a war party to avenge a Pawnee attack on their village's herd of horses and returning with a scalp. Afterward, in the victory celebration, Hunter was awarded the highest O-don for giving justice to his Osage sisters who had been tending the horses in the pasture at the time of the raid.[6]

He had been completely surprised by what came next. A procession of elders danced toward him and encircled him, singing his praises as a provider and a protector. Then one of them stepped forward to bestow the adult name that had come to him in his dreams. The naming ceremony was the most sacred of Osage ceremonies, particularly for an outsider like him, whose new name signified his rebirth as Osage. His name was woven into his identity, and expunging it threatened his very being: "I therefore determined on retaining that [Hunter] as my patronymic." However, he settled on a compromise. He adopted the forename of a local resident, John Dunn, who had taken an interest in him and treated him respectfully. Perhaps having his name might quiet the other students and keep him in school.[7]

When the term was over, he went up the Missouri to trade for furs, and an entrepreneur was born. In St. Louis, he traded his packs of furs for hemp and tobacco and then piloted his own flatboat to New Orleans. He joined the hundreds of vessels transporting lead and flour from Missouri, lumber from New York and Pennsylvania, threads and needles from Ohio, corn from Illinois and Indiana, tobacco, hemp, and whiskey from Kentucky, cotton bales from Tennessee, and furs from Michigan and Wisconsin.[8] He called to mind the intrepid American boatman of so many songs, paintings, and tales, the folk hero who tamed the river with each decisive sweep of his rudder, steering through rapids and past bobbing sawyers that wrecked many a boat and fortune. In an age of expansion and steam power, the boatman was already becoming a throwback to an earlier time of rugged individualism.[9] Landing in New Orleans, Hunter sold his tobacco and hemp "on advantageous terms," further evidence of his enterprising spirit, and invested in his future by purchasing a plot of land on the White River.

The end of his narrative purposively reads like a resume of the generous people who had helped him along the way. He was pleased to pay them "the homage of a public acknowledgment." However, he was also making a preemptive strike against the doubters who would inevitably question the truth of his story, and so he provided the names of individuals who could verify different parts of it. There was Philip Sublette, whom he met in the Missouri River town of Franklin in the fall of 1819. Sublette had followed Daniel Boone from Kentucky to Missouri, and he took Hunter to visit the "celebrated Col. Boone" at his cabin near the family saltworks west of town. We are left to wonder what things they talked about that afternoon.[10] Shortly after Hunter returned downriver, Boone passed away. "His memory will forever remain dear to me," Hunter stated.

Franklin was a busy river junction with over 1,000 people, where travelers stocked up for their journeys to the Rockies or, in a few years to come, to the Southwest over the Santa Fe Trail. Franklin was the sort of frontier outpost where Hunter and Manuel Lisa would not have been too surprised to cross paths again. Lisa, spotting him on the landing, recognized him instantly as the ringleader of the Osage and Kansa crew who had deserted his expedition a few years earlier. According to Hunter, Lisa tried to ruin his trading relationship with a group of Native peoples by accusing him of being a liar and thief, but his attacks did nothing to shake the confidence of Hunter's

Figure 6 "The Jolly Flatboatmen." Oil on canvas, by George Caleb Bingham, 1846. George Caleb Bingham's painting captures the spirit and camaraderie of young men, like Hunter, navigating their flatboats down the Mississippi and Missouri Rivers.
Source: Courtesy of the National Gallery of Art. https://www.nga.gov/collection/art-object-page.75206.html

partners. Suspicious of Lisa's motives, they evidently judged Hunter to be an honest broker and stood by him.

Hunter also had to account for the fact of his authorship of such a singular book. It should be remembered that there was no free public education in the United States during the early 1800s. Children who had the advantage of a formal education in private academies and colleges were largely from wealthy families; everyone else learned what they could at home or pursued other types of education, typically in church schools, apprenticeships, charity schools for the poor, and Sunday schools. Hunter pursued the same piecemeal education as so many of his contemporaries. When he took time away from school to work on the river, he read everything he could get his hands on. "During the recess of my school employments," he remarked, "I seldom went anywhere without a book," sounding much like a more famous flatboat pilot, Abraham Lincoln, who also was largely self-educated. So, too, was David Walker, a free Black man from Boston, who wrote in 1829 *An Appeal to the Coloured Citizens of the World,* which historian Daniel Walker Howe called the "most incendiary political pamphlet in America since Tom Paine's *Common Sense*."[11] Like so many of his largely self-educated contemporaries, Hunter read an enormous amount, and he enjoyed the advantage of having personal references that enabled him to borrow books from wealthy patrons: "I had access to some respectable libraries, and became literally infatuated with reading." With the aid of his teachers, he learned and absorbed information at a dizzying pace.

In the intervals between the hunting and trading seasons, he attended school and threw himself into his studies with singular determination. He documented his formal schooling as best he could because, as his friends had repeatedly warned him, some people would question his ability to write and reason. He estimated that his terms added up to about two and a half years. By comparison, the Pequot author William Apess, who wrote five books between 1829 and 1836, had around six winters of schooling and was also largely self-taught. Apess, too, came from humble beginnings, growing up in abject poverty in Rhode Island before the state eventually took custody of him and indentured him to several white families in New England. He learned how to read and write in their homes and at church schools. He joined the US military as a drummer boy in the War of 1812, experienced a religious awakening, and subsequently wrote the autobiography that certified him as a Methodist minister in 1829.[12]

Hunter's earnings from the river trade provided him with opportunities to invest in his education. In addition to studying with Madam Mashon on the St. Francis and with Mr. Simpson in Cape Girardeau, Hunter spent a six-week term, "in the autumn of 1821, at Mr. Samuel Wilson's academy, near Walnut Hills, Mercer County, Kentucky." Father Wilson was a Dominican friar from Belgium, with a reputation as a philosopher and theologian. Shortly after coming to Kentucky, he and his fellow priests founded St. Thomas Aquinas College, the first Catholic college west of the Appalachians.[13]

Much of Hunter's schooling took place at a seminary near the Pearl River in a western crook of Mississippi Territory, where he studied under Robert Currie, a "very respectable teacher," and his successor, John Lewis. He was nearly denied a place because of a bad first impression he had made on Currie. Hunter's experience in Cape Girardeau had taught him to be guarded and taciturn around the other students, and Currie was about to send him on his way when he received from Missouri a sterling letter of recommendation from Philip Sublette that changed his mind. With this friend of "highly respectable character and standing," who had introduced him to Daniel Boone, vouching for his character and ambition, Hunter was allowed to stay in school, and thus was saved from what would have been a difficult setback.

His narrative ends in this pragmatic way, with him corroborating his schooling and listing his teachers and references. The last word comes in the form of an important letter that he transcribed in its entirety. It was from George P. Watkins, the fur trader whom Hunter had saved from an Osage ambush three years earlier. They had run into each other in New Orleans in the spring of 1821, a serendipitous and emotional encounter Hunter remembered as "sincerely affecting to us both." The letter, Hunter explained, "alludes to the circumstances of my preserving him and his party from destruction by the Osage Indians, as previously detailed."[14] This letter was the only document in his possession from someone who saw him living with the Osages. It was invaluable testimony that Hunter hoped would satisfy anyone who was skeptical of his personal history.

The same impulse had motivated Watkins to write it. After Hunter left the city before Watkins could provide him with the letter, Watkins made inquiries about his journey and learned that Hunter was recuperating from an illness in Shawneetown, on the Illinois banks of the Ohio. The letter arrived as he was preparing for his departure for the East.[15] Watkins worried that without his letter, it would be even more difficult for Hunter to defend himself against the attacks on his intelligence and credibility that were sure to come. He promised Hunter that if and when it was necessary, he would also validate, in public, that Hunter had been living with the Osages and had saved his life: "I am willing to certify upon oath, at any time, if required, my delivery from inevitable destruction, by your timely and hazardous undertaking."[16] Both were prescient in sensing the potential value of the letter. Watkins wrote it fully expecting controversy; Hunter transcribed it in the hopes of averting controversy. The truth was that no letter, no further explanation, and no additional references were ever going to protect his reputation from the attacks leveled by his detractors.

In the final sentences of his autobiography, Hunter kept mum on how it might have felt for him to be back in Illinois, the land of his birth, where the Kickapoos had taken him from his family and later fled with him across the same prairies. That was in the past. In the grand American tradition of looking to the bright future, he only envisioned the man he was destined to become. He carried with him letters from, in his words, "some of the most respectable people in the Western States," who had instructed him to "journey eastwardly as far as Baltimore, Philadelphia, and New York."[17] Their letters would put him under the tutelage of teachers and philanthropists who would show him how to achieve his dreams, which he humorously noted was "nothing less than the subjugation of science and literature." His patrons told him that what he carried in his head, his knowledge of the land and peoples west of the Mississippi, was in high demand. He should plan to publish his life story. "With my mind thus filled with lofty expectations," Hunter wrote in conclusion, "I crossed the Alleghany Mountains, and, as it were, commenced a new existence."

PART II

A New Existence

CHAPTER SEVEN

White Indian

WE CAN THANK THOMAS JEFFERSON for clearing up Hunter's whereabouts after setting out from Kentucky on his eastward journey. There had always been rumors that he showed up on Jefferson's doorstep, but firsthand evidence of their meeting was missing until I discovered a letter from Jefferson to James Madison. Jefferson had dashed it off the afternoon of Hunter's visit and given it to him for delivery. "The person who hands you this letter is an interesting subject of curiosity," Jefferson wrote to his friend up the road at Montpelier:

> He was taken prisoner by the Kickapoos when he supposes he must have been about 3. or 4. years of age, knows not whence taken nor who were his parents. He escaped from the Indians at about 19. as he supposes, & about 7. years ago. He has applied himself to education, is a student of Medicine, & has assumed the name of Hunter as the translation of that given to him by the Indians. To a good degree of genius he adds great observation and correct character. He has been received with great courtesy at N. York & Philade. by the literati especially and also by the gens du monde. He has been long enough in this neighborhood to be much esteemed. He is setting out for the Medical lectures of Philade. & asked me to give him a

> letter to you which I do, satisfied that the enquiries you will make of him, and to which he will answer with great willingness will gratify you to the full worth of the intrusion. He has prepared a very interesting book for publication.

Jefferson certainly knew how to compose a persuasive letter of introduction. The bright and accomplished young man at Madison's door used to be an Indian captive. He had lived most of his life with them, but he had returned to America and received the blessings of progress and republican society. He was now studying medicine and would soon be a successful author. How could Madison not have wanted to sit down with such an extraordinary visitor?[1]

The letter is indispensable in filling in an eighteen-month gap in Hunter's life story. First off, Jefferson placed Hunter at Monticello in the fall of 1822, a full year *after* he was assumed to have stopped there for the first time. The timing is important because the letter reveals that Hunter had already achieved some fame as the white Indian, the eloquent survivor of captivity. He already had been received with high praise by the literati in New York and Philadelphia and by Jefferson's friends and colleagues in Virginia, where Hunter had been visiting for weeks, perhaps months, and making the rounds of dinners and parties. Jefferson had not decided to spend the afternoon with some unknown traveler who had stumbled to his doorstep. He welcomed the opportunity to meet with Hunter in his library and was more than happy to introduce him to Madison. Hunter carried with him a draft of his eagerly anticipated book, which Jefferson may have read or at least discussed with Hunter, because he described it to Madison as "very interesting."

Jefferson assured Madison that he would not regret opening his door to Hunter. A visit from this former captive of the Kickapoos was "well worth the intrusion." Jefferson wrote over

Figure 7 Thomas Jefferson, c. 1821. Oil on wood, by Gilbert Stuart. Known as the "Edgehill Portrait," this painting of Thomas Jefferson by the Rhode Island artist Gilbert Stuart was begun around 1805 and completed in 1821.
Source: Courtesy of the National Gallery of Art. https://www.nga.gov/collection/art-object-page.69391.html

20,000 letters during his lifetime. He seemed to really enjoy writing this one.

The letters of introduction in his satchel opened doors for Hunter, but what explained his rise to fame was the era's obsession with Native peoples and their histories. What made Hunter a phenomenon, however—an "interesting subject of curiosity," in Jefferson's understatement—was that he stood as an exception to an old rule in North America. White people who had lived among Native peoples were supposedly sullied by the experience and lost forever to respectable society. They were looked on with mixed feelings of fear, pity, and loathing. As Colin Calloway shows in his study of these pariah figures, generally they were considered even more degenerate and vicious than their Indian companions. But there were the few and unusual cases of white Indians who had "gone native" and survived without being corrupted by the experience.[2] Calloway specifically identifies Hunter and Daniel Boone as two white Indians who were not despised for crossing into the Native world. They had never forgotten their whiteness, lost their moral compass, or otherwise been degraded by living with the Indians.[3] Quite the opposite, in fact. These unusual men had acquired some of the best traits of the Indian's character. They were courageous, intensely jealous of their liberties, and completely at home in the American wilderness. They were role models for a frontier democracy that no longer needed to look to Europe for direction and inspiration.

Hunter arrived in New York in 1821 with a precious gift coveted by the leading lights in the city: the Indian's knowledge of plants and animals.[4] He came to the attention of the eminent physician and botanist David Hosack, who was known for mentoring gifted students from meager circumstances.[5] A child of the American Revolution, Hosack saw it as his patriotic duty to serve the common good. He was revered for bravely ministering to the sick and dying during the yellow fever epidemics of the late 1790s, which took the lives of thousands of New Yorkers. He taught botany at Columbia University and published groundbreaking papers on breast cancer, tetanus, obstetrics, and infectious diseases. His mission to establish the botanical laboratory called Elgin Garden nearly bankrupted him. He stood so far above the partisanship of the era that his close friends Aaron Burr and Alexander Hamilton agreed that he must serve as their attending physician at their duel. As a leader in several organizations, including the New-York Historical Society, the American Philosophical Society, the New York Horticulture Society, and the American Academy of Arts and Sciences, he dedicated his life to building the institutions necessary for a vibrant democratic society.

Much of what is known about Hunter during his time in New York comes from the scattered references to him in the correspondence among Hosack and his acquaintances. Hunter rubbed elbows with them at Hosack's celebrated Saturday gatherings. He exchanged ideas with Benjamin Silliman, the Yale geologist and founder of the *American Journal of Science*, who became a loyal supporter. He indulged the linguist and philosopher Peter Stephen DuPonceau by speaking Osage for him and answering his questions about vocabulary and syntax. Given his reason for being there, he probably compared notes on medicinal plants with the many physicians who were regulars at the gatherings and talked seeds and planting practices with the gardeners, nurserymen, seedsmen, and other members of the horticulture society.

Hosack's driving ambition was to create an American scientific community as independent as the nation itself. It was past time to break free from European standards and orthodoxies. Early in his medical career, Hosack had started researching and cataloguing the flora of North America, which he thought was an untapped source for new medicines and treatments. It was an idea, a fixation really, born out of his agonizing experience during the yellow fever pandemic of the late 1790s. Able to recite European theories and practices better than any physician in the city, he dispensed the standard cure of bloodletting and mercury purgatives, then stood helplessly at the bedsides of his suffering patients and watched them weaken, turn a ghastly yellow, and die. He was devastated and eventually rebelled against his European training. If the nation was going to survive and prosper, he believed, it must develop its own drugs and treatments from indigenous plants.[6]

He set out a vision of a magnificent garden that would ensure the health of the body politic. He modeled it after the private garden established in 1728 by the naturalist John Bartram on the west bank of the Schuylkill River just outside of Philadelphia, which Bartram's sons John and William had transformed into one of the largest collections of North American plant species in the world. Hosack believed the nation needed, in the words of Victoria Johnson, his biographer, "a new kind of garden—a botany classroom, chemical laboratory, apothecary shop, plant nursery horticulture school, and lovely landscape all rolled into one."[7] In 1801, he purchased twenty acres from the city, where Rockefeller Center sits today, and broke ground on his dream garden. Soon he was cultivating over a thousand species of indigenous plants from seeds sent to him by his contacts from around the country. He taught his students on the grounds. Together they researched the chemical properties of medicinal plants and created drugs and treatment protocols. He hosted visitors from around the world. A Hosack lecture at Elgin Garden was considered a must-see event in the city.

American scientists were every bit as obsessed with Native peoples and their knowledge of the land as their counterparts in the arts were. Across the Northeast during those years, physicians, botanists, and naturalists were following Hosack in researching the healing properties of indigenous plants.

Believing Native peoples held the secrets to this mysterious world, they pored over ethnographic studies and conducted field work with the Native healers. Their work culminated in 1820 with the publication of the first national pharmacopeia. Of the over 300 drugs listed in the *U.S. Pharmacopeia*, which included instructions for preparation and dosage, at least 200 were derived from roots, plants, and herbs commonly used in the botanical remedies of Native peoples. Its publication spurred widespread interest in Native healing practices, and by the next decade, all sorts of medicinal lotions, potions, pills, and powders were being marketed "under the banner of Indian healing."[8] Like the Indian tales and legends that captivated the public imagination, the *U.S. Pharmacopeia* also claimed the Indian in the wilderness as the source of a uniquely American identity.

John Dunn Hunter, widely respected for his knowledge of Native healing practices, seemed to have walked out of the pages of the *U.S. Pharmacopeia*. In the ethnographic section of his book, he documented fifty-five of these botanical remedies in all, most of which he knew from personal experience. Seneca root was an expectorant that alleviated respiratory problems. Goldenseal was used to treat digestive disorders, eye irritations, and skin problems. The oak tree's bark was the base for several antiseptic tonics. Black walnut was taken for colic, anise for flatulence, flax weed for asthma, and charcoal for indigestion. The salicylates found in the willow tree's bark made it an effective pain reliever. The bitter bark of the dogwood tree contained quinine substitutes and could be mixed with various plants and roots to lessen the effects of malaria.[9] The slippery elm's bark was added to concoctions to soothe sore throats and mucous membranes, but in a memorable aside, Hunter remarked that the bark was also the ultimate survival food when traveling through enemy territory.[10] His apology for laying out this "dry record of facts," as he called it, did not sit well with Richard Drinnon, who praised the deceptively modest chapter as "Hunter's monument to the intelligent concern of tribal peoples to lessen human distress and pain."[11]

Recall that Hunter had found his own calling as a healer in Flee's Settlement, where he resided for a short time after leaving the Osages. When a virus swept through the community, the French and American inhabitants asked if he would accept the responsibility of treating the sick. When he stammered that he was no healer, they brushed him off, reminding him that he came from the Osages, famous for their medicine, and he must have learned some of it. And it was true. He came from a place where everyone was schooled in medicinal flora and the treatment of illnesses, and he proudly noted that he successfully concocted a remedy that relieved their illness.

It would have been difficult for physicians to miss his veiled criticism of their profession. He implied they had much to learn from the practices of Native healers, who were in no way inferior to their white counterparts. In Hunter's experience, they were respected elders, were selflessly devoted to their people, and did not practice medicine in the name of vanity or in the "hope of gain." They rejected payment for "all their services, deprivations, and sufferings," other than the gift of a ceremonial robe or a special pair of moccasins. They bonded with their patients, patiently listening to them describe their ailments "with the most profound attention and silence." They stayed by their side day and night, heeded the slightest of changes in their breathing and color, and quieted their fears. Aware of common prejudices, he conceded there were sorcerers among the less advanced tribes, but Osage and Kansa healers were rational thinkers and showed sound judgment—he pointedly called them "Indian physicians." Their strength of character glowed in the darkest moments. He could still hear the awful cries of failure: the healer, unable to save their patients from death, would "cling to them till their last gasp" and plead to the Great Spirit for a better cure, as human beings have done from time immemorial.

During his time in New York, Hunter put himself at the vanguard of the American scientific and medical community, along with Hosack and the other intellectuals with whom he was mixing. He presented himself as both a curious student and an expert teacher who could instruct them in the practices of Native healers and in the astonishing biological diversity west of the Mississippi, which the Americans were only beginning to fathom.

Another glimpse of Hunter in New York comes from a lecture by Samuel Akerly, the superintendent of the New York Institution for the Instruction of the Deaf and Dumb. He began speaking that afternoon with an amusing anecdote about a curious visitor who kept turning up at the school for reasons he could not guess: "Mr. John D. Hunter, the white Indian who has been restored to civilized society."[12] Hunter, Akerly recounted, had stood quietly off to the side and watched the gestures of the students with that "apparent indifference peculiar to the Indians of this country." Fascinated by his visitor, Akerly had studied him just as closely from across the hall, wondering what exactly had captured his attention. Then one day the white Indian was gone, and Akerly had missed his opportunity to ask him.

That afternoon at the Lyceum of Natural History, Akerly used his encounter with Hunter as an entertaining introduction to his topic. At the time, what is now known as American Sign Language was in its infancy and heavily influenced by French gestures, vocabulary, and grammar; like their counterparts in science and medicine, deaf educators in America looked toward Native peoples in their effort to break free from the Old World.[13] For months Akerly had puzzled over Hunter's visits until the mystery was finally solved by the publication of the

Figure 8 David Hosack. An 1816 engraving based on oil paintings by Thomas Sully and John Trumbull.
Source: Courtesy of The Miriam and Ira D. Wallach Division of Art, Prints and Photographs: Print Collection, The New York Public Library. https://digitalcollections.nypl.org/items/510d47da-f86a-a3d9-e040-e00a18064a99

account of Stephen Long's expedition to the Rocky Mountains.[14] Long and his men had made a stunning discovery: a sign language that was the lingua franca of the many different peoples on the Great Plains. As Akerly read the incredible glossary of over 100 signs, he recalled the white Indian lost in study, gazing at his students, and suddenly Akerly "could explain his frequent visits" to the school. By God, Hunter could speak in this language of signs! He had not been merely gawking at the students, as Akerly had assumed. "His repeated calls at the school were the indications of a more than common interest," Akerly realized, "excited by seeing instruction imparted through the medium of signs, to those who could not hear."

It was an engaging opener for a lecture on the discovery of an Indigenous sign language. Akerly followed with a clever reversal that must have drawn smiles from his audience: the white Indian who had journeyed to his school in their city was a dead ringer, a double, for the explorers and travelers who had been studying Indigenous languages and customs for centuries. Setting down Long's glossary on the lectern, Akerly declared that their great republic had inherited more than land from the Indian tribes. He then pantomimed his favorite signs in the glossary—those for *truth, lie, lodge, man, woman, brother, sister, good, death, pretty, eating, drinking, sleeping, bison, fish, fool,* and *snake*—and, after pausing theatrically, announced that these Indian signs were "the same as those employed in the schools for the deaf and dumb." Even the many intricate variations in both sets of signs for *see—look, gaze, behold, stare, discover, view*—were alike. Akerly had solved the mystery of the white Indian's visits: He could not stay away from the school because he had discovered the etymological roots of their common language of signs.

One of the great debates of the era was about the origins of language. Akerly expressed a popular view that human expression began with physical gestures and evolved over time into oral languages, which gradually lost their authenticity and expressive freedom as they drifted away from their moorings in nature. Sign language was thought to be the remnant of a purer form of expression that existed before the advent of Western civilization and the development of linguistic processes. In their fieldwork, the members of the Long expedition had relied on a questionnaire about Indian vocabularies and grammars created for them by the American Philosophical Society, under the direction of Peter Stephen DuPonceau, the same linguist who had taken notes as Hunter spoke Osage for him at Hosack's gathering (and who later, after Hunter became a scandal, would backtrack and claim he had suspected all along Hunter was a fraud). Akerly praised the Long expedition for their spectacular findings. They had proven that the Native peoples they encountered were unique in human history: They had acquired the power of speech while never losing their original language of signs. They were the perfect model for the creation of an American sign language free from European corruptions.

When one is reconstructing the life of a marginalized person, a stray document can be as significant as a trove of state papers in the biography of a statesman. In addition to offering a rare sighting of Hunter in New York in 1822, Akerly's lecture suggests the presence of another language in Hunter's book that had been there all along but remained unseen for over two centuries until a perceptive scholar, Robert Gunn, found it. He combed through every page and discovered Hunter's references to three manual signs that had never been seen in print before 1824: the signs for passage of a day, a fierce wind, and hands aloft in an appeal to the Great Spirit. Gunn came to the groundbreaking conclusion that "Hunter's knowledge of PISL [Plains Indian Sign Language] could not have come from a printed source."[15] This discovery debunks the allegation made by his adversaries, and then repeated by historians, that he merely copied his ethnographic material from existing sources, including the James account of the Long expedition, which was published later that year. Furthermore, the new evidence of PISL in Hunter's narrative, hiding in plain sight for all these years, reveals the depth of his knowledge of Indigenous culture. Gunn found even more evidence in Hunter's writing. On their journey to the Pacific, Hunter's party encountered a group of people on the Platte River "with whom we were obliged to communicate wholly by signs."[16] After walking away from Manuel Lisa on the upper Missouri, Hunter and his Osage companions sought information from some English fur traders about the dangerous path ahead. "By signs," Hunter wrote, "we made them understand our apprehensions of the hostile Sioux, which were settled lower down, on the Missouri."[17] And there was the frantic warning of an ambush that he gave to Watkins: "My gestures and features spoke in a language not to be mistaken."[18]

Then there was the day when Tecumseh arrived in his Osage village and implored them, in a storm of words, signs, and gestures, to join his war against the whites. Hunter's transcription of the speech can still be found in history books (often without attribution of the source) as a rare record of Tecumseh's eloquence. Here is an excerpt from the fiery speech:

> *Brothers*—We are friends: we must assist each other to bear our burdens. The blood of many of our fathers and brothers has run like water on the ground, to satisfy the avarice of the white men. We, ourselves, are threatened with a great evil; nothing will pacify them but the destruction of all the red men.[19]
>
> . . .
>
> *Brothers*—My people are brave and numerous; but the white people are too strong for them alone. I wish you to

> take up the tomahawk with them. If we all unite, we will cause the rivers to stain the great waters with their blood.
>
> . . .
>
> *Brothers*—The Great Spirit is angry with our enemies; he speaks in thunder, and the earth swallows up villages, and drinks up the Mississippi. The great waters will cover their lowlands; their corn cannot grow; and the Great Spirit will sweep those who escape to the hills from the earth with his terrible breath.

Hunter confessed that the translation was lacking because words were inadequate to accurately transcribe something that was more of a performance than a speech. You had to watch Tecumseh in action, see his hand gestures and facial expressions, shudder at the sound of his exclamations, to truly feel his power. With only a pen, Hunter was resigned to the fact that he could never capture the electrifying physical performance he had witnessed that day. He could only sketch "the shadow of the substance" of the great warrior.[20]

In retrospect, these linguistic artifacts buried in Hunter's book help disprove the attacks on his identity. For instance, Lewis Cass claimed that this account of Tecumseh's visit to the Osages was yet more evidence of a hoax. It was very personal for Cass, who faced Tecumseh at Moraviantown in the battle that took the Shawnee's life. Cass was offended by Hunter's glorifying of an archenemy who had fought with the British during the war, butchered settlers, and obstructed the peace process.[21] Cass denounced Hunter's image of a gallant Tecumseh as a dangerous and unpatriotic falsehood. Determined to set the record straight, Cass examined every document in the War Department referring to Tecumseh. He studied every map of his movements before the war. He read every field report that might expose the hoax. In the end, Cass stated confidently that all the evidence supported him: "No Shawnese had, in 1812, ever visited the Osage as a friend, nor was Tecumthe ever within many hundred miles of a party of that nation."[22] This conclusion turned out to be untrue, but at the time, it served Cass's purpose of disputing Hunter's account of his Osage childhood.

Nearly two centuries passed before historians showed just how wrong Cass had been about Tecumseh.[23] John Sugden, in the best biography to date of Tecumseh, did not rely exclusively on War Department records. He drew from a wide range of sources, including the oral histories of Indian tribes and accounts from fur traders and travelers. It seems Tecumseh was very good at evading the surveillance of American officials. In his campaign to organize Indian tribes on both sides of the Mississippi, he had traveled far more widely than anyone had previously known, and it seems reasonable that he would have attempted to recruit the powerful Osages into the resistance. Sugden believed that it was very likely that Tecumseh's travels had taken him to Hunter's village, just as Hunter remembered it.[24]

CHAPTER EIGHT

Celebrity

WHEN WHALE OIL RESERVES were being quickly depleted in Philadelphia during the War of 1812, an inventor by the name of Edward Clark proposed lighting the streetlamps with tallow and old fat, but the city rejected the plan as too costly.[1] Clark was best known for inventing an ingenious contraption for moving a boat against the current. It was a special tow boat, fitted with paddle wheels, windlasses, and friction rollers, and anchored at the head of a rapids. The way it worked was that an approaching boat was attached to the tow boat, and as the tow boat's paddle wheels churned in the flow of the river, enough power was generated to pull the other boat upriver.[2] Clark claimed his invention would revolutionize commerce and travel, and at a far lower cost than turnpikes, canals, and steamboats. The *Port Folio* commended his "patriotic undertaking" for reflecting the "greatness of a nation" and its enterprising spirit.[3]

In 1822, when Clark wasn't working on his contraption or debating the best way to pump clean water into the city, he was helping Hunter prepare his manuscript for publication. In the opening pages, Hunter fully acknowledged his "ignorance of book-making" and expressed his gratitude to Clark for taking time away from his experiments to assist him. Clark's influence on the book will never be fully known, but there were rumors that he was the ghostwriter. How else to explain how someone raised by Indians could have written a work of such intelligence and merit? The rumors were demonstrably false, as we'll see, but they raised doubts about Hunter's authorship and his identity. There were no such doubts about the former captives Mary Jemison and John Tanner—they were illiterate and dictated their life stories to white editors, who then transformed their voices and experiences into as-told-to autobiographies for a mass audience. However, Hunter claimed to be the sole author of his work, with some editorial assistance from Clark, which gave his detractors an opening to accuse him of lacking the ability to write a book in coherent English.

The truth has always been hiding in plain sight. We can set aside for the time being the fact that Hunter wrote additional chapters the following year in London, in his room at Halloway House. In 1822, he was already the author of two articles in New York medical journals, which were never mentioned by Lewis Cass, so Hunter already had provided enough proof to any doubters that he could think and write on his own. Regarding his book, there were few, if any, signs of a heavy editorial hand. Not once did Clark intrude in the book to offer interpretations, corrections, or clarifications. He seems to have fulfilled the duties of a traditional editor by commenting on style, structure, and content; correcting grammar and punctuation; and, above all, making necessary changes while maintaining the originality of the author's voice. Clark and Hunter were often seen together in Philadelphia, and it remains a mystery why Clark, after seeing his friend attacked in the press, never stepped forward to defend Hunter's integrity.[4]

Hunter's book was published in Philadelphia in early 1823 with a long and scholastic title common to the era: *Manners and Customs of Several Indian Tribes Located West of the Mississippi; Including Some Account of the Soil, Climate, and Vegetable Productions, and the Indian Materia Medica: To Which Is Prefixed the History of the Author's Life During a Residence of Several Years Among Them.* The title appealed to a learned audience with an interest in natural history, geology, botany, and ethnography. The sensational part of Hunter's story, his Indian captivity, was relegated to the background with a plain reference to his "residence" among them. However, a London firm, seeing much wider appeal in Hunter's captivity, quickly published its own edition, giving it the more eye-catching title *Memoirs of a Captivity Among the Indians of North America, from Childhood to the Age of Nineteen: With Anecdotes Descriptive of Their Manners and Customs. To Which Is Added, Some Account of the Soil, Climate and Vegetable Productions of the Territory Westward of the Mississippi*. The book was an instant success. A second London edition was released later in 1823, and a third edition in 1824; German and Dutch editions followed that same year, and a Swedish edition two years later.

The reviews of the book were exhaustive, and enthusiastic about a new figure in American letters. Reading Hunter was an experience unlike any other, his "striking and singular" voice an unprecedented fusion of the Indian and the white man. According to a writer in London's *Monthly Review*, "in everything but his actual birth and parentage" this unusual white man was very much an "Indian, imbibing their feelings, practicing their manners, and living their life."[5] The Indigenous world he rendered so vividly might seem peculiar, perhaps even fictitious, but the consensus was that he drew from a deep well of personal experiences. "The internal marks of authenticity are so strong," concluded a writer in the *Eclectic Review*, "that we entertain no suspicion whatever of its substantial genuineness and accuracy."[6] After predicting that the book would be deemed a fake by some people, a reviewer in the *British Critic* praised its historical accuracy and reiterated that "we by no means intend to express any disbelief."[7]

A book by an unknown author, and about such a controversial subject, was bound to elicit questions about the role of the editor. A writer in London's *Quarterly Review*, after putting every line under scrutiny, finally determined there was "nothing suspicious in the composition of the narrative."[8] Quite the contrary. He had come away with a deeper appreciation of the way Hunter's "imperfect" understanding of English had created a distinctive voice: "The style is that of a man unaccustomed to write: not altogether free from embarrassments and vulgarism; but it is simple and precise, and in the story of his own adventures, warm, animated, and natural." For instance, whenever Hunter reminisced about the loved ones forever lost to him, his prose "abounds with beautiful and natural touches." At least in this writer's judgment, Edward Clark had been a superb choice for editor. He had clearly fixed the most egregious and embarrassing mistakes while letting stand many of the idiosyncrasies and thus preserving the authenticity of Hunter's voice.

The writer from the *Monthly Review* did not simply dismiss the rumors that Hunter was an "ingenious imposter." He pinpointed the bigotry that fed the rumors:

> It may well excite astonishment, indeed, that a person kidnapped in his infancy; torn away from all civilized society before he cold lisp his mother's tongue or articulate his mother's name; plunged into the deep forests of America by a tribe of savages, and learning no other than their barbarous and imperfect language; following for nearly twenty years the wandering life which they passed, roots and wild buffalo his food, and the skins of hunted animals his clothing;—it must excite astonishment, we say, that a person so brought should in the short space of a few years from his escape, have been able to compose a volume in the English language, in which terms of arts and science are frequently and appropriately used, and subjects relating to physics, morals, jurisprudence, natural history, commerce, manufactures, &c. are introduced as occasion requires.[9]

Hunter's accomplishment was astonishing, but that did not make it implausible. The reviewer appreciated how he had anticipated any doubts about his identity and truthfulness by listing the names and locations of his teachers and benefactors. The reviewer even included new details about how Hunter conducted himself in society. He had arrived in London with excellent letters of recommendation "from gentlemen of the highest character and station in the United States." Several friends of this writer were "well acquainted" with Hunter, who struck them as sincere, honest, and incapable of deception. They had not the "slightest doubt that he is exactly what he represents himself to be." Other writers who mixed with Hunter in London also spoke to his high character. The reviewer for London's *Literary Gazette* recalled the "pleasure" of debating Hunter about how to help the Indian tribes.[10] The reviewer for Philadelphia's *National Gazette* claimed to know Hunter well and vouched for him as a "person of uncommon intelligence and a lively sense of honour." He was an honest witness to history: "The intercourse which we ourselves have had with him has inspired us with the most favourable opinions of both his intellectual and moral character."[11]

It was the power and originality of Hunter's book that had so many reviewers raving. They compared it favorably to the leading works on the land and peoples west of the Mississippi, which ultimately put a target on his back. Those works included Henry Marie Brackenridge's *Views of Louisiana; Together with a Journal of a Voyage Up the Missouri River, in 1811*, which recounted his trip to the Mandan villages with Manuel Lisa of the Missouri Fur Company; John Bradbury's *Travels in the Interior of North America in the Years 1809, 1810, and 1811*, which included an account of traveling to the Pacific with William Hunt's expedition; Thomas Nuttal's *A Journal of Travels into the Arkansas Territory, During the Year 1819*, which detailed his botanical excursion along the Arkansas and Red Rivers; both

Henry Rowe Schoolcraft's *Narrative Journal of Travels Through the Northwestern Regions of the United States in the Year 1820*, which documented an expedition led by Lewis Cass, and his *Journal of a Tour into the Interior of Missouri and Arkansaw Performed in the Years 1818 and 1819*; and two books by members of Stephen Long's expeditions of 1819–20 and 1823, Edwin James's *Account of an Expedition from Pittsburgh to the Rocky Mountains Performed in the Years 1819, 1820* and William Keating's *Narrative of an Expedition to the Source of St. Peter's River.*

Hunter's book was judged by many to be far superior to these works. One reviewer applauded him for "offering incomparably the best account which we have ever seen of the Indian tribes."[12] His intimate view of Indigenous life made his book a landmark achievement in North American letters, and this was not just the opinion of British reviewers, far removed from the American frontier. In the *Cincinnati Literary Gazette*, an anonymous author claimed that Hunter was the historian and the poet that Native peoples were desperately in need of:

> The Indians of our country have never had an opportunity of describing themselves; they have had no historian to represent their own nation in the fairest light, to dignify their barbarities with the name of just and lawful vengeance on their enemies; to magnify the courage and deeds of their warriors, or celebrate the virtues of their sages. They have had no poet to bind the laurel and the brow of the hero, to represent rudeness as amiable simplicity; or by vivid description of the beauties of nature, to excite the respect we insensibly feel for the possessors of things beautiful.

With Hunter's arrival on the scene, a knowledgeable insider could finally depict Native peoples in a more edifying light. He shunned the worst stereotypes and prejudices about them, respected their beliefs, touted their achievements and resilience, cherished the wisdom of the elders, and documented their brave struggle to maintain their way of life in the face of an American invasion.

According to this prescient reviewer, Hunter represented a new way of writing and thinking about the history of Native peoples in North America. Dating back to early colonial times, the accounts of explorers, soldiers, settlers, clergymen, and captives glorified the clash between settlers and savages and created "the contemptuous light in which we are accustomed to regard the aborigines of our country." After all, the victors write the history, and the reviewer could not think of one nation or society that had ever been represented fairly and accurately by their enemies, "by men who had done them injustice, and felt the hatred that is felt towards those we have injured, and the contempt excited by manners widely different from our own."[13] Like any other victorious nation's, the American historical tradition was a thicket of resentment, confusion, distortions, and myths about the original occupants of the land. Americans had trouble recognizing Native peoples as fellow human beings because from a very early age, "we are taught to shudder with horror at the bare mention of their names." The reviewer concluded with an impassioned plea for what today is called discursive equity. Until that day when Native peoples seized the power of the pen as Hunter had just done, they would never change the ugly and false narratives about them: "Those who are so unfortunate as to be without literature are without the means of conciliating our friendship, or exciting our sympathy."

However, it was risky for any author to challenge, in even the most minor of ways, the false narratives about Native peoples. The mere act of depicting their humanity and their struggles under colonialism often made the authors targets of criticism and abuse. To be sure, this was especially true for Native authors, such as Samson Occom (Mohegan), William Apess (Pequot), David Cusick (Tuscarora), Elias Boudinot (Cherokee),

John Ross (Cherokee), George Copway (Ojibwe), Black Hawk (Sauk), and Peter Jones (Ojibwe), whose counternarratives were inherently subversive.

These authors lived and wrote in the precarious borderlands of North America—"contact zones," as anthropologist Mary Louise Pratt defines them, where "peoples geographically and historically separated come into contact with each other and establish ongoing relations, usually involving conditions of coercion, radical inequality, and intractable conflict."[14] Their autobiographies were the textual equivalent of contact zones, dynamic and disruptive, contesting unequal power relations, interjecting tribal histories into national discourse, and envisioning a future less defined by racial and ethnic absolutism.[15] As the reviewer in the *Cincinnati Literary Gazette* suggests, Hunter's anticolonialism also came from his experiences in the borderlands. By providing a history as he experienced it with the Kickapoos, Kansas, and Osages, Hunter challenged the dominant discourse of the Indian experts in the United States. If he was right about the missionaries who confused the respectful silence of the Osages for their conversion to Christianity, then how accurate were the reports on Indian tribes from soldiers, officials, company clerks, fur traders, and travelers? How accurate were their accounts of tribal rituals, customs, and beliefs? How reliable were their maps of Indigenous lands or their lexicons of Native languages? How well did they understand their political structures? Was it true that fur traders treated Indians fairly and discouraged the use of alcohol? Were American officials really revered by chiefs and warriors?

The high praise for Hunter's book was ultimately the kiss of death because it pitted him against the day's leading authorities on the Indian tribes. In addition to Governor Cass and Agent Schoolcraft, there was Major Stephen Long and his band of explorers. Even before they left St. Louis for the Rocky

Mountains in 1819, their expedition was being hailed as a milestone in the history of American progress and ingenuity. For the first time, a team of trained scientists was being deployed to the western frontier to gather information about the land and tribes. Thomas Say, the zoologist, doubled as the chief ethnologist. Titian Peale, the naturalist, sketched botanical specimens and wildlife. Samuel Seymour, the artist, drew landscapes and Indian pastimes. Edwin James, geologist and naturalist, collected mineral and plant samples. Their expeditionary account included the glossary of 100 signs and gestures, some of which, as mentioned earlier, Samuel Akerly had pantomimed for his audience at the New York Lyceum of Natural History.

The scientists and thinkers aboard the *Western Engineer* were led up the Missouri by 1,000 soldiers. Major Long, the West Point engineer, had designed the seventy-five-foot-long steamboat, with its unique stern paddle wheel, so that it could move through the Missouri River's notorious currents, snags, and shoals. Fearing hostile attacks from Indian warriors, he had fortified the pilot house in armor, mounted a cannon on the bow, and stationed howitzers port and starboard. He even thought of giving the vessel a menacing look. The figurehead of a massive black serpent appeared to rise out of the water, looming above the bow, its upturned mouth hissing and spewing steam into the air. It was the perfect symbol for their coercive diplomacy: the threat of force as an instrument of peacekeeping. The expeditionary flag, raised high above the scaly black serpent, sent the same message. As an observer on the St. Louis wharf commented in the *Missouri Gazette*, "The *Western Engineer* is well armed and carries an elegant flag representing a white man and an Indian shaking hands, the calumet of peace and the sword."[16]

When their account was published in early 1823, around the same time as Hunter's book, Long's expedition was widely criticized for failing to live up to its lofty promise. In comparison with Hunter, the best-and-brightest team of scientists and scholars looked like outsiders, far from their comfortable libraries back east. There were topographical blunders, defective instruments, missed landmarks, lost notebooks, a bogus theory of a Great American Desert, and an errant trip down what the explorers believed was the Red River only to later discover they were on the Canadian. A reviewer in *The Monthly Review* had initially praised the expedition's account but immediately repented after reading Hunter's book and being mesmerized by his intimate view of Indian life. After reading Hunter, the flaws in the expedition's account became glaringly obvious to the reviewer. For instance, Edwin James, who wrote the account of the expedition, claimed that the tribes they encountered were woefully "negligent of their old people, and indifferent to their deaths."[17] But this conclusion now seemed wrong, even absurd, considering Hunter's description of the reverence people felt for their elders, like the beloved Tshutchenau who entertained the Kansa children with stories and taught them how to live an honorable life.

In a stunning footnote, this same reviewer provided a rare glimpse of Hunter at several social gatherings, where he was questioned about whether it was true that Native peoples neglected their elders and felt nothing when they died. His response more than satisfied his interrogators:

> We find that Mr. Hunter has repeatedly assured his friends here in conversation, that the greatest possible reverence is paid to old age among all the tribes with which he is acquainted; and so far are they from being indifferent to the decease of those belonging to their tribe, that, if any engagement they find it impossible to bring away those who are killed, they will traverse immense distances, even after a lapse of years, if no earlier opportunity occurs, for the purpose of exhuming their slaughtered warriors, and of bringing them to their native territories for burial.[18]

It must have required a great deal of patience and goodwill for Hunter to answer their questions. (It's the only instance I have found of Hunter engaged in debate in a social setting.) The gentlemen arrogantly wanted him to reassure them of the simple truth that Native peoples were human beings just like them and not ignorant and unfeeling savages. Hunter, apparently sounding as calm as he could possibly be, simply told them that Native peoples were the same as anyone else in cherishing their elders and honoring their memories. The reviewer hoped that his anecdote would set the record straight.

Native peoples had been traveling to Britain as envoys, dignitaries, curiosities, and slaves for centuries. Manteo, the Croatan chief who aided the Roanoke colony, came to London to meet with Sir Walter Raleigh in 1584. Pocahontas, accompanied by a Powhatan delegation, was presented to the royal court in 1617. Tisquantum, also known as Squanto, arrived in London around the same time; several years after being captured on Cape Cod by an English explorer and sold into slavery in Spain, he was trying to obtain passage home to his Patuxet people. There were several diplomatic missions to Britain during the eighteenth century, none more celebrated than the "four Indian Kings" from the Iroquois nations who delivered a wampum belt to Queen Anne at St. James Palace in 1710. A stream of ballads, chapbooks, broadsides, and paintings reported on their sojourn in London. They enjoyed a performance of *Macbeth,* took a more lowbrow excursion to the cockfights, and visited with the paupers at a workhouse. Samson Occom, the Mohegan minister and one of the first Native authors, traveled to England in 1786 to raise money for an Indian school. His charismatic preaching drew large crowds and large donations. (Once back home, his white partners, without his knowledge, ignored his plan and instead used the funds to establish Dartmouth College.)[19]

Figure 9 "War Dance in the Interiour of a Konza Lodge." Cephas Grier Childs, engraver, and Samuel Seymour, 1822. The artist Samuel Seymour documents the scene of Kansa Indians dancing inside their lodge, as the members of Major Long's exploring expedition watch from the perimeter.
Source: Courtesy of the Library of Congress. https://www.loc.gov/item/2007683612/

In 1804, John Norton, a Mohawk chief and the son of a Cherokee father and a Scottish mother, had traveled to London to obtain the land deeds promised to the Iroquois for fighting with the British during the American Revolution. Norton, also known as Teyoninhokarawen, was educated, cultured, and refined, disappointingly so for British aristocrats, who wondered if he was not too educated, too cultured, and too refined to be an authentic Indian, sparking rumors that Norton might be an imposter. The doubters in Britain were unacquainted with the cultural mingling in North American contact zones, where, as Fulford notes, "cross-cultural partnerships and mixed-race children were not uncommon."[20] Because he was in England to attain the promised land deeds, it was politically necessary for Norton to satisfy the Romantic expectations of the British by playing the part of a "real" Indian, and so he often broke out into an entertaining war dance at his lectures and let out chilling war cries in posh parlors.

In the spring of 1823, John Dunn Hunter, the Indian captive, was the latest curiosity from the New World to appear in Britain. Like his precursors, he would be presented at the royal court, invited as an honored guest to lavish parties at country manors, summoned to the coffeehouses for debates, and introduced to men of rank. Britons were fascinated by the white Indian. Being raised so close to nature and so far from the vices of modern civilization seemed to have given Hunter an innate sense of gentility and honor. This was the age of British Romanticism, after all, and he had come to the metropolis of London from the wilderness of America.[21] Representing the best virtues of white and Indian worlds, Hunter bore a marked resemblance to the noble savage in the poetry of Wordsworth, Coleridge, Southey, and Heman.

During his little more than a year in London, Hunter resided at Mary Halloway's boardinghouse, located in Charing Cross. Her house was popular with American authors. Washington Irving had written *The Sketch Book of Geoffrey Crayon* in the drafty ground-floor apartment.[22] John Neal, the novelist who ultimately turned against Hunter, and whose story is yet to come, took up residence in Irving's old apartment a few months after Hunter's arrival. Hunter shared an upstairs room with Elias Norgate, an amiable twenty-five-year-old from outside of Norwich. They were kindred spirits and became fast friends. They explored the city, took their meals together, attended parties, and read together by candlelight. Hunter spent the holidays at Elias's family estate in Norfolk. The elder

Norgate was a gentleman farmer and horticulturalist, and he contributed regularly to the journals that reviewed Hunter's book. He probably enjoyed getting to know the exotic American who had caused such excitement in London.

Shortly after Hunter's arrival in London, a procession of callers began inquiring for him at the house at 7 Warwick Street. One was an anonymous acquaintance from America, probably from in or around New Orleans, who reported on his visit in a letter to the *Natchitoches Courier*. Upon entering the main vestibule, he was stunned to see all the cards for Hunter left by well-to-do callers: "His card rack was crowded with notes and cards, from persons of the highest distinction."[23] A quick perusal indicated that Hunter was recovering from a shoulder injury and had been very well looked after: "I saw one of two very sentimental notes of condolence from the Duke of Sussex to Hunter while the latter was confined to his room, by a dislocated shoulder: which, by the way, was attended to, in behalf of the Duke, by his surgeon, Dr. Petingale." Hunter's standing was such that the Duke of Sussex himself—Prince August Frederick, the son of King George III—had ordered that he be given the royal treatment. The curious visitor also noted that Hunter was sought after as a dinner guest by an intellectual circle, which included the eminent botanist James Smith and the horticulturalist Joseph Sabine, two fellows of the Royal Society. Also taking notice of the stir created by his countryman was the US ambassador, Richard Rush. After inviting Hunter to several gatherings at his residence in the West End, Rush presented him to King George IV and his court as part of his effort to improve diplomatic relations.[24]

It was during the spring and summer of 1823 that Hunter first emerged as a public figure. Reports of him could not agree on what he looked like. He was described as either short of stature, swarthy, scrawny, and not very handsome or as middle-sized, fair-skinned, athletic, and very handsome. The only surviving picture of Hunter was drawn by the English painter Charles Leslie, an acquaintance from Rush's gatherings. Preserved as the frontispiece in the London edition of Hunter's book, the picture shows an attractive young man with a cleft chin, straight nose, full lips, and charcoal eyes. He is well dressed in a waistcoat with a fashionable cravat around his neck, but the white Indian does not look like an ordinary gentleman. His skin tone is darker than that of the average Englishman, and his dark hair is slicked into what appears to be a mohawk coiffure, a stylistic insignia of his Indianness. He does not gaze directly at the artist. He looks past him with a pensive expression.

There was general agreement about Hunter's personality. He was as serious as a Puritan minister on the Sabbath. He was reserved, often listening intently and saying very little, until the subject turned to the Indian tribes of North America, at which point memories flooded out of him. He was modest and uninterested in fame and fortune. He was an idealist with a dream of helping the Quapaws in Arkansas stay on their land and stave off removal, and he was single-minded in the pursuit of it. He studied the latest agricultural methods and traveled to experimental farms around Britain. He was also very shrewd, refusing offers of gifts so that he wouldn't give anyone a reason to question his motives. He was aware of the long history of fraudsters and charlatans who suddenly appeared in London proclaiming to be African princesses, Indian chiefs, and rulers of foreign kingdoms.

Hunter made other important friendships at Rush's residence in the West End. One that merits special attention was his relationship with an up-and-coming American artist named Chester Harding. Born into poverty in Massachusetts in 1792, Harding was the son of an inventor who could not put enough food on the table for his twelve children. When Harding turned fourteen, the family sought a fresh start on the western frontier of New York. He remembered thinking, as his body ached from clearing the forest for their patch of crops, that there must be an "easier way of making a living." He followed his brother Horace into chairmaking for a spell, then tried cabinetry and drum making, but the trades did not suit him. One day in 1815, Caroline Woodruff in a dark crimson dress took his breath away and he "fell in love at first sight." They married three months later and before long were blessed with a child, but he could not support his family with his earnings from managing the local tavern. Small loans to get by grew into a mountain of debt.

They were soon fleeing down the Allegheny River to escape the creditors who threatened him with jail. In Pittsburgh, Harding did odd jobs, earning money as a house painter, as a busker with his clarinet, and with a tightrope dancer for a partner, but the money was never enough to keep his family from going hungry. At his lowest point, he borrowed money for brushes and stencils and tried his hand at sign painting. When he received payment for his first sign in gold leaf letters, he threw the bills into Caroline's lap, and they rejoiced at their good fortune. Skilled with the brush, he enjoyed a steady income for the first time in his life, but as fate would have it, he saw the portraits of a local artist in a shop window and tired instantly of his stencils. He persuaded Caroline to sit for him, began sketching her face in charcoal on a discarded board, and then added hints of crimson to her cheeks and shades of brown to her hair. As her beautiful likeness emerged on the board, Harding could hardly control himself, and he became "frantic with delight," staring in disbelief at what his hands had done. He took his first client, a kindly baker, who paid $5 for a portrait of himself. His third client, his landlord, accepted a portrait as payment for their overdue rent. Harding had found his calling.

It just so happened that Harding's brother Horace, the chairmaker, had also taken up portrait painting. He had a

Figure 10 Caroline Woodruff (Mrs. Chester Harding). Chester Harding's drawing of Caroline Woodruff, the woman who stole his heart at first sight. When her family moved away after their brief encounter, Harding could not stop thinking about her and did the only sensible thing—he set out on foot, walking fifty miles to find her, and proposed as soon as he did.
Source: From *A Sketch of Chester Harding, Artist, Drawn by His Own Hand,* 1890. https://archive.org/details/sketchofchesterh00hard/page/n50/mode/1up

flourishing studio in Paris, Kentucky, a morning's carriage ride from Lexington, and wrote to his brother that he could not keep up with the demand. Harding sold off the family's belongings and purchased an old keelboat that carried him and his family down the Ohio to the Limestone junction. In Paris, he was an instant success, a better painter than he had even imagined; by year's end, he had completed nearly 100 portraits at $25 a head. Never again would he have to plead with the butcher for scraps. They lived comfortably in Paris. "Here it was that I mingled for the first time in 'tip top' society," he recalled, with a tinge of guilt about adopting the local custom of taking a bourbon julep or two before breakfast. But there were only so many portraits to paint in Paris and Lexington. When business slowed, he pawned his wife's favorite gold watch and their silver spoons and booked steamboat passage to St. Louis.

In St. Louis, after Governor William Clark sat for a portrait, a line of clients began greeting him outside his studio door. One session was interrupted by the governor, who had brought a delegation of Osage chiefs to see his portrait. One of the chiefs, riveted by the likeness to Clark, insisted on having his portrait done. Not long after this Daniel Boone sat for him in his cabin just before he died. His career could not have gotten off to a more promising start. Harding was supremely confident of his talent—"I already painted better pictures than any artist in this country, and probably better than any in Europe"—but his lack of formal training nagged at him. He came up with a plan to go to England to hone his craft. He moved his family back to western New York, making sure to pay off the creditors who had given him up for dead, and then he headed to Boston to open a studio to raise funds for his trip. He made a handsome sum of money, doggedly painting eighty portraits in six months, and sailed to England in the summer of 1823.

He was welcomed into the London art world and joined the weekly processions of artists to exhibitions, museums, and private collections. Charles Leslie, who had drawn Hunter's portrait, was their guide. They discussed artistic techniques and debated the relative greatness of the masters. Of all the painters they were studying, Harding's favorite was the Flemish artist Anthony Van Dyck, whose mesmerizing portraits, with their incredible silver hues and precise features, were more beautiful than any work Harding had seen by Rembrandt, Titian, or Rubens (whom he judged to be overrated). Harding practiced what he was learning back in his studio.

Harding and Hunter grew close during these heady days. It aggravated Harding how some of their countrymen joked about Hunter behind his back, mocking him as a novelty act. He thought they were simply envious of what they lacked. In his journal, Harding expressed his admiration for his friend:

> I am often vexed to hear the Americans abuse Mr. Hunter in the manner they do. I have spent much time in his company, and I think him one of the most remarkable men I ever knew. His opinions of men and things are entirely natural, free from the errors and prejudices that a conventional education is liable to give. . . . His society is courted by the great, partly, no doubt, because he is a wonder; but the very thing that makes him wonderful is that which reflects his greatest honor. I think him an honor to the country that claims him, and I am happy to find that he is devotedly attached to that country.[25]

Harding and Hunter were perfectly matched as friends. They shared a similar background, education, and outlook. They had lived in Kentucky and Missouri around the same time, traveled over the same roads and rivers, knew the same landmarks, and stopped at the same ports, villages, and cities. And, of course, each of them had sat with Daniel Boone in his cabin. They were self-educated and had used their wits and talents to pull themselves out of poverty. They had captured the imagination of the British public as twin wonders from the American frontier.

Harding was grateful to Hunter and credited him with his help in making him a success. It was Hunter who had looked out for his friend by introducing him to the Duke of Sussex at Kensington Palace. There was no greater distinction for an artist in Britain than painting a member of the royal family. "For this honor," Harding wrote in his journal, "I am indebted to my friend Hunter." After word spread, Harding suddenly had many sittings in his studio, including commissions by prominent friends of Hunter's—Thomas Coke, Archibald Hamilton, and Robert Owen.[26] By some accounts, the finest portrait he ever painted was of Hunter, which the Duke of Sussex had commissioned. A decade later, the duke showed it off to George Catlin, the American artist whose gallery of Indian paintings was drawing raves in London. As they gazed up at Hunter's portrait at Kensington Palace, Catlin might have shared his reminiscence about an earlier encounter on the Great Plains with some Osages who fondly remembered Hunter as one of their own. After the spendthrift duke passed away, his choicest possessions, including his prized portrait of Hunter, were sold off to cover his substantial debts. The portrait went missing and has never been found.

I like to think Chester Harding repaid his debt to Hunter by documenting their time together. In the journal he kept for his family, there is the rare sighting of Hunter in a private moment with a friend. It was a ramble on a bright spring day, one of Harding's favorite memories of London. Delighted to see and feel the sun shining down on them, they roamed through the streets, weaving through throngs of pedestrians and around coal wagons pulled by massive draught horses, and eventually found themselves in the colorful gardens of Kensington Palace. They called on the duke, enjoyed tea together on the terrace, and continued their ramble to the Thames. Hearing the wherryman's bellow at Waterloo Bridge, they were inspired to rush aboard the boat and go wherever the evening might lead them:

Figure 11 Self-Portrait. Oil on canvas, Chester Harding. Chester Harding began painting this self-portrait around the time when he and Hunter were becoming close friends in London.
Source: Courtesy of the National Gallery of Art. https://www.nga.gov/collection/art-object-page.34102.html

On the Thames we had a most beautiful view of the city. The sun was just setting, but still shone bright up on St. Paul's stupendous dome, and some of the prominent points of the city, such as Somerset House, the Adelphi, etc.; and, as we floated along under the several bridges,

> concluded it would be many years before our country could boast such monuments of art.

The artist framed the picturesque scene: the sun setting, its rays vanishing but still touching "St. Paul's stupendous dome," a pantheon of the empire's monuments. As the wherry crept toward Iron Bridge, they compared England and America and gave many compliments to "the land of our birth," which Harding did not elaborate. They talked about what the future might have in store for them. The self-professed best painter in America envisioned himself leading an artistic renaissance back home. He left no hint in his journal about what his friend may have been contemplating as they floated along the Thames. Hunter would soon be leaving for Arkansas with a plan for helping the Quapaws hold on to their land, and he may have been anxiously wondering if he was too late.

CHAPTER NINE

Dreamers

HUNTER HAD ARRIVED in London as a novelty, but the white Indian was soon known and respected for his plan to help the Quapaws of Arkansas transition to settled farming.[1] His personal story gave him credibility as someone with insight into how to bring about social change among Indian tribes. The New England Company, the oldest missionary organization in England, turned to him for advice in turning around its failing settlements in eastern Canada. That summer, in his upstairs room at Halloway House, he put his plan into writing for the board. He described how, after immersing himself in the study of agriculture, he would return to Arkansas to build a model farm on his land along the White River. He imagined his farm shining like a beacon of hope to the nearby Quapaws, many of whom had already started their new lives as farmers. They were led by a "brave and manly chief," whom Hunter knew personally and clearly admired: "He is a man of talent: His glory is fallen, but his spirit not sunk; his lofty mind, still elastic, rises under pressure, and lifts him above the frowns of misfortune. His influence is felt beyond the little remnant of his tribe, and is felt by the neighboring whites." Although Hunter does not name the chief, it was most likely either Heckaton or Saracen, who were the principal chiefs of the Quapaws and whom Hunter appears to have known during his time in Arkansas. As Hunter imagined it, the chief and his people would visit his farm, smoke a pipe with him in his comfortable house, and inquire about his methods and tools. He would take them to see the plow horses in the stables and the fat cattle in his pastures. He would walk with them down the irrigation furrows and share the agricultural principles he had studied in England.[2]

Hunter was responding to an unfolding catastrophe across the Mississippi in the new federal territory of Arkansas. Public pressure was building to seize the land of an estimated 600 Quapaws and remove them from the valley. In 1818, when Hunter had last been there, Quapaw chiefs had agreed to a lopsided deal with William Clark and the United States. They ceded nearly all of Arkansas south of the Arkansas River and most of present-day southern Oklahoma in exchange for hunting rights on those lands, a sizable annuity, and a strip of land along the river where their villages were located.[3] Their only hope of keeping their land depended on how quickly they adapted to the American nation closing in around them, a change that must, by a de facto government mandate, begin with them giving up their hunting grounds and taking up farming like the Americans.

The Quapaws intended to follow the example of the Cherokees, their neighbors, who had been migrating west for many years. The Cherokees were held up as a success story of the government's policy of "civilizing" Indian tribes. Their farms, orchards, and fenced pastures stretched along both banks of the Arkansas, above the pine bluffs, and along its northern tributaries. Like their relatives in Georgia, their farms were prosperous, their children healthy and strong, and their houses handsomely furnished. They liked to add Western accessories to their traditional style of dress. They were learning how to read and write. On his research trip up the Arkansas in 1819, the botanist Thomas Nuttal was both stunned and pleasantly surprised to see the Cherokees making such a "happy approach to civilization."[4] Their future looked bright, particularly since larger groups of Cherokees were trickling in from Georgia.

This transition to settled agriculture was also happening in other Native communities across North America, none more successful than the Shawnees in western Ohio. In their village of Wapakoneta, around 500 Shawnees had chosen to stay and fight peacefully for their land rights rather than follow Tecumseh to Indiana and join the resistance against the Americans. After losing nearly all their territory in the Treaty of Greenville (1795) and then watching helplessly as hundreds of thousands of white settlers spread into Ohio over the next twenty years, the Shawnees who remained behind were determined to do whatever it took to retain the last vestige of their land. On several occasions, Chief Black Hoof, or Catahecassa, traveled to Washington to meet with officials and negotiate for more tools, seeds, and assistance. His people modified their traditional farming practices by planting potatoes, turnips, and cabbages along with their staples of corn, beans, and squash. The men began hunting less and working more often in the fields with the women. They plowed furrows behind Pennsylvania workhorses, raised pigs and cattle, and cultivated apple and pear orchards. The Shawnees kept their communal fields, but they were also fencing off acres for family farms. They constructed and operated a sawmill with the help of a Quaker farmer. They lived in cabins, drove coaches, and began wearing articles of Western clothing.

Another Quaker neighbor expressed amazement at how the Shawnees seemed less Indian after exchanging "their Indian way of life for the life of a white man."[5] It was, and is, a mistaken belief endemic to settler societies. Black Hoof and his people had not abandoned their culture after supposedly experiencing some epiphany about a superior civilization. Like Indigenous peoples across history, they had not suddenly become less Shawnee because they were shrewdly borrowing

Figure 12 "Ca-Ta-He-Cas-Sa-Black Hoof, Principal Chief of the Shawanoes. Drawn, printed & coloured at I. T. Bowen's Lithographic Establishment." United States, 1838. After the passage of the Indian Removal Act in 1830, President Andrew Jackson pressured Shawnee leaders to cede their remaining lands and move their people west. Chief Black Hoof steadfastly refused to sign any removal treaty. He stayed behind in Wapakoneta and died in early 1832.
Source: Courtesy of the Library of Congress. https://www.loc.gov/item/95502230/

from and compromising with the newcomers surrounding them. By taking this path, they had not disavowed their beliefs, language, ceremonies, or ancestors. According to the historian Colin Calloway, Wapakoneta was like other reservations that would soon appear across the United States: "cultural refuges, places where Indian ways persisted and Indian communal values survived." Their culture was under constant attack from the Americans, but even as settlers, speculators, and missionaries cut through Wapakoneta like clouds of locusts, the Shawnees never lost the sense of who they were: "Despite the efforts to change them completely, reservation communities like Wapakoneta remained islands of Indianness within a sea of white American life."[6]

Hunter did not present himself as a white savior who would rescue a vanishing tribe from destruction. Rather, he saw a role for himself as someone knowledgeable about Native life who could assist the Quapaws in a transition to settled agriculture already underway. Farming in the manner of American settlers was the key to the same strategy—survival by adaptation—that had proven so successful for the Shawnees and Cherokees, as well as many other groups of Native peoples across North America. The Mohawk chief Joseph Brant, who himself had traveled to London in 1786, pursued a similar strategy for the Six Nations Confederacy; it was Brant who sent John Norton, another Mohawk chief, to Britain to obtain a land grant so they could adopt white agriculture and protect themselves against settler encroachments.[7] This context of survival by adaptation is essential to clarifying Hunter's misunderstood motives: he never advocated for the sort of "civilizing mission" idealized by many Americans, whereby a total conversion to white society erases every trace of Indianness. Rather, his plan for helping the Quapaws followed the strategy of the Shawnees, Cherokees, Creeks, Choctaws, Mohawks, and many other tribes. The nonnegotiable element in their strategy was that Native sovereignty and land rights were sacrosanct and must be protected from violation. Hunter did not propose any role for white people in his imagined community of Quapaw farmers because his experience had shown him how white people abused these rights. His plan did not call on missionaries to convert the Quapaws, on creditors to leverage them, or on officials to oversee them. Nor did his plan separate children from their families and force them to labor as indentured servants, which the New England Company was doing in Canada, or compel them to reside at a boarding school and to labor in the fields, which was happening, with the consent of the Cherokees, at the new Dwight Mission in Arkansas. He had come to England to prepare himself for his mission.

❖ ❖ ❖

He found an important mentor in Robert Owen, the socialist reformer and one of the most famous individuals in all of Europe. Born into a laboring family in Wales in 1771, he was ten years old when he was sent away to work for a linen draper in England. He first learned the trade by delivering yards of cloth to seamstresses and tailors, then eventually graduated to rolling out and cutting linens, wools, and silks for the fashionable women who frequented the shop. When he was nineteen and had at last had enough of his lot as a draper, he took out a loan and started his own business making clothes. He instantly turned a profit, and before long he moved up to managing a spinning factory in Manchester. He grew rich, carried along by the tide of the cotton boom, but he was disturbed by the wretched working and living conditions of the mill workers. They were poor, gaunt, and crowded into filthy slums and barracks. Far too many were women and children. They labored for twelve or fourteen hours a day on a factory floor as dangerous as any coal mine or whaling vessel. The pounding shuttles mangled their limbs, the loud machinery damaged their hearing, and infections and illnesses ruined them. He was troubled by the thought of their misery nurturing his growing fortune. He worked out his feelings of guilt and responsibility at the Manchester Philosophical Society, reading Jean-Jacques Rousseau, Jeremy Bentham, and Adam Smith, attending lectures on the free market and moral philosophy, and debating theories of government and social organization. He thought there might be a more humane way to organize society. As he made up for the education he had lost after being sent away as a boy, he developed his core belief that human potential had not been preordained at birth. Every individual was indelibly shaped by their environment. He filled his notebook with ideas for a social revolution that he aimed to launch in the lives of his workers.[8]

A fortunate marriage in 1799 to Caroline Dale, whose father was open to selling his textile operation in Scotland, gave Owen the opportunity to pursue his vision. Along with several investors, Owen purchased the New Lanark complex and began revolutionizing the industry that had made him and his partners rich and powerful. He immediately banned the practice of hiring orphans from poorhouses. He established an eight-hour workday and created safer working conditions. He set up an insurance fund for sick and injured workers. He built sanitary housing for 1,500 people, opened a free medical clinic and a daycare, and prohibited corporal punishment. He barred the company store from gouging workers for coal and food. He provided gardens where workers could get outside, enjoy the fresh air, and cultivate potatoes, turnips, carrots, squash, beetroot, tomatoes, peas, and beans. He started a school where children took courses during the day, while their parents filled the classrooms at night after work. Statesmen, reformers, and industrialists from across the world came to New Lanark to see this new society for themselves.

Owen is remembered today, along with Charles Fourier, Henri de Saint-Simon, and Étienne Cabet, for initiating an early stage of socialism that came to be derided by the label "utopian." In *The Communist Manifesto,* Marx and Engels criticized them for being naively unaware of the class struggle and coming revolution, arguing that their experiments in communal living were an escape from reality and not even a minor annoyance to the capitalists who controlled the modes of production. Marx and Engels believed they were perfectly content to maintain the material conditions of inequality by fiddling around with "small experiments, necessarily doomed to failure." These dreamers certainly did not go as far as Marx and Engels would have wanted. But despite what later socialists might have thought of them, their ideas for creating a cooperative and peaceful society, where workers enjoyed the fruits of their labor and the necessities of life, spread across the globe during the nineteenth century. Over 100 utopian communities were established in North America, including Owen's own New Harmony on the Indiana frontier, now a state historical site for schoolchildren to visit and learn about the utopian impulse in the evolution of American democracy.[9]

Owen and Hunter met that summer in London, with a hand from John Adams Smith, scion of the former president and secretary to the US legation at London. After Hunter and Smith called on Owen but did not find him home, Smith wrote to him to say that Hunter would be attempting another visit on his own:

> I beg leave to recommend to you my countryman Mr. Hunter. I called with him to present him to you last week but had not the good fortune to find you. He is going out of town tomorrow but will himself, before he goes, make another attempt at finding you at home. It will give me great pleasure to know that he has seen you as he is, as I am, much interested in the present prospect of improvement in the degraded condition of civilized man.[10]

There is only a sparse record of their time together in Britain, but it shows that the two men quickly became friends. Owen gave Hunter access to a circle of progressive thinkers, most notably William Godwin, the renowned author of *Political Justice*, philosopher of anarchism, and novelist; Jeremy Bentham, the political reformer, philosopher, and critic of imperialism and religious institutions; and Anna D. Wheeler, the feminist and reformer, who wrote to a friend that in her home "Mr. Hunter will always be welcome."[11]

Hunter's growing confidence as a writer and social critic was on display in the pamphlet he had been commissioned to write for the New England Company of London. Mindful of the power of his image as the white Indian, he made every attempt to control that image. Many people were eager to celebrate him as a triumph of the civilizing project, but he objected to being held up as an endorsement of the virtues of empire. He wanted the great nations of the world, "where civilized man has received his highest polish," to confront their complicity in the ongoing destruction of Native lands and peoples. There were "evils too tedious to name" still being done in the cause of progress and enlightenment. It was a miracle he had survived to tell his story:

> Thousands, perhaps I might say millions of these people have perished within the boundaries now claimed by the United States, since their intercourse with the first adventurers to this part of our continent. Numerous nations, which before that period were powerful and happy in their pursuits, now cease to exist. Many others have become feeble, and are so rapidly diminishing, that in a short time, unless the proper measures be adopted to prevent it, very little will be known of them except their names.[12]

He made it clear that it was the American nation's desire for conquest, and not fate or natural law, that had destroyed so many Indian tribes and threatened to wipe the rest of them from the face of the earth. Each wave of settlers across North America drove them from their homes and into a corner between "two enemies, the whites on one side, the hostile tribes on the other," and they had no choice but to fight for their survival. Legions of fur traders carried out a staggering slaughter of animals, "only for the sake of their skins," leading to more wars, hunger, and displacement. Whiskey traffickers profited from their distress and were impervious to pleas to stop their lethal trade. The theft of their ancestral lands lay at the root of the catastrophe. They had been "duped out of their lands" by cunning officials, cast out into a wasteland with "no country to call their own." Hunter, who had fled Illinois with the Kickapoos, knew of what he spoke: "Witness the Natchez, the Choctaws, the Kickapoos, and a hundred more tribes, once the glory of their race, and pride of the West, to whom history has scarcely given a name in her pages!!"

He ended his jeremiad by imploring his fellow Americans to live up to their republican values. Their wayward nation, which "has become great and powerful as it were on the destruction of the Indians," must redeem itself by protecting them. He was a patriot eager to do his part:

> I look forward with pleasure to the task I have undertaken voluntarily. The motives are no less than the preservation of a high-minded, noble race of the human family, who have been debased, cheated, and slandered, from a destruction which inevitably awaits them, unless some kind arm be interposed to arrest the causes which are rapidly hurrying them to oblivion. The very thought that such a people, inheriting such distinguished gifts from nature, should eventually become extinct, without records even to tell their melancholy fate, must be truly affecting to those who think seriously on the subject. To me, whose

> liveliest associations and earliest impressions were derived amongst them, its indescribably painful. I cannot reconcile it to my feelings to believe it.[13]

His grief nearly overwhelms him in this passage. It pains him to think that his fellow Americans would avoid responsibility for a catastrophe that had worsened under republican government. He shared again his childhood memory of hearing Tecumseh call for war against the invasion, if only to underscore how drastically their world had changed. Armed resistance now seemed futile and only incited the Americans to retaliate by taking more from them. He reported that the death of the "brave and gallant Tecumseh has damped the ardor and crushed the hopes" of so many Native peoples, but there remained a path to survival. They must transition to farming at once: "Now the wise and experienced are conscious they must either become tenants of the soil, or be soon lost in the sea of forgetfulness!"[14] This was how chiefs and warriors would honor Tecumseh: simply by doing everything possible to keep their people alive and on their land.

Hunter finished the pamphlet on August 2, about a month after meeting Owen for the first time.[15] Hunter's trenchant analysis of settler colonialism and his call for agrarian reform makes it easy to see why he was welcomed into Owen's circle. Drinnon rightly claims that Hunter was emboldened by Owen's secular view of human nature—we are born good and not ruined by original sin—which pointed to the social causes of that misery. In his last published work, Hunter understood more clearly than ever that, as Drinnon put it, "what was wrong was not the nature of man but the nature of imperialistic societies."[16]

By month's end, Hunter had gone to see Owen's experiment at New Lanark for himself. "John D. Hunter of Mississippi. American," he wrote in the visitor's log on August 29, 1823.[17]

They would have had much to discuss. Owen's ambitions had grown beyond industrial reform; for years he had been advancing his vision of "villages of cooperation" in the countryside. Each village would have between 500 and 1,200 people from the poor and working classes. They would live together in a group of buildings in the shape of a parallelogram, which included their apartments, communal kitchen, medical clinic, school, and artisanal workshops. Like Hunter, Owen saw farming as the path to happiness and social harmony, so the residents would be taught how to farm and raise stock. The dignified labor would give the urban poor and working classes the means for achieving happiness and becoming complete human beings.

The next stop on Hunter's educational pilgrimage was the famous estate of Thomas William Coke of Norfolk, a leading figure in the agricultural revolution—the innovator of new methods for rotating and fertilizing crops, cultivating corn and turnips, draining and irrigating fields, and crossbreeding sheep. Hunter did not come to the estate on his own. He arrived in the esteemed company of the botanist James Smith, founder of the Linnaean Society, and a great admirer of Hunter's. In a letter to a friend, Smith had touted Hunter's plan for agrarian reform among the Indian tribes as having "the noble design of improving them on the wisest and best principles."[18] He envisioned an auspicious meeting between Hunter and Coke, the great man who had developed those principles, with Hunter sharing his unique knowledge of North American plants and Coke the latest agricultural methods.

Smith could not have been more disappointed by Hunter's poor first impression on Coke. There he stood, in the presence of the visionary whose "Norfolk agriculture" attracted visitors from around the world, staring mutely at his shoes. Of course, anybody would have been a little intimidated by the surroundings. The main entrance to the Palladian manor

Figure 13 Robert Owen, Esq. In this portrait, Robert Owen is surrounded by the rake, scythe, and other farming tools—symbols of the agricultural ideals and the dignity of labor at the core of his reform movement.
Source: Courtesy of The Miriam and Ira D. Wallach Division of Art, Prints and Photographs: Print Collection, The New York Public Library. https://digitalcollections.nypl.org/items/790e9d48-4852-8455-e040-e00a1806752e

ushered visitors into a majestic room with a colonnade supporting a fifty-foot gilded dome ceiling and then led them toward a flight of alabaster stairs leading up to the crimson saloon, the statue gallery lined with Roman figures, the library filled with rare manuscripts, the dining room with secret corridors to the kitchen, and luxurious bedrooms and sitting rooms. Hunter may have clammed up for a moment, but he fared much better than his friend Chester Harding did a few months later. Harding was so unnerved after entering Marble Hall that he hid in his room and put off meeting Lord Coke until breakfast. And Harding did not have to contend with another rather daunting guest, the Duke of Sussex, who very much wanted to meet the white Indian he had heard so much about.

It did not take as long for Hunter to get comfortable and open up. He was soon regaling them with stories "of all his extraordinary experiences," a guest related in their diary entry, "on his sensations upon first beholding a city, on his astonishment at the first sight of the Pacific Ocean and a ship, and of his surprise on entering London."[19] Smith, breathing a sigh of relief that his friend had come to life, reported that the "Duke of Sussex and Mr. Coke were delighted with him."[20] Hunter stayed several days at Holkham, perhaps even weeks, soaking up as much as possible from Coke. He showed the "keenest interest" in all facets of Norfolk agriculture, scribbling in his notebook, passing along rows of corns and turnips, inspecting the drainage work in the pastures, examining the livestock, and handling the newest farming implements.[21] When Coke presented him a gift of one of them, Hunter surprised him by politely declining to accept it. He explained that he valued his independence more than anything in the world and did not wish to be beholden to anyone. It was nothing personal, he assured him. He had said the same thing to friends in New York who had offered to pay for his education: "No, if you educate me, you will expect me to think as you do. I have money, I like to think and judge for myself."[22] Coke was delighted by what he regarded as this American attitude to be independent in all things.

It is worth pausing on Hunter's refusing a gift from Lord Coke. After he had his reputation destroyed by Lewis Cass and then passed into history as a mysterious figure, there remains a persistent assumption that Hunter, if not a swindler, must have motivated by pecuniary self-interest, like one of the "professional Indians" who gained their income from the lecture circuit, government, church, or wealthy benefactors. If there is evidence to support this belief about Hunter, then it has yet to be found. However, the evidence we do have amply proves that offers of gifts, money, and charity made him very uncomfortable and he rarely accepted them. In the single instance I have been able to identity, which will be introduced shortly, Hunter borrowed some travel money from Robert Owen and promptly sent him a letter with instructions to see a friend of his in Philadelphia, Elliot Cresson, who would repay him out of Hunter's personal funds. Hunter mixed with some wealthy people, in New Orleans, Philadelphia, New York, London, and Mexico City, and none of them left behind a record of complaint against him for exploiting, manipulating, or cheating them. Rather, they noticed a personal code of ethics based on his desire to pay his own way and be independent of others.

Norfolk agriculture was about more than technological innovations. Reformers came there because Coke's tenants and farmers, by all accounts, were treated fairly and enjoyed a high quality of life. Robert Owen, in a toast at Coke's summer festival in 1821, had offered some advice to anybody thinking of trying their hand at Norfolk agriculture. The essence of it was as simple as it was elusive: This noble man cared as much for his people as he did for his property, and he cultivated their hidden potential as intensely as he did the light soils of the

Norfolk coast. Coke gave them a "fair and liberal portion of his wealth" out of respect for the true value of their labor. They lived in comfortable houses and sat down at full tables for supper. They had control over their lives and were not at the mercy of competitive capitalism. Everyone gathered in the hall well knew Owen stridently opposed the landlord system, but he refrained from attacking the wealthy men before him. Probably even more surprising for them was that he was holding up Holkham Hall as the microcosm for the ideal England, cheekily claiming Coke as a kindred spirit. He ended his toast by inviting every patriot in the hall to follow their honorable host in building a more cooperative society.[23]

The next word on Hunter came from his own pen, in a letter to Coke after returning to London. He thanked Coke for his hospitality and updated him on his plans. He had been getting ready to sail for America, but he decided to delay his trip a little longer. He wanted to finish a new course of study he was taking in botany, chemistry, and mechanical philosophy. He felt it necessary to acquire as much "useful knowledge" as possible before breaking ground in Arkansas. He shared with Coke the progress reports he was receiving from friends in the United States, such as the new turnpikes and canals that were connecting the Atlantic coast with the Great Lakes and accelerating travel across the continent. He told him about an invention by his friend and editor Edward Clark, an ingenious contraption that could move a vessel against the current with the aid of paddle wheels. The trial had been a triumph. Hunter quoted from Clark's letter: "Never was the march of Human intellect more rapid than in America at the present time." America was truly a land of dreamers.

His visit to Holkham Hall had been a pivotal moment for him, and he wanted to memorialize it. He had managed to persuade Coke to have his portrait done by Chester Harding, so that Hunter could carry it with him to Arkansas as a way of honoring him and spreading his ideas far and wide. Hunter was happy to report that the portrait was finished, and he was not alone in calling it a masterpiece. Everyone who had seen it was astonished by how Harding had captured his likeness. The Duke of Sussex himself had praised the painting to Hunter over dinner at the exclusive Beef Steak Club. The innovations of Norfolk agriculture had not yet reached the frontiers of North America—it came as no surprise to Hunter that "beyond the mountains and across the Mississippi, our frontier brethren should not be acquainted with you." But that would change when he returned to Arkansas, after he built his farm as Coke had taught him, and then reaped the harvests. The example of his farm promised to "have a very happy effect on our countrymen."

It would be a glorious day on the American frontier. "Your example and friendship are treasure to me," Hunter confided, "and I hope the time will ere long arrive when a seat of hospitality will be found by your countrymen under my homely roof. It will be my delight to hail them welcome." Coke had been an idealistic dreamer a lifetime ago, famously raising his drink high to General Washington and the republican experiment in the former colonies. He always regretted never crossing the ocean to see it for himself, but Hunter promised that his name would one day ring beyond the Mississippi. The letter closed with the reformer's creed: "Misery be banished from our planet!"

Hunter expected to sail very shortly for home, but the portrait would not be going with him straightaway. For the inaugural exhibition at its Suffolk Street gallery, the Royal Academy wanted to exhibit an American painter and asked Harding for his portraits of Coke, Owen, the Duke of Sussex, and Hunter. The portrait of Coke never did make it to Arkansas. Today it hangs in a stairwell of Holkham Hall, mistakenly ascribed to an unknown artist in the British School.[24]

CHAPTER TEN

Forest Shadows

EVER SINCE READING Hunter the year before, Felicia Dorothea Heman, a leading poet of the Romantic movement, had been trying to write a verse about his extraordinary life. Her poems exulted in the exploits of common people with a hunger for freedom and the courage to fight for a righteous cause. Her heroes often hail from distant lands and stand up to tyrants. In *The Forest Sanctuary*, a father and son escape from the Spanish Inquisition and find freedom in the American wilderness. In her collection *The League of the Alps*, mountain fighters liberate Switzerland from Austrian tyranny. In *Records of Woman*, women fight back against patriarchy and refuse to submit to the faithless men in their lives. In the words of her American contemporary William Cullen Bryant, Heman's poetry "tells us of the high purpose of patriotic souls."[1] This was liberation poetry, made for an age of democratic movements and heroes, which is why her ode to Hunter was so curious.

Her feelings about Hunter finally crystallized in a poem just before his departure for America. In "The Child of the Forests," the narrator pleads with him to stay in London and resist the pull back to the wilderness.[2] This sentiment went against the grain of a Romantic movement, so familiar to us today, that valued nature as a therapeutic retreat from modern civilization, a mystical place where a searcher discovered truths about the universe and themself. Nature was usually not to be avoided, as Heman's poem has it, but a closer look reveals why she treated Hunter differently than her other subjects. The narrator immediately engages him in an intimate, and edgy, one-sided conversation, beginning with a not so innocent question about his state of mind:

> Is not thy heart far off amidst the woods
> Where the red Indian lays his father's dust?

The narrator knows full well he misses his people. His memories, against his will, have transported him over the ocean and across the infinite plains, into a thrilling buffalo chase with his Indian brothers, but the narrator then jolts him out of his reveries:

> And where art thou, the swift one in the chase,
> With thy free footstep and unfailing bow?

Where art thou, John Dunn Hunter? Where art thou when your people need you, "the swift one in the chase," to fly over the plains after the herds? Where art thou when "the hunter's work is done"? Where art thou as "the night-fires blaze beneath the giant pine" and your brothers "hear the tales of old" and enjoy the camaraderie of a successful hunt? Where art thou, John Dunn Hunter? It is a refrain of tough love that rings out through the couplets. Hunter is scolded for thinking he can recapture his past life after joining "civilized" society. He has been gone too long, replaced by another around the fire: "And there a place is fill'd, that once was thine."

The poet warns Hunter not to board the ship for America. If he returns to his Indian people, then he will inevitably spiral down into a savage state. The narrator reminds him that his conversion to civilization has changed him; if he manages to find his people, they might not welcome him back or even recognize him:

For thou art mingling with the City's throng,
And thou has thrown thine Indian bow aside,
Child of the forests! Thou art borne along
Ev'n as ourselves, by life's tempestuous tide!
But will this be?—and canst thou *here* find rest?—
Thou hadst thy nurture on the Desert's breast.

The narrator, after praising Hunter for handling the pen just as skillfully as he once did the bow and arrow, perceives his inner turmoil. His conversion seems tragically incomplete. He feels like an actor playing the part of an anxious gentleman, haunted by the memories of his old life, able neither to forget his Indian home nor to find comfort in his exile. He is a wreck, disoriented by the "forest's shadow on thy dreams," tormented by the "murmurs which none else may hear," but the narrator reassures him, in a whisper, that he has not lost his mind. She, too, hears the "wild voices" calling him "back to thy free and boundless woods again!" He must ignore their siren song, she tells him. He cannot return to the past.

Another farewell to Hunter, an essay in the *New Monthly Magazine*, took the opposite perspective on his imminent return to the western frontier. The unknown writer praised him for bravely rushing back to help his people survive the invasion of their country. He was going back to a frontier where unspeakable acts of violence—"the murders, robberies, injustice, and oppression of the native Indians, the kidnapping and carrying them off for slaves, the assembling them under peaceful pretenses and betraying them, men, women, and children, to destruction, together with the occupation of their hunting grounds and native soil"—had made a mockery of the American republic and its celebrated ideals. Hunter would find a deteriorating situation in the West, but he had prepared diligently for his mission: "Mr. Hunter is gone again to the woods of the

Figure 14 Felicia Hemans. One of the most popular poets of her era, Felicia Hemans was a literary celebrity whose work was admired by Wordsworth, Byron, and Scott. Many of her poems were memorized, anthologized, and even set to music.
Source: Courtesy of The Miriam and Ira D. Wallach Division of Art, Prints and Photographs: Print Collection, The New York Public Library. https://digitalcollections.nypl.org/items/510d47df-de9b-a3d9-e040-e00a18064a99

Missouri with the advantage of much knowledge acquired both in England and America, to attempt some amelioration of [the Quapaws'] condition." His education had opened his mind and his heart and made it impossible for him to ignore his duty. The writer portrays Hunter as a pathfinder for progress.[3]

The last documented sighting of Hunter in England was at the residence of US ambassador Richard Rush. It was a dinner party along with Chester Harding and Robert Owen that ended with a spirited debate, lasting several hours, between Rush and Owen over the principles of social reform. Harding left no other details in his journal, and Hunter sailed for America not long afterward. The voyage across the ocean, depending on weather conditions, generally took between fifteen and forty days from Liverpool, giving Hunter plenty of time to take stock of his time in Britain. He had grown as a writer and thinker. Two new chapters in the London editions of his book provided a cogent critique of territorial expansion and the crisis facing Native peoples in the United States. His studies had taught him about the innovative practices of Norfolk agriculture. His acceptance by a circle of reformers had fired his imagination and sharpened his plan for the Quapaws.

Hunter resurfaced in Philadelphia in July 1824. The United States had only grown larger and more powerful during the two years he had been gone. Over 2 million of its approximately 10 million people now lived west of the Appalachians. Indiana, Illinois, Mississippi, Alabama, and Missouri were new states. A transportation revolution of steamboats, canals, and roads was accelerating expansion, settlement, and the growth of the market economy. It had been four years since the Missouri Compromise divided the nation between free and slave states, and universal suffrage for white men was now the rallying cry for a whites-only democracy. In its 1823 ruling in *Johnson v. McIntosh*, the Supreme Court emboldened this belief by giving the federal government broad sovereignty over the land, declaring that Native peoples were merely occupants who were free to use the land but could never own or sell it. Around this time the United States surpassed India as the largest cotton producer in the world, which was partly due to southern states and slaveholders confiscating the lands of the Cherokees, Choctaws, Chickasaws, and Creeks and turning them into cotton plantations. That same year, in a speech remembered as the statement of the Monroe Doctrine, President Monroe warned Europe not to interfere with the rising destiny of the American hemisphere.[4]

In Philadelphia, Hunter took a room at Elizabeth Linn Brown's boarding house at 98 South Third Street, around the corner from the old statehouse.[5] He had not planned on a lengthy visit, but a yellow fever outbreak in New Orleans delayed the next leg of his journey. When the mosquito-borne illness subsided in the autumn weather, as it always did, he intended to travel by sea to New Orleans and then head up the Mississippi to his land in Arkansas. There is little information about his five months in the city, but we know that he reunited with friends and acquaintances after his absence, fought over royalties with his Philadelphia publisher, and attended various lectures. It is easy to imagine, given his earlier fascination with the signing Deaf students in New York, that he paid a visit to the Pennsylvania School for the Deaf on the corner of Eleventh and Market Streets, a short walk from his lodging. A popular excursion that summer was to the new Fairmount Water Works on a scenic bend in the Schuylkill, and Hunter might have gone with friends to watch the waterwheels spin and pump water into the city. He also could have taken a packet boat down the Delaware to Newbold's Landing, where the main attraction was the crew of a thousand laborers digging the Chesapeake and Delaware Canal and hauling away the dirt and stone.

It would have been strange if he was not part of the huge crowds welcoming the Marquis de Lafayette to the city. The

French hero of the Revolutionary War had embarked on a grand tour of the twenty-four states to celebrate the fiftieth anniversary of American independence. On September 23, Lafayette was escorted into Philadelphia by a procession of officials, military officers, soldiers, aging veterans of the Revolution, clergymen, and a boisterous band. Thousands of cheering spectators packed the viewing stands along the parade route, lined the rooftops, and perched high in the trees so they could catch a glimpse of the returning hero. The freedom and dignity he had fought for were showcased along the way by shoemakers, silversmiths, cabinetmakers, printers, blacksmiths, carpenters, clockmakers, and other tradesmen, who had set up their workshops in the street, beneath giant placards of Lafayette and Washington that read "To their wisdom and courage we owe the free exercise of our industry." The printers' apprentices grabbed copies of the "Ode to Lafayette" off the press and handed them out to parade-goers and to the dignitaries as they made their way to the old statehouse.[6] The festivities lasted a week with balls, speeches, concerts, and banquets around the city. It was the major event of the year in Philadelphia.

A fascinating letter from Hunter to James Madison provides the clearest picture of him that fall. He had planned to visit the former president, whom he had met two years earlier after appearing at his door with a letter of introduction from Thomas Jefferson. Unfortunately, Hunter's plan fell through after stopping in Richmond to take care of some business that took longer than expected, and he had to rush back to Philadelphia to finish his preparations for his journey: "I hope to embark for the Western Country in a few weeks."[7] It must have been a difficult decision to bypass Montpelier. He had been all potential on his first surprise visit to the "Father of the Constitution"; now he was an acclaimed author with many distinguished friends and admirers. He asked if Madison had received a copy of his book. Hunter informed him that his publisher had "treated me with much injury" by not sending copies to a few of his selected friends, as per their agreement. "I fear you are among those neglected," he wrote. "If not will you let me know?" The gift was meant to signify Hunter's great regard for Madison. Only a few years removed from the wilderness, Hunter had tapped his natural gifts and validated the aspirations of the revolutionary generation. He would be honored if the book could find a home in Madison's library.

What was this important business that took Hunter to Richmond and caused him to miss out on a triumphant return to Montpelier? There are clues in his letter to Madison. Hunter had told him to keep an eye out for the delivery of a package of seeds—sharing seeds was (and still is) a common practice among the world's farmers, horticulturalists, and botanists. Most of the seeds on their way to Madison, such as those that produced giant white turnips measuring thirty inches in circumference, were gifts from Coke of Norfolk. Hunter proudly noted that "I spent some weeks" at Holkham Hall and then described a few of the tools and machines being used on Coke's estate. Hunter himself was taking to Arkansas a "new Machine for dressing flax without watering and other valuable mechanic improvements." It seems very likely that the purchase of this machine—called a scutcher, for beating and breaking straw—was the reason for his trip to Richmond, a manufacturing center.

Madison wrote back five days later. The turnip seeds had come and were waiting to be planted. He had received the book and was grateful to Hunter for solving the mystery of who had been kind enough to send it. "The work will give pleasure to every reader," he said flatteringly, "who takes an interest in the subject of it." Mrs. Madison was touched by Hunter's remembrance of her kindness. They would have been delighted to have seen him on his trip to Virginia and "shall be so whenever

Figure 15 James Madison, c. 1821. Oil on wood, by Gilbert Stuart. *Source*: Courtesy of the National Gallery of Art. https://www.nga.gov/collection/art-object-page.56914.html

your movements make it convenient to you." Then Madison wished him every success in his western endeavors.[8]

Not everyone in America thought he should be going back to the western frontier. As word spread of his plans, a bittersweet love poem about Hunter appeared in the fine arts magazine *The Atlantic*. In a preface, the author, known only by the initial C, shared the disappointing news that Hunter had turned his back on civilization and soon would be "returning to the simplicity of Indian life and manners." The poem takes the form of a complaint by the mistress abandoned by him. She complains that she did everything possible to please him, and it was not enough. She had doted on him and taught him social graces and etiquette. She had nurtured his virtues and improved his character. She had led her changed man into regal halls "where bright jewels shone around" and praise rained down on him from the nobles. And he was going to leave her despite it all. The sweet melodies she had breathed into his ears had not calmed his wild nature as she had thought. The faraway look in his "vacant eye" told her he was already gone, already finished with the "pomp and glare" of the "gay scene" and poised to leave her for one of the thousand rapids and waterfalls roaring in his head. He was returning to the wild.

The long-standing assumption has been that Hunter's fall from grace commenced with Cass's accusations in the *North American Review*. However, as the poem shows, Hunter's reputation had taken a hit before Cass accused him of being an imposter. The poem's narrator can hardly believe he would spurn such a beauty just as he was starting to enjoy the pleasures of civilized life:

> —Thy lip has scarcely prest the sparkling shine,
> And canst though the delicious draught resign?
> Slaked is thy thirst so soon, for light divine?
> —See how she bares her breast, and offers free,
> The deep rich draught, exhaustless as the sea,
> From that bright dazzling fount, to nurture thee.

The temptress who offers herself to the white Indian is an allegory of the nation's civic and moral ideals. This was a very popular trend at the time. The iconography of neoclassical women, such as America, Liberty, Columbia, and Minerva, was emblazoned everywhere: in poetry, novels, paintings, music, and sculpture; on coins, medals, and banknotes; in woodcuts, engravings, cartoons, and magazine illustrations; on maps, newspaper mastheads, and broadsides; and on the stage. White women were being assigned new roles in the new nation as "the nurturers, educators, and moral compasses of a nation of public-spirited citizens."[9] Sometimes they failed in these roles. In the poem's story of unrequited love, the nurturing narrator gave everything of herself to the white Indian, and it was not nearly enough to save him from his savage instincts.

Hunter did not leave as planned for his journey because he fell seriously ill. We know this only because Robert Owen sailed into New York Harbor on November 4 and immediately sent word to Hunter at his boardinghouse in Philadelphia.[10] Owen was on his way to Indiana with his son William and Captain Donald Macdonald of the Royal Engineers to consider purchasing 20,000 acres on the Wabash River. His surprise arrival had created a stir in New York. At one of David Hosack's Saturday gatherings, where Hunter once had mingled with the city's leading lights, Owen was an honored guest and shared his vision of cooperative community on the Wabash without private property and exploitation. He took an excursion to a Shaker village outside of Albany and came away feeling heartened that his dream would become reality in the New World.[11]

On the morning of November 18, the Owen party stood on deck as their steamboat headed out of the harbor, bound for New Jersey. They sailed down the shores of Staten Island and through the twisting Kills, then up the Raritan to New Brunswick, where a four-horse coach was waiting to carry them to Trenton for the night. They boarded a second steamboat at dawn for the three-hour trip down the Delaware to Philadelphia and passed cottages, farms, and villages that made them think they were in Dutch country. A fellow traveler first pointed out the estate of Joseph Bonaparte, former king of Spain, brother of Napoleon, who cohabitated scandalously with a girl sold to him for $10,000 by an opportunistic mother, and then slyly gestured to the far end of the dining room, where the same woman just so happened to be having breakfast with another of her daughters. They passed by the villages of Bristol and Burlington, the villa of the well-known actor Thomas Cooper, and two imposing ships owned by the banker Stephen Girard, one of the richest men in the country. They heard the din of Philadelphia's wharf through a thick cloud of smoke. A porter with a wheelbarrow took their bags to the Mansion Hotel while they marched down the street to surprise Hunter at his boardinghouse.[12]

"He was delighted to see Mr. Owen and gave us all a hearty welcome," wrote Macdonald in his journal, but Hunter was looking grim. He showed the telltale signs of a bout of yellow fever: He was "sallow complexioned," laboring to breathe, and gaunt. For the next several days, Owen stayed by Hunter's side and entertained many of his friends who were eager to meet one of the most famous men in all of Europe. They welcomed callers all day and into the evening, sipped digestifs, and talked in the parlor. One evening after returning from a walk, they found Hunter's friend Edward Clark, the inventor, waiting for them. Owen had heard all about his apparatus for moving boats against the current, and so he gladly unspooled his blueprints for his cooperative village across the table and brought his vision to life for the "eminent civil engineer."[13] On another evening they met a small group at the house before walking over to the Athenaeum to hear Owen speak about his project to "a large circle of scientific men," including Major Stephen Long, just back from his exploring expedition to the Red River. In a few short and lively days, Owen had laid the groundwork for recruiting an exceptional team of settlers for his cooperative community on the Wabash. The following year, around forty scientists, engineers, educators, and artists would settle their affairs in the city and follow him to southern Indiana.[14]

If Hunter had not fallen sick, then there would be no record of this exciting moment in his life. He would already have been sailing down the coast by the time Owen arrived in Philadelphia, with no friends on board to document the journey. But Owen convinced him to change his travel plans and head west overland with his party, which included two dutiful diarists, William Owen and Donald Macdonald, who kept a meticulous record of their journey. They boarded a steamboat for Baltimore on November 23. Also with them were a pair of siblings from Illinois, George Flower and Mary Katherine Ronalds, whose father, Richard Flower, was brokering the deal for Harmony. It was a pleasantly warm day as they steamed by the Navy Yard and the city receded behind them. A few miles downriver, Captain Macdonald, with an interest in and an eye for military landmarks, pointed out the sandy elevation on the left bank where the Continental Army had defeated a few thousand Hessian mercenaries in the Battle of Red Bank in 1778. The victory, after a string of defeats and blunders, lifted the spirits of the colonists and made them believe they could possibly win the war. The travelers disembarked at Newcastle, shuttled by stagecoach fourteen miles to Frenchtown on the eastern shore of Maryland, then transferred to a steamboat that carried them through the night to Baltimore. A man snoring loudly could not be roused and kept them awake for hours.

They landed at Baltimore as the sun was rising and were fortunate to find accommodations at the Indian Queen Hotel. Visitors had been flocking to the city for two big events, the annual livestock exhibition and a parade in honor of Lafayette. They headed to the exhibition, where they were impressed by the plows, corn shellers, straw cutters, and other contraptions on display at the fairgrounds. They walked every part of the city. The First Unitarian Church seemed to them far superior to the massive Roman Catholic cathedral designed by Benjamin Henry Latrobe. They stopped to have coffee and read the papers at the Merchant's Exchange, also a Latrobe project. They walked over to Calvert Street to see the Battle Monument commemorating the soldiers who died during the British attacks of 1814. They peered up at the names of the dead carved into a marble base thirty feet high, atop which stood Lady Baltimore wearing the crown of victory and grasping the rudder of a British warship. They headed north of downtown to see the nearly finished monument to George Washington, a 178-foot Doric column created by Robert Mills, who later designed the even taller Washington Monument in the US capital.

They had tea later that evening at the home of Robert Goodloe Harper. The veteran of the American Revolution and the War of 1812 had also served in Congress as a representative from South Carolina (1795–1801) and as a senator from Maryland (1816). Even though Harper was waiting on Lafayette's imminent arrival, he did not want to pass up the chance to meet Owen, who probably would have stayed for the festivities if not for a busy slate of meetings in Washington. They set out the following afternoon, changing horses three times along the thirty-eight-mile route, and entered Washington with a beautiful view of the Capitol building aglow in moonlight.

PART III

Exodus

CHAPTER ELEVEN

"Singing the Corn Songs"

THE MORNING AFTER THEIR ARRIVAL in Washington, Robert Owen made the rounds in search of federal funding, pitching his vision to Secretary of State John Quincy Adams, Secretary of War John C. Calhoun, and Secretary of the Treasury William Crawford. With a free day, Hunter and his companions went to see the Capitol building, its reconstruction nearly complete ten years after British forces had tried to burn it to the ground. They stepped around the "busily employed" laborers and "wandered all over the building." They strolled through the empty chambers of the Senate and House of Representatives and looked inside the ground-floor chamber of the Supreme Court. They passed a "great many committee and clerk rooms" where the essential and often mundane work of the people's government was being done.[1]

The US Capitol was designed to serve as the symbolic heart of the nation. Washington and Jefferson had chosen the architectural plan, in 1793, because they believed that it promoted better than any other design their revolutionary principles to the world. With its domed roof, sandstone walls, tall columns, symmetrical shapes, and triangular pediments, the Capitol building was a neoclassical monument to an experimental republic that could collapse at any time. The architecture was all boast, proclaiming the permanence, legitimacy, and inevitability of the Revolutionary government, and naming their young nation as the true heir to Greek and Roman civilization. It's why the Rotunda was built in the style of a Roman temple. In this ceremonial space, the nation pays final tribute to its most prestigious citizens, receives foreign dignitaries, and commemorates important events in its history. It had been completed just in time for the reception of the Marquis de Lafayette.

Hunter and his companions were also witnessing the construction of national memory. The primary purpose of the architecture and artwork was to shape public attitudes and beliefs about the distant and recent past. In a side room, they admired a canvas depicting the Declaration of Independence being submitted to the Second Continental Congress and another one depicting the surrender of Lord Cornwallis and the British army at Yorktown. These were two of the four paintings that Congress had commissioned from John Trumbull in 1817. The canvases—*Declaration of Independence, Surrender of General Burgoyne, Surrender of Lord Cornwallis,* and *General George Washington Resigning His Commission*—are fabled scenes from the Revolutionary period: Thomas Jefferson, with his esteemed committee standing behind him, presenting the first draft of the Declaration of Independence to John Hancock and the Second Continental Congress a week before its adoption on July 4, 1776; General Burgoyne surrendering his forces to General Horatio Gates at Saratoga, in 1777, which caused France to enter the war on the American side; Lord Cornwallis surrendering his sword to General Benjamin Lincoln at Yorktown, in 1781, in the last major campaign of the war; and General George Washington, in military dress at the Maryland State House in 1783, resigning as commander-in-chief, and thus establishing the highest principle of republican government, the supremacy of civilian over military rule.[2]

In this early phase, the Capitol was not yet spilling over with paintings, statues, sculptures, murals, and other artistic pieces, but it was on its way to becoming the cluttered site of national memory that it is today. Hunter and his companions were told that Trumbull's paintings would soon be installed in the "magnificent circular" Rotunda.[3] The artwork displayed there would define the events and people worth remembering by the nation. Whereas Trumbull's paintings show the patriots who gave birth to the nation, four sculpted relief panels told an equally important story: *Preservation of Captain John Smith by Pocahontas* (1825), *Landing of the Pilgrims* (1825), *William Penn's Treaty with the Indians* (1827), and *Conflict of Daniel Boone with the Indians* (1827). Unveiled simultaneously with Trumbull's paintings, these by now very familiar scenes introduced four other foundation stories for the settler nation: Pocahontas, covering the body of the prostrate Smith, pleading with the warriors to lower their clubs and spare his life; a Pilgrim father being welcomed by a kneeling Indian with an ear of corn in his outstretched hand; William Penn holding his famous treaty and shaking hands with two Native men under the legendary elm tree; and Daniel Boone, with one dead Native warrior underfoot, fighting for his life against another. Complementing these panels were the sandstone busts of the explorers Christopher Columbus (1824), Sir Walter Raleigh (1824), John Cabot (1828), and Sieur de La Salle (1829).

The artwork in the Rotunda conveyed the view that the American people were the rightful heirs of the continent. There were no hints of ambivalence about the devastation that followed the arrival of Europeans, only a clear choice Native peoples had between submission and death. The "good Indian" bowed their head, welcomed the European with an ear of corn, put their mark on parchment, and pledged eternal friendship under the elm tree. The "good Indian" was open to the grace of God. The "bad Indian" looked defiantly at the newcomers, rejected every olive branch, and unleashed their rage on innocent settlers. The "bad Indian" was an agent of evil and destruction. The artwork, even the simple busts of the explorers, has the same general theme: The United States justly occupied the expanding territory it had claimed for itself. Just down the hall a year earlier, the Supreme Court had ruled in *Johnson v. McIntosh* that the discoveries made by European explorers and their claims on the continent had been handed down through time to the American people. A walk across the Rotunda floor assured visitors of the divergent destinies of a rising America and the disappearing Indian tribes.[4]

At the bottom of the Senate staircase, Hunter and his companions stood in front of the six "corncob" columns that had survived the fire of 1814. The vertical fluting on each of the classical columns resembled stalks of Indian corn and were topped by capitals surrounded by ornately carved ears of corn. They had never seen anything like it in Europe, "a new order of architecture formed from Indian corn," Macdonald exclaimed in his journal.[5] Of all the many stylistic features the architect Benjamin Latrobe could have chosen, Indian corn, or maize, was an especially significant one.[6] In every colony, Native peoples had saved the Europeans from famine by introducing them to the grain. After half of the Plymouth colony perished during their first winter, Squanto appeared with a bushel of seeds and taught the Pilgrims how to plant the grain and how to fertilize it with fish parts. In the fall, they joined together in a corn feast with the Wampanoags and other local tribes to celebrate a successful harvest and give thanks to the Great Spirit for watching over them. The relief panel in the Rotunda, *Landing of the Pilgrims,* whitewashed this history for the settler nation. An Indian with an ear of corn welcomes ashore the Pilgrims, as if the chronology had been magically reversed and they had been given the knowledge of sowing and reaping corn before that first starving winter.[7]

According to our national mythology, the abundance of corn manifested the promise of the frontier, pulled settlers westward, and made them self-reliant and jealous of their freedoms. There were good reasons for the faith in corn. A small patch of the fecund crop could sustain impoverished families through the winter. Corn required less labor and attention than wheat, oats, and rye, the grains familiar to Europeans; this meant more time for hunting and fishing and thus improved nutrition. The crop typically yielded a surplus, which was fed to chickens, cattle, and hogs. Corn improved the overall quality of life in early America by increasing the food supply, fattening livestock for market, and making farming more profitable. Corn was a major trade item commonly used to pay taxes, rents, and debts. Almost everything depended on the crop, and as we know from history, the availability of a nutritious grain has always determined the rise and fall of empires.

Bountiful corn inspired dreams of becoming freehold farmers, convincing settlers they would not only survive hard times but eventually prosper. It was the corn growing outside their forts, and the corn they stole from their Native neighbors, that saved Boone's settlement from starvation. Territorial expansion would have gone much differently without corn. The crop's profitability facilitated settlement, raised the value of western lands, created an international market for corn and its many byproducts, and expedited the building of roads, canals, and railroads. The Indian tribes said to be standing in the way of this progress were expelled from their lands. Corn made slavery even more profitable by expanding the cotton belt, since southern planters could never have sowed nearly every acre in cotton without importing corn to process into a staple mush for their enslaved laborers. In an age before the dominance of fossil fuels like coal and oil, solar energy created the renewable resources that sustained human existence and forged powerful nations. In North America, the solar energy being converted into corn (and other grains) was creating possibilities for a new kind of democratic politics and society, albeit a racially exclusive one. It's no exaggeration to say that corn was as important in creating American democracy as any set of laws or theories.[8]

Hunter knew something about the promise of corn. In a bittersweet memory of his childhood, he recalled the corn ceremony that took place in late summer at harvest time:

> No occasion with which I am acquainted, displays in a more manifest degree its social effects than the corn feast. The heart dilates with pleasure even to overflowing, and the guests give utterance to their joys in songs and dances, and continue the hilarity for the remaining part of the day and night, and frequently for the whole of the succeeding day. No people, I am persuaded, experience the mirthful scenes of life in a higher degree than they do. In fact, the old gray-headed men and women are seen to commingle in the sports, and seem to re-enjoy with increased zest the scenes of their youth.[9]

It bears repeating that such an intimate and poignant account of Native life was very rare for the period. The ceremony's "social effects" were profound: the joy felt as people danced and sang, the merriment as they reminisced with relatives, and the delight in watching the old heads trying to recapture their more athletic days. In sharp contrast to stereotype, these Native people were not sullen, drunk, weak, sick, or deranged. He described in detail the leading role of women in the ceremony. They exercised "almost unlimited authority" and made the important decision of giving one matriarch among them the honor of watching the plant mature and ripen until the time was right for "her children, as she calls her tribe . . . to commence eating the green corn."[10] After she decorated her lodge door with corn husks—the invitation to the ceremony—word spread quickly to their neighbors and preparations commenced for the feast. After their relatives had come in from their villages in the valley, there would be several days of dancing, singing, and feasting. Hunter reminisced about seeing everyone "joyfully skipping and dancing to their respective fields," singing the corn songs in thanks for the sun and rain, chasing each other through the tall rows, and picking armfuls of corn to carry to the fires. After roasting husks over the flames or burying them in the embers, they seasoned the colorful kernels with bear oil or marrow and would "partake of the rich though simple repast with joyful gratitude."[11]

Many decades after Hunter wrote about the corn ceremony, ethnographers and anthropologists corroborated many of the details in his account, albeit without referencing him. We know now that in many corn songs, by different Native groups, there are the recurrent footsteps of a mysterious and powerful woman. She rises at dawn, paints her hair red, and heads to the field with her planting stick and bag of seeds. She arranges seven mounds and drops seeds into each one. As she tamps down the soil with her foot, she chants and sings until a sun shower falls from the sky and green shoots break through her footprints and flower into abundance. According to Paula Gunn Allen, the Laguna Pueblo poet, this version of the story is about how food was given to the people: Corn Woman sacrifices herself for her children, planting a piece of her heart in the ground to nourish the seeds so they will have enough to eat.[12] The Osage women whom Hunter remembered being central to the feast were continuing the sacred work of their foremothers. They were strengthening their bonds to each other and their ancestors, preserving harmony with the natural world, and honoring the Great Spirit. Corn rituals are essentially about the rebirth of the people.

This story about Indigenous rebirth was never going to be told in the US Capitol, the ceremonial heart of the settler nation. It would not make any sense at all. Latrobe's memorial to corn, his "new order of architecture," proclaimed the birth of a people who were neither European nor Indian but

Figure 16 "Push-ma-ta-ha: A Choctaw Warrior." This portrait of Pushmataha shows him dressed in a similar style as that afternoon in the Dennison Hotel. The military epaulets on his shoulder represent his status as both a distinguished Choctaw chief and U.S. Army officer.
Source: Courtesy of The Miriam and Ira D. Wallach Division of Art, Prints and Photographs: Picture Collection, The New York Public Library. https://digitalcollections.nypl.org/items/510d47e1-1ac4-a3d9-e040-e00a18064a99

American.[13] The ear of corn handed to the Pilgrim by the kneeling Indian was like the signed treaty William Penn held in his hand—both marked the transfer of power and title to the Europeans and the death and vanishing of Native peoples. The American nation has never been able to tell the exceptional story of itself without its imaginary Indian, always a dying race withering away like corn stalks in the autumn field.

Hunter and his companions had entered a fantasy world of ancient and vanishing Indians, but outside of the Capitol building, a Choctaw delegation was in town, fighting for the future of their people. In treaty talks four years earlier, General Andrew Jackson had given an ultimatum to Chief Pushmataha: either trade 5 million acres in Alabama and Mississippi for land in Arkansas or General Jackson would obtain the requisite signatures from some Choctaws already living west of the Mississippi. The deal would be made one way or the other. Pushmataha accepted the devil's bargain, known thereafter as the Treaty of Doak's Stand, but when the Americans already squatting on their land refused to leave and the government refused to evict them, the treaty was effectively null and void. Pushmataha, along with Apuckshunubbe and Mushulatubbe, had no choice but to come to Washington in 1824 in the hopes of revising the treaty and convincing the United States to enforce its terms.

The chiefs received a steady procession of dignitaries at the Dennison Hotel, including Robert Owen. He wanted to introduce them to Hunter, but when Owen went to the Indian Queen Hotel to pick him up, Hunter was feeling sick after having three teeth extracted that morning, so Owen, his son William, and Captain Macdonald went to meet the Choctaw delegation without him. In any treaty conference, there are social settings beyond the official meeting in which the participants form personal relationships, build support for their policy aims, and promote their nation's achievements.[14]

Public diplomacy, as it's called, involves direct engagement with well-connected people. That afternoon, the Englishmen were ushered into a drawing room where the Choctaw delegation was "sitting in council." The parties exchanged solemn handshakes and took their seats around the circle. Sweet cakes and whiskey were served to put everyone at ease and provide time for small talk. Then Chief Pushmataha, dressed in a military uniform with gold epaulets, a red sash, and a hat adorned with feathers, stood to deliver a welcoming speech. He was a seasoned diplomat and the interpreter at his side hardly seemed necessary, in the opinion of William Owen. The chief, talking clearly with his hands, was "saying with a good deal of gestures that he was happy to see us and to shake hands with his white brethren."[15] After he sat down, one of the other chiefs—it isn't clear which one—rose to extend his greetings through the interpreter. The Choctaws had been surrounded for many years, first by the Spanish, the French, and the English, and now by the Americans. The Choctaws adapted to every situation and were "very friendly to them all."

The chief then invited Robert Owen to address the gathering. Owen told them how he had traveled across the great water with the important message that the British people were gravely concerned about the poor Indians. If they did not make peace with the whites and convert to civilization, then they would be gradually "extinguished" from the face of the earth, and what a pity that would be for such a noble race of people. It was not the first time the chiefs had been offended by the ignorance of white men, but they sat respectfully and did not interrupt Owen as he lectured them to change their ways. At least he had the virtue of being unusual. His ideas for helping them depended on the Americans also curbing their hunger for land and changing some of their other destructive habits. In this early version of the melting pot theory, Owen envisioned combining the best features of both cultures into a dynamic new social order and indoctrinating the next generation of white and Indian children in its values, ideas, and practices. He saw a future in which the "white and red" races were united and living harmoniously together. He was about to make a major address on the topic, and he wanted to know if the Choctaws shared his vision. Would they assimilate or separate? Did they "prefer amalgamating with the whites, or forming a separate body quite distinct from them"?[16]

The Americans had been asking them versions of this questions for many years, so the Choctaw delegation was more than prepared for it. One of the chiefs rose to praise Owen's remarks. He did not scold their esteemed visitor for revealing his profound ignorance about the Choctaws and their long history of adjusting to foreign interventions and settler intrusions. The three chiefs had been asked the very same question by Tecumseh and answered memorably by rejecting him and fighting alongside the Americans against the British.[17] In the years after the war, as whites continued to infiltrate their land, they made strategic adjustments. As Philip Deloria memorably put it about the real-world resistance to settler colonialism across the nineteenth century, "Real Indian people continued to challenge American expansion and steadfastly refused to vanish."[18] For the Chotaws, their American houses, large farms, and herds of livestock were but a few of their latest achievements. They also grew a variety of crops, used the newest methods and tools, erected grist- and sawmills, built more roads to transport their goods to market, established schools, tried to ban the alcohol trade, and created new legal codes in accordance with federalism.[19] Yet here they were again in Washington, trying to hold on to the fruits of their labor, listening politely to another white man full of ideas.

The Choctaws were engaged in an elaborate performance of their successful adaptation to American civilization. Dating back to the colonial period, this performative tradition, as many scholars have shown, was a strategic way for Native peoples to set the agenda in diplomatic meetings with European and American officials, challenge the myths about their savagery, and assert the complexities of their cultures and identities.[20] In Washington, the Choctaw delegation treated every meeting as an opportunity to introduce themselves to their visitors and advance their agenda. They had rehearsed the story of their progress many times, in the hopes that it clearly demonstrated how they were changing and meeting the demands of American society. At the moment the chief began speaking about their investments in education and their many young people who had gone off to school, two smartly dressed young men stepped into the middle of the room and addressed the group in perfect English. The Englishmen gawked at the two men, who "looked very much like sunburnt Americans," and wondered if they were truly Indians. Indeed, they were future chiefs, David Folsom and Daniel McCurtain, the sons of white fathers and Choctaw mothers. Macdonald accepted them as "proofs that Red Indians could be brought up to appear like the White people," but Robert Owen was not interested in producing imitations.[21] Unable to contain himself, he interrupted the performance to say that he aimed to make "the red brethren superior to the whites." Their closeness to nature had given them a special aptitude for republican living. Perhaps if Hunter had been there rather than nursing his swollen mouth, Owen might have introduced him as the ideal fusion of nature and civilization.

Even the interpreter had an important part to play in Choctaw pageant of progress. John Pitchlynn, a white farmer adopted by the Choctaws forty years earlier after the deaths of his parents, first entered the historical records as a translator for George Washington during his negotiations with the Choctaws. Pitchlynn married Sophia Folsom, the daughter of a Choctaw mother and white father, and they had ten children.

(One of them, Peter, attended the University of Nashville, was an envoy to the United States, and became chief of the Choctaw Nation of Oklahoma in 1864.) In addition to farming and raising many hundred head of oxen and hogs, Pitchlynn owned an inn on Gaines Trace that was popular with travelers on the Natchez Trail. When Macdonald quizzed him about living with the Indians, Pitchlynn's answer surprised him—"he much preferred their honesty, sincerity, friendship, & behaviour, to those of the white settlers."[22]

Neither Owen nor Macdonald fully understand the performance they documented in their journals. The Choctaws aimed to dispel the stereotype of the Indian, but the journals of Owen and Macdonald reveal how challenging this objective could be to achieve. The Englishmen had never met a "real Indian" before, and what little they knew of their cultures came largely from the tales of Romantic literature. They were confused by the conduct of the Choctaws at the Dennison. These Indians did not seem very authentic to them, especially the old chiefs. They were dressed in assorted pieces of the uniforms of American and British officers, each of the chiefs sporting a trademark accessory—a cloak of Stuart tartan, an oversized greatcoat with a billowing cape, twin gold epaulettes. Macdonald thought they looked ridiculous. That night in his journal he wrote scathingly of how the chiefs "deform themselves by wearing a costume."[23] It was "quite a masquerade" that debased them, a pathetic demonstration of how the march of progress had permanently damaged the Choctaws. Macdonald insinuates that an authentic Indian chief belonged in the wilderness, not in a hotel drawing room.

His description of the chiefs brings to mind a famous portrait by the artist George Catlin, who spent eight years traveling through the West and painting picturesque scenes and portraits of Native peoples. In St. Louis in 1831 Catlin had stood on the banks and watched as a delegation of Indians,

Figure 17 "Assinneboine Chief before and after Civilization." Oil on card mounted on paperboard, by George Catlin, 1836.? A liquor bottle in Wijunjon's back pocket completes Catlin's image of his deterioration after crossing into American society.
Source: Courtesy of the National Gallery of Art. https://www.nga.gov/collection/art-object-page.50341.html

on their way to Washington to meet with President Andrew Jackson, came ashore. Among them was a majestic Assiniboine chief named Wijunjon or Pigeon's Egg Head, who agreed to have his portrait done by the painter in his studio. Eighteen months later, the chief passed through St. Louis on his way back home. Catlin wrote in dismay that the chief had traded in "his native costume, which was classic and exceedingly beautiful," for the modern dress of an American gentleman.[24] Catlin, joining him aboard the *Yellow Stone* for the final thousand-mile stage of the journey, was stunned by his metamorphosis into a dandy. Here was Wijunjon sporting a top hat and suit coat and "strutting and whistling Yankee Doodle about the deck of the steamer that was winding its way up the mighty Missouri."[25]

Six years later, Catlin painted his metamorphosis in *Assinneboine Chief before and after Civilization*. The portrait is divided vertically into two parts. Before the journey to Washington, Wijunjon stands in profile on the left side of the panel, traditionally dressed in mountain-goat leggings and shirt, a headdress made of porcupine quills, and ornamental scalps taken from his enemies. After the journey to Washington, Wijunjon stands on the right side with his back turned to the viewer, foppishly dressed in a blue military uniform with boots, scarlet sash, gold epaulettes, and stovepipe hat. He wears white gloves and holds a fashionable folding fan in his right hand. He left for Washington with a peace pipe in his left hand; he returns with a furled umbrella. A liquor bottle is about to fall out of his back pocket. The portrait turned Wijunjon into "a living caricature," as one Catlin biographer put it, like the racist cartoons denigrating the achievements and aspirations of free Black people in the North by comparing them to apes.[26]

The Choctaw chiefs in the Dennison Hotel were also easy targets for mockery. It did not occur to the Englishmen that the chiefs were playing an important role in a diplomatic performance and had dressed tactically, with a higher purpose in mind. Their uniforms signaled their respect for the Americans and for their history as allies during the war against the British and the Creeks. To be fair, perhaps the Englishmen would not have viewed the uniforms as ridiculous if Pushmataha, mumbling and listing in his chair, his eyes shut, his fine beaver-skin hat tumbling to the floor, had not distracted them. The great chief appeared to be flat drunk, but nobody in the delegation seemed to pay him any notice. Pushmataha's stirring oratory once had rallied his people to reject Tecumseh in favor of the Americans, but he was clearly not the man he used to be. The Englishmen hardly needed to spell it out in their journals: Pushmataha in a drunken stupor made a farce of the Choctaw pageant of progress.

It would have been unusual if the Englishmen had not fixated on the drunken Indian. The stereotype, then and now, deflects attention away from some of the devastating consequences of colonialism.[27] For centuries, the whiskey trade had exploited and subjugated Native communities by burying them in debt and dependency. The Choctaws, like so many others, had tried and failed to ban the trade, and they could not prevent the whiskey peddlers from selling to their people. Sometimes, as was the case with the Choctaws at the Dennison, the peddler was the federal government itself. There was extravagant public spending on hosting Indian delegations, with a large portion of the budget devoted to the supply of whiskey. For instance, the bar bill for hosting the Choctaws was an estimated $67,000 in today's dollars according to the expense account uncovered by the historian Angie Debo.[28] Endless sanctimony from officials about the virtues of sobriety did not make them any less cunning or ruthless in treaty negotiations. In his analysis of the treaty conference between the Choctaws and the United States, the historian Richard White concluded that American officials "gladly provided enough whiskey to lubricate Choctaw negotiators" as a means of gaining every advantage possible over them.[29]

As the Owen party left the Dennison, they met John Dunn Hunter hurrying across the avenue. He was not going to let his throbbing jaw deny him the chance to sit down with the Choctaws. Their meeting was an emotional experience for Hunter. He confided to Macdonald and William Owen that in the six years since leaving the Osages, "he had never felt so pleasantly at home as with [the Choctaws]" that afternoon at the Dennison.[30] William recalled that "Hunter was so much affected by meeting them that he longed to hasten westward." He was so overcome by the desire to see his people that he suddenly felt "quite uneasy" and "anxious" to get on his way. The Englishmen said nothing more and did not speculate in their journals about the depths of his anxiety. It seems reasonable to think that Hunter was also troubled by what the Choctaws probably told him about the deteriorating situation for Indian tribes across the West. The government's refusal to protect treaty rights must have worried him and left him wondering about what he would find in Arkansas.

Pushmataha became ill and died only a few weeks after Hunter and the rest of the Owen party had started their journey west. He had lived long enough to agree to the Treaty of Washington City, which obligated the Choctaws to renounce their claims on the land now occupied by American settlers in exchange for an annuity, some debt forgiveness, and pensions for the Choctaw veterans of the War of 1812.[31] On his deathbed, Pushmataha reportedly whispered to Andrew Jackson, his former commander in that war, that he wished to be buried in his US Army uniform with military honors. And so a Christmas Day procession of several thousand people trailed after Jackson and the chief's casket to the Congressional Cemetery, where Pushmataha was buried alongside statesmen. A monument, engraved to a great warrior and true friend of the American people, was erected on his grave. Chiefs Pushmataha, Apuckshunubbe, and Mushulatubbe had managed to hold their red line by refusing to surrender any more of their territory in Alabama and Mississippi other than the land already lost to the whites, but their resistance proved to be fleeting. General Jackson was president five years later, the Indian Removal Act was the law of the land, and the first group of some 15,000 Choctaws was marched to the new Indian Territory in what is today Oklahoma.

CHAPTER TWELVE

Overland and Downriver

ON NOVEMBER 28, the day after meeting with the Choctaw delegation, Hunter and his companions set out on their journey. It took them two days to travel the seventy-five miles through Rockville and Fredericktown to Hagerstown, where they switched to long-distance coaches and picked up the new National Road traversing the Appalachian Mountains and Pennsylvania. Soon after rumbling over the new Conococheague Bridge, with its five stone arches, they were twisting through limestone and shale valleys and lurching up the Maryland mountains. Finally, here was the "wild and beautiful" landscape, ablaze in reds, browns, and yellows, that the Englishmen had been waiting to see. Not content with watching the scenery pass by his window, Macdonald bounded from the coach and hollered for Hunter to walk ahead with him. Macdonald peppered him with questions about the forest canopy, and Hunter obliged by pointing out varieties of oaks, sycamores, hickories, beeches, elms, chestnuts, walnuts, and persimmons, plus the pines and cedars that added splashes of green to the autumn scenery. He also named the many varieties of plants and pulled up some sassafras sprouts with which he made a delicious afternoon tea. It was a memorable day for Macdonald, who rhapsodized about Hunter being his spiritual brother. The two of them were awed by the "sublime but simple beauties" wrought by "Nature's hand"—not even the blight of ramshackle cabins and paltry farms that occasionally interrupted their view could "check our flow of spirits."

They passed over Town Hill and Green Ridge as night fell, crossed Nicholas Mountain by moonlight, and just before midnight reached the bottom of a gorge carved by the waters of the Potomac River and Wills Creek. They had reached the Cumberland junction, where they feasted at the communal table in their inn and then fell asleep next to a large blazing fire, which the Americans seemed to favor. They left Cumberland at daybreak along a road that climbed over Haystack Mountain toward Frostburg and Uniontown, following the course of an Indigenous trail that had been widened into a military road by General Braddock and a young officer named George Washington during the Seven Years' War.[1] By the time Hunter and his companions were traveling across it, Irish and German timber cutters, quarrymen, and diggers had cleared the trees, hammered through the rocks, graded the roadbed, and extended the national turnpike from Pittsburgh to Wheeling on the Ohio River.

Hunter and Macdonald ambled up ahead through a thick fog. They heard the clanging of wagons, the jangling of pots and pans, and the shouts of the drivers before they could see the travelers. The Ohio-bound families, "plain and friendly in their manners," had sold their farms "with the hopes of a larger and better establishment in a new country." After conversing with one family and wishing them good luck, Hunter and Macdonald continued over Big Savage Mountain, named after an early surveyor in search of the headwaters of the Potomac, and down into the village of Alleghany. After a fourteen-mile trek, they had the pleasure of sitting down to a hearty breakfast of wheat and rye bread, broiled chickens, pears, apricots, honey, venison steaks, and pork sausages, along with coffee and sassafras tea made from the sprouts Hunter had picked. The rest of their party arrived in time to join them. The long table crowded with an assortment of dishes was often remarked upon in travelogues as an indication of the splendid abundance of the American frontier.[2]

The country's abundance could be seen every day on the National Road. Along the way, they encountered droves of snorting and squealing hogs, some as large as 500 or 600 head, being driven from western farms to eastern markets. The hogs gorged themselves on the copious stores of Indian corn procured at roadside farms and stands. It was this "wholesome food of the forest," in Macdonald's opinion, that made the American hog's "flesh much sweeter & delicate" and less fatty than their British cousins. Of course, the landscape was also abundant, changing from valley to valley, from towering pines to iron deposits to lush limestone soils to coking coal beds. The travelers meandered toward the banks of the Youghiogheny River, crossed over the new Great Crossings Bridge, which was inundated with the construction of a reservoir and today is occasionally visible when water levels are low, and climbed through the Laurel Hills and along Chestnut Ridge, where the once plentiful chestnuts would be eliminated by blight in the 1920s.[3]

The road funneled them into Smithfield, at the bottom of a deep hollow of the Youghiogheny. A small crowd surrounded a wiry old man with a thick mane of gray hair and, to Macdonald's eye, a "stern but pleasing expressive countenance."[4] It was Andrew Jackson, on his way to Washington to await the results of the contested presidential election of 1824 and, although he could not know it yet, to sit at the deathbed of Pushmataha. Seeing Jackson holding court, Robert Owen rummaged through his file trunk for the letter of introduction given to him by DeWitt Clinton, governor of New York, who had guessed the two men might cross paths on the western road. Owen parted the crowd with his lively greeting, presented his letter to Jackson, and introduced William, Macdonald, and Hunter. Regrettably for historians, our scribes said nothing about the encounter other than that everyone went inside the inn and enjoyed a delicious meal together.

They continued the next day and night over the Laurel Ridge and along switchbacks that kept them on edge and fully awake until they were finally out of danger and rolling across farmlands with a beautiful sunrise at their back. They did not stop until sundown, when the horses were changed out, and then pushed on to Brownsville on the Monongahela, taking advantage of the "clear starry night & bright moon" illuminating the road ahead of them. Nobody was awake at the inn when they arrived, so they sprawled uncomfortably in chairs or curled up on the floor for a few hours of sleep until they were roused by the smells of coffee and pork sausage. After another hearty American breakfast, they ferried across the river and traveled through a flourishing country with European-style houses and barns. They reached the junction of Little Washington around midday. They ate, dozed, washed, read the papers, and dozed some more. In the morning, they piled into the mail stage and pitched along a rough trail over the steep hills of the Allegheny Plateau and down past one coal pit after another to where the Allegheny and Monongahela Rivers converge to form the Ohio. On the other side of the covered bridge over the Monongahela was Pittsburgh.

They could not shake the taste of soot. Every "poor and miserable house" in Pittsburgh was caked in it, the people clothed in it, the streets choked in it. Yet the city was not in as bad a shape as they assumed. The canopy of black smoke was a welcome sign to locals that their city was recovering from the postwar depression that had shuttered its factories and crashed its economy. A contributor to the *Pittsburgh Gazette* had reported recently that most of the factories were back in production, adding cheekily that the smoke and soot problem was once again "intolerable."[5] It was also early December, and as one travel guide remarked about the bleakness, "even snow can scarcely be called white in Pittsburgh."[6]

After freshening up at Darlington's Hotel, they called on some of the leading citizens in Pittsburgh, which then was known as America's Glass City. They visited the manufacturer Benjamin Bakewell, the first in the nation to make fully cut glass; his exquisite glassware graced the White House tables of President Monroe. They visited with George Sutton, another important glassmaker, and enjoyed tea with former congressman Henry Baldwin, an ardent champion of protective tariffs for the glass industry, whom President Jackson would appoint to the Supreme Court in 1830.

By amazing coincidence, George Rapp, whose Indiana property, Harmony, Owen was going to see, was also in town. Over breakfast the next morning, Owen and the German-born Rapp found they had much in common. Both had come to a country where huge parcels of land were readily available and affordable to them. While they championed different ideologies—Owen was the secular utopian and Rapp the leader of a Christian sect—both were disillusioned with the social ills caused by industrial capitalism. For years the two visionaries had been methodically refining their ideas and establishing communities where the elimination of poverty, drudgery, ignorance, and exploitation was the purpose of life. Owen was delighted to accept Rapp's invitation to visit his new settlement, Economy, about a day's ride outside of the city.[7]

Their caravan departed Pittsburgh by crossing the Alleghany via another "handsome wooden bridge" and then heading down a thin, muddy road cut into the right bank of the Ohio. After slipping through the aptly named Narrows, a spot where only a single coach could pass, Hunter and Macdonald stopped at a roadside tavern. The owner, a shoemaker by trade, brought them mugs of cider and submitted to Macdonald's questions about the history of the region. There was an edge in the shoemaker's voice as he told the British captain about the "barbarous proceeding" in the late war, by which he meant England sending "the Savage Indians" to slaughter white families. That put an end to talk about the war. The shoemaker told them about the many opportunities pulling people clear across the Mississippi, including "one of his sons [who] had gone down the river to take possession of some lots of land on the Arkansas river which he had purchased from American soldiers."[8] This was important information for Hunter, but he appears to have kept silent about his own plans in Arkansas. The shoemaker had shown that he was no friend of the Indian.

They reached Economy after dark and were able to make out a few good frame houses with several more under construction. The Harmonists, as the sectarian pilgrims were known, were preparing themselves for Christ's second coming. They had established three towns—Harmony and Economy in Pennsylvania and a second named Harmony in Indiana—each with about 800 people. They should not be confused with pie-in-the-sky utopians. Industrious and practical, they built cotton mills, wool factories, sawmills, tanneries, grinding mills, breweries, distilleries, and granaries. They operated stores, inns, taverns, and repair shops and invented new designs for wagons and boats. They exported a variety of goods to ten countries and over twenty American states. On the caravan's way to Economy, Rapp had pointed out the *William Penn*, their new eighty-ton steamer, being towed upriver to the Pittsburgh shipyards.

The Harmonists were also accomplished in literature, music, and the fine arts. They set up the first independent printing press in the state of Indiana. They published a newspaper, books of religious, philosophical, and social inquiry, and collections of poetry and essays. They practiced a communal socialism guided by the scripture of the money changers being cast out of the temple by a righteous Jesus. All property was held in common, and the profits of their collective businesses were deposited in the town coffers.[9]

That evening at Rapp's house, as his daughters prepared an impromptu dinner for their guests, the men huddled around a map of Posey County, Indiana. They drank "some very good Harmonie wine" and listened to Rapp's lecture on the many improvements on the land made by his people. Owen then laid his blueprints over the map and explained the additional improvements he planned to make, if they could agree on a fair price for the property. The two reformers went on to engage in a spirited debate about the "proper arrangement of society." We can only imagine what was going through Hunter's mind. It was not the first time he had stood intently by as Owen debated the principles of reform, but Rapp must have been a revelation to him. The man had founded three towns in North America and could point to his many achievements in agriculture, trade, and manufacturing. He knew how to achieve his dreams in America.

The next morning, a melodious psalm, played on a keyed bugle and French horn, summoned everyone to the chapel. About 100 men and women filed in, took their spots on opposite sides of the room, and broke into a rousing hymn to friendship, which was followed by a lively sermon on the same subject by the sixty-seven-year-old patriarch. Afterward, Rapp and Owen exchanged copies of their writings and went over Owen's blueprints again. Rapp assured him he was selling his Indiana property only because God had told him that he should await the second coming of Jesus Christ in western Pennsylvania. According to William, Rapp promised them they would enjoy similar success on the land along the Wabash River, "should my father be induced to purchase it."[10] Friendship was the refrain of the morning for a very practical reason: Rapp predicted that the rising number of steamboats on the rivers would nurture a profitable relationship between their villages. After the musicians played several parting songs, the visitors climbed into their carriages and went back up the Pittsburgh Road.

On a frosty December 6, after waiting several days for the river to rise high enough for steamboat passage, they boarded the *Pennsylvania* and were seen off by some of their new friends. The Ohio River, before being tamed by locks and dams, was very difficult to navigate and sometimes dangerous, particularly at the end of the fall travel season. The *Pennsylvania* crawled along at seven or eight knots to avoid snags, ice floes, and frozen channels, but the forty passengers and crew were still knocked around by the hull scraping the river bottom and by sudden heaves to port and starboard as the pilot steered them down the foggy river. After clearing Deadman's Ripple, they saw one steamboat aground, then another, then another, and they feared the *Pennsylvania* might be next. Macdonald, sitting beside the hot coal stove, followed their route in Zadoc Cramer's *The Navigator*, a popular guidebook for boatmen and travelers on the Ohio and Mississippi Rivers. Published in Pittsburgh, it provided maps for navigation; directions and mileage; soundings of the river's depth; markers of channels, islands, sandbars, rapids, and eddies; details on local history and commerce; and descriptions of landmarks, harbors, towns, and settlements. "It cost me a dollar," wrote Macdonald, "and proved extremely well worth its cost."

The pilot hit the chute between sandbar and snag at Indian Logstown and they ran to Legionville with little problem. The army of General "Mad" Anthony Wayne had encamped there before the "total defeat of the northern Indians" at the Battle of Fallen Timbers, and Macdonald directed everyone's attention to the chimneys of the army's moldering cabins still visible on the high plateau. They continued past Beaver River, with Harmony, Pennsylvania, just above its falls, and before long came upon the manufacturing center of Beavertown, with its large brewery that exported ales to Natchez and New Orleans. They stayed safely between the breakers near Raccoon Creek, sailed by the two-tavern village of Georgetown with bituminous tar sands bubbling up on the opposite shore, and hours later rounded a sharp bend with blast furnaces, forges, tanneries, and cotton-spinning mills along the banks. At some point they cut through the invisible knot of state lines between Pennsylvania and Virginia on one side and Ohio and Pennsylvania on the other.

The deceptive current at Baker's Island concealed sunken boulders, but their pilot read the ripples and maneuvered them through the crooked channels around Nealy's cluster of islands and into an easy stretch of river. They came up on Steubenville, 73 miles below Pittsburgh according to *The Navigator*, with 2,032 inhabitants, 453 dwellings, 3 churches, 27 stores, 16 taverns, a courthouse, steam-powered paper, flour, and cotton mills, a brewery known for superior ales and porters, a woolen factory producing "cloths of the finest texture and most brilliant and lasting colors," and many more industries and professions. Further downriver, Mr. Bakewell's son, from Pittsburgh, who was traveling with them, may have pointed out his father's stoneware manufactory atop the bluffs of Wellsburgh, a town with 80 dwellings, a courthouse, a jail, and a pillory—the last of these disgraceful, in the view of Zadoc Cramer. Wellsburgh was the flour depot for the New Orleans market, and passengers could stand at the railing and watch teams of workmen lower barrels of flour by pullies and windlasses from the top of a four-story warehouse and onto barges at the incredible rate of three to five barrels a minute.

After cruising by tiny Warren and its single flour warehouse, they veered into the middle channel to avoid a logjam along the left bank just above the old frontier outpost of Wheeling. The Nail City was a boomtown at the end of the National

Road. It teemed with nail mills, blast furnaces, shipyards, warehouses, coach works, textile mills, freight companies, and the tobacco rollers who rolled the "stogies" smoked by the Conestoga teamsters who transported over 10 million pounds of cargo annually to the town and the surrounding Ohio Valley.[11] It was pitch black, so the *Pennsylvania* anchored in the harbor "until the moon rose and then continued course" through the night.[12] At sunrise they had a near miss with the *Congress*, which had run aground in the shallows; its stranded passengers shouted to come aboard, but the *Pennsylvania*'s captain, not wanting to further embarrass his fellow commander, ignored their calls and sounded the whistle as he left them behind. They experienced another close call later that afternoon, brushing by a steamboat stuck on a reef at Amberson's Island, twice grounding for a terrible instant before being rescued by the current.

After dark they laid to until a bright yellow moon rose to light their way. One of their fellow passengers was Samuel Drake, the pioneer of theater in the West, whose troupe was entertaining them with a performance of singing, dancing, and comedy acts when the watchman bellowed. Everyone rushed to the port bow and looked down at a small group waving frantically from their beached flatboat, which was immediately followed by joyful shouts of recognition, for here were the other members of the troupe, including Alexander Drake Jr., his famous wife, Frances Ann Denny, and their children. Since the low river had slowed steamboat travel, they had taken a flatboat out of Pittsburgh so that at least part of the troupe would make their upcoming performance in Kentucky. "Taking this party on board," Macdonald wryly remarked, "occasioned quite a theatrical bustle."

They slept through miles and miles of unbroken sheets of silvery river that Zadoc Cramer thought were as beautiful as any stretch between Pittsburgh and Natchez. They passed the Rock of Antiquity and its etching of an Indigenous man with a pipe in his hand, which William Owen had been hoping to see; the villages of Point Pleasant, Gallipolis, Burrsburgh, and Adamsville; and the salt furnaces blazing along the banks. They finally reached Maysville, at the mouth of Limestone Creek, just as the sun dipped behind its picturesque hills. Drake and his troupe bade them farewell, climbing into several of the coaches that ran the Lexington-Frankfort route, and the through passengers took the opportunity to stretch their legs. At a dry goods store, Hunter and Owen purchased mittens, and Hunter watched his friend engage in a "bantering conversation with the storekeeper regarding money and labor notes." When the moon appeared a few hours later, the *Pennsylvania* steamed out of the harbor into a clear and cold night.

They were walking through the wide streets of Cincinnati before sunup. William was impressed by the progress of the city: "Twenty one years ago there was hardly a house standing. Now it contains about 13000 inhabitants" and handsome brick buildings.[13] Cincinnati had been built upon Indigenous ruins, and William and Mary Ronalds broke off from the group to follow the trail of earthworks to the enormous burial mound between Race and Walnut Streets. Daniel Drake, no relation to the theater impresario, had written about the mounds in the area and his book included a map to many of them.[14] One of the most respected historians of his day, Drake had plundered the graves for beads, tools, shells, and the skeletal remains of over twenty human beings. Applying some of the new principles and techniques of phrenology, he took the measurements of the "fossil skulls," compared them with a Wyandot skull in his collection, and arrived at the conclusion shared by every reputable American antiquarian: Current Native peoples could not have descended from this lost race of Mound Builders. With the aid of his calipers, Drake had given pseudo-scientific credibility to a foundational myth of the settler nation. An ancient civilization had once existed in North

America before the barbaric ancestors of current Native peoples had invaded their lands and wiped them out; this act of conquest had been superseded by the conquests of the Europeans and then the laws of the Americans, which meant that the current Indians possessed no title to the lands they claimed as their own. Those lands were currently being acquired for and redistributed to the American people by lawful treaties, the details of which Drake described in his book.

They enjoyed a pleasant stretch from Cincinnati past the Big Miami and the Licking. After tea the deck and cabin passengers crowded around the stove, sang songs, and told stories until bedtime. They were awakened at dawn by the Falls of the Ohio thundering in the distance. The gauntlet of rapids, dropping twenty-six feet over two miles, was impassable for steamboats except in very high water, so the pilot, his eye fixed on the most important navigation marker on the river, turned the *Pennsylvania* up Bear Grass Creek to the Louisville landing. (The canal soon to be dug around the falls was still in its planning phase.) They trudged through the cold rain and mud to the Washington Hotel. When the rain let up, they explored the town and saw how it was thriving from being located at the break in the river. Some streets were paved, taverns and dining rooms were crowded with travelers, and stores were busy with customers. Dozens of buildings were in various phases of construction. On their walk to Shippingport, below the falls, Hunter described for them some of the flora along the path. There was the honey locust tree, its sweet pulp used in the remedies of Native healers, and the flowering milkweed, its silky, fibrous pods part of many other remedies and also used to make rope, baskets, and textiles.

As much as they liked the city, they were troubled by the large number of enslaved people there. Enslaved stevedores loaded and unloaded ships. Enslaved porters lugged cargo to both sides of the falls. Enslaved chauffeurs transported white passengers through the city. Their enslaved waiter told them, under their questioning, that his owner had purchased him for $750 and recently refused $1,500 for him. It was a shrewd response to his inquisitors, praising his owner for a wise investment in such a valuable worker. "He said he liked this place very much," William commented, perhaps to ease his conscience. The barber who had given them a shave and haircut was not enslaved—he told them how he had purchased his freedom for $1,000 and then worked relentlessly, "nearly night and day for years," until he had saved enough to purchase the freedom of his wife and child. It was a lot to process for these English reformers. In a speech the next day, Owen veered from his prepared remarks and called for abolishing slavery in a responsible way. He had an idea for a "negro settlement" based on his cooperative model, which would educate those whose enslavement had kept them ignorant and help them to develop their natural abilities. It would not take them long to save enough money, as the barber had done, to fairly compensate their former owners for emancipating them. William reported that his father's remarks were applauded.

Two days later, they pushed aboard *The Favorite* at Shippingport with such a throng of passengers that the ship nearly sank before the crew hastily rearranged the cargo and the 380-ton sternwheeler finally crawled into the current. Both William and Macdonald blamed the slave trade for nearly sinking the ship, and they were not merely being bombastic—the heavy cargo was forty-seven enslaved persons "going down to be sold" on the auction blocks of Natchez and New Orleans. A distressed Macdonald protested that these poor souls, his fellow human beings, different from him only in color and circumstance, were "treated like beasts going to market." He was disturbed by the way everyone around him talked so naturally, and callously, about the price each human being would bring at auction. Accepting the horrors of human bondage had done irreparable damage to these Americans: "There could be no doubt that their feelings must be greatly impaired, and their minds deranged by such barbarous and irrational customs."

That night Hunter fell asleep alongside William and Macdonald near the stove. After the crew adjusted the length of the paddle wheel's bucket planks, they made 150 miles the next day down the heavily forested banks of the Ohio and anchored after nightfall because the moon was no longer bright enough for "night sailing." Several of them took the yawl ashore and built an enormous bonfire in the woods; the steward soon appeared with a crate of steaks, pork fillets, and bottles of brandy and porter. Hunter cut some three-pronged sticks and showed them how to roast the meat in the Osage fashion. The gentlemen passed the bottles, ripped into the meat with their teeth, and danced around the bonfire. As the leaping flames found a hollow tree and turned it into a spectacular flume of fire, Hunter suddenly sounded the war whoop, and everyone tilted their heads up, raised their fists, and tried to copy him. Then they heaped more logs near two other hollow trees and balls of fire and sparks started shooting out the tops like roman candles. At last, the blazing trees fell—"very grand, well worth waiting for"—and the revelers whooped into the night sky.

It was a rare moment in the life of this staid and sober young man. Richard Drinnon called it "an unforgettable night and one that at last revealed Hunter not to have been all high-minded seriousness."[15] While William Owen certainly revealed a hidden part of Hunter's personality, his lavish description of the bonfire should be read with a skeptical eye. "Hunter was quite in his element," William said about the white Indian who seemed to be guiding them through a rite of passage into the American wilderness. Urbane gentlemen diminished by city life and modern society and finding their primitive manhood in nature—this was a cliché even at the time. However, the rite of passage Owen had in mind worked differently for the white

Indian, whose conversion to civilization would be tragically undone if he heeded the call of the wild, just as the bittersweet poem in *The Atlantic* had prophesied.[16] And as in the poem, there in his journal William singled out Hunter as the one who turned into a savage in the wilderness, an insensitive comment by the owner of the land where they had built the bonfire apparently setting him off. Mildly annoyed by the intrusion of the revelers, the landowner flippantly thanked them for clearing the brush and leaving less work for his two slaves. Hunter, instantly riled by the comment, muttered that they should grab him and "duck him" in the river, an old common-law punishment still occasionally used in Kentucky at the time.[17] If this indeed happened as William remembered, then it seems out of character for Hunter. Perhaps the brandy hit the teetotaler hard, or the landowner's words were more offensive to him than his companions could understand. William wrote that he finally managed to calm him down, but they kept clear of the water until rowing back to the boat long after midnight.

The morning was a meander down a stretch of river that seemed to bend toward every point in the compass. After winding past Hendersonville and channeling to the right side of Diamond Island, they landed at Mt. Vernon at a horseshoe bend in the river, about 1,000 miles from Pittsburgh. Here was where Hunter left the Owen party, which was taking a short ride up the road to Harmony. It was not a final farewell, since they fully expected to see each other again, after they had broken ground on their respective dreams.

CHAPTER THIRTEEN

Exodus

PASSENGERS CROWDED THE DECKS as they approached the confluence of the Ohio and Mississippi in anticipation of experiencing one of nature's brilliant panoramas, but many of them were disenchanted by the bleakness of the scene. It was ridiculed as a "vile sewer," "the dullest, dreariest, most uninviting region imaginable," and a gloomy ditch of "solitary desolation." On his American tour, the novelist Charles Dickens had stood at the rail in shock upon seeing the two great rivers, appalled by the "slimy" and "intolerable" scenery. Another disappointed traveler remarked that the conquistador Hernando de Soto should have exercised some discretion and kept his discovery to himself.[1] We can only imagine what John Dunn Hunter was thinking as he gazed across the dingy landscape, but he may have been feeling nostalgic about his experience on those muddy waters. They had changed his life forever, giving him independence and direction after leaving the Osages. He had piloted his flatboat, loaded with goods and merchandise, through these same currents and down the Mississippi, and parlayed his earnings into an education and a parcel of land to begin building his future.

All of what we know about the brief interval between Hunter's return to New Orleans and his departure for Arkansas comes from two letters he wrote to friends. In a letter to Robert Owen, which he wrote after arriving in New Orleans, he hailed the marvel that was *The Favorite* for covering the 1,000 miles from Cairo to New Orleans in an incredible six days, which seemed unimaginable to the former flatboat pilot. The letter clarifies why he chose to travel all the way to New Orleans rather than leave the Mississippi 600 miles earlier and take the short jaunt up the White River to his land in Arkansas. He planned to purchase the supplies for his farm with the money he had lent out to a friend in New Orleans. But there was a problem: "The man who owes me money is not in town yet." Although frustrated, Hunter was confident his good reputation in town would give him access to all the credit he required: "My disappointment can be no material obstruction to my ultimate proceedings for I can obtain what I want here. My credit is good for any amount I may be in need of." Hunter was slightly embarrassed because he also wanted to repay a small debt to Owen for the traveling expenses that Owen had loaned him. Hunter assured Owen that his predicament was but a slight obstacle. Whenever Owen returned to Philadelphia, Hunter instructed him to go directly to the residence of Elliot Cresson, his close friend, who was safeguarding Hunter's money and would pay Owen back. Personal banking in the nineteenth century depended on trustworthy intermediaries.[2] Hunter asked about the status of the deal for Harmony, unaware that Owen had taken possession of it at the same moment Hunter was writing to him.

In a second letter from New Orleans, written to a friend in England, Bessy Walker, Hunter dropped his guard and shared his burdens and fears. He was setting out for a conflict zone, and he rightly worried that he might never return. His words were wrenchingly prophetic of his fate:

> I am now about to bid Adieu—perhaps forever! to the kind friends with whom I have been blessed for the last six or seven years of my life. Heaven knows: but human

> foresight cannot look into futurity, and what may await me in the yet almost trackless wilds, we cannot say; even if every thing turns out to the utmost of my wishes, it is impossible for you conceive the situation in which I am placed. Scarcely can I pourtray to you the pleasures I anticipate from again enjoying the rustic scenes of the chase, the gun and the endeavor to improve the little knowledge I have already acquired in the Arts and Agriculture."[3]

Hunter left New Orleans in early January, just after writing farewell to Walker, who confided in Neal that the determined Hunter would not be deterred from his laudable mission. A few weeks later he resurfaced at the Dwight Mission on the edge of the Arkansas frontier. Given the short duration of his trip, it seems probable that he had left the city by steamboat for a nearly 900-mile journey up the Mississippi and Arkansas and through bayous blanketed with bright yellow lotuses and vast swamps guarded by funereal cypresses with ragged beards of Spanish moss.[4] This had been the heart of Quapaw country since the 1500s. Their migration from the Ohio Valley had given them their name, which translates as "the downstream people" in their Dhegia-Siouan language. They had been key allies of the French and the Spanish during the 1700s because of their importance to trade and diplomacy in the valley. The "Arkansas," as the Europeans called them, shared their knowledge of the surrounding hills and rivers, served as intermediaries with other tribes, and adopted elements of French and Spanish cultures.[5]

Their world unraveled in the aftermath of the Louisiana Purchase, during the new era of American rule. The Quapaws were estimated to be between 600 and 1,000 people, so they were too small to pose a threat to American interests or to serve as a useful ally; besides, the United States didn't require their help in keeping the peace or controlling trade. In 1818, the Quapaws agreed to a treaty that allowed them to stay in the valley in exchange for giving up nearly all their land, approximately 30 million acres, but they held on to the land around their villages, retained some of their hunting rights, and received a comparatively large annuity payment. Not content with their near total surrender, American settlers in the region howled in objection. In petitions to President Monroe, the US Congress, and the legislature of the newly established Arkansas Territory, they protested that the presence of the Quapaws deprived the settlers of their freedom and undermined their mandate to improve the land and make it productive. If the treaty was not revised, then some "of the best soil" west of the Mississippi for cotton cultivation would remain in Quapaw hands, and everyone knew what that meant: It would lie mostly fallow, impeding progress and prosperity and slowing the path to statehood for Arkansas.[6] They wanted every acre of Quapaw land.[7] The only way to accomplish it within the bounds of the law was to convince Washington that most of the Quapaws actually desired a fresh start somewhere else. Over the next few years, officials in Arkansas commenced "a campaign of deceitfulness and half-truths," as Baird described it, that duped the government into believing the Quapaws wanted to leave Arkansas for a barren strip of land in northwestern Louisiana.[8] The mendacious campaign was successful, and the Quapaws had little choice but to accept an even worse treaty in 1824, which expelled them from their land.

News of the treaty likely reached Hunter after he had left New Orleans for Arkansas, since there was no hint of it in the letters he wrote from the city. The Quapaws were forced to cede the last remnant of their homeland in exchange for land farther south, on the Red River in Caddo country, and were given until the end of the year to vacate their homes in the valley.[9] Hunter probably heard the news on his trip to Arkansas, and he must have been stunned both by the devastating blow to the Quapaws and by the collapse of his plan before he had even broken ground. Around 600 Quapaws remained in their villages on the Arkansas when Hunter would have stopped there in late January, but he did not find the people he was looking for; his inquiries into their whereabouts sent him upriver and past the pine bluffs into Cherokee country.

He reached the Dwight Mission on the twenty-eighth of January.[10] Founded by the American Board of Commissioners for Foreign Missions, this was a new type of missionary institution in the United States: a manual-labor boarding school for children built on Native land and backed by federal funds. The evangelists, teachers, farmers, and their families lived on the property and were supposed to serve as the model of a Christian community.[11] When visitors landed at the mission, on Illinois Bayou, they were usually greeted by the director, Reverend Cephas Washburn, and his assistant and brother-in-law, Reverend Alfred Finney. After offering thanks for their safe arrival, the evangelists took their visitors on a well-rehearsed tour of the Zion they had cleared out of the swamps. There was a simple, elegant chapel, several log cabins with verandas and gardens, a schoolhouse for 100 children, a large dining hall, the stables with corn crib and farming equipment, and fenced pastures for their cows and hogs.

Every appearance of visitors at the mission was treated as an opportunity to promote not only God's work but also the vanguard ideas of the American Board of Commissioners for Foreign Missions. Visitors were told how the Cherokee children were removed from their homes at a very young age, preferably as infants, "before bad habits formed," and placed with the American families at the mission. Every day was praised as another step toward civilization for the children dressed in clothes donated by churches across New England. The children practiced their letters and numbers. They learned moral and religious lessons from their *New England Primer*. They performed all the different kinds of labor on the farm. The boys planted crops, fenced the fields, dug irrigation ditches, felled trees, cared for the livestock, and harvested the plots. The girls were not spared from this labor, but they were also taught to sew and spin. In sum, the missionaries implemented the noxious doctrine of "killing the savage in order to save the child," which would become the norm at Indian boarding schools in the United States and Canada.

Hunter's appearance at Dwight Mission was an exciting event. The missionaries, fully aware of who he was, sent an enthusiastic account of his visit to the *New York Religious Chronicle*. They wrote that the "striking and singular" history of their visitor should be well known to the readers of the paper. He was the very same man who had been taken captive as a boy and raised by the "Missouri Indians"; after returning to American civilization and acquiring an education, he had written a book that earned him many admirers on both sides of the Atlantic. The missionaries were impressed by his plan for assisting the Indians, but his zeal for the cause was the young man's distinguishing trait: "The recollection of the wrongs and outrages they have suffered fills him with generous indignation, and he is determined to exert all his influence in every way to meliorate their condition. His efforts for their good are to commence with the Quapaws."

It was an accurate picture of Hunter, but then they went too far by claiming his endorsement for their practices at Dwight Mission, saying that he hoped for similar success with the Quapaws. However, he knew better than anyone how absurd the idea was that the Cherokees could not survive and prosper without the aid of Christian missionaries. They were thriving by any standard measure of progress. The naturalist Thomas Nuttall, traveling up the Arkansas in 1819, marveled at the banks

> lined with the houses and farms of the Cherokees, and though their dress was a mixture of indigenous and European taste, yet in their houses, which are decently furnished, and in their farms, which were well fenced and stocked with cattle, we perceive a happy approach towards civilization. Their numerous families, also, well fed and clothed argue a propitious progress in their population. . . . Some of them are possessed of property to the amounts of many thousands of dollars, have houses handsomely and conveniently furnished, and their tables spread with our dainties and luxuries.[12]

Unfortunately, these few thousand Cherokees now faced the same problem that had dogged them and their relatives east of the Mississippi. Their farms and prosperity proved nothing to the Americans and could not quiet the demand for their land. When they had been pressed yet again to show their eagerness to assimilate as quickly as possible, the Cherokees made the Faustian bargain by inviting the missionaries into their territory and putting their children under their care. It would not have been lost on Hunter that the Cherokee were compromising and doing everything they could to hold on to the world they had built for themselves.

The missionaries who deemed to speak for Hunter seemed to be oblivious to his skepticism about Christian conversion. They had apparently not read his book very closely, because if they had, they surely would have remembered the scene where Hunter mocked the evangelist who came to his village for his ignorance of Osage culture, his inability to speak the language, and his arrogant assumptions, all of which caused the evangelist to miscount every bowed Osage head as another soul converted.

The directors of the Dwight Mission had committed the same error by mistaking Hunter's civility for his approval of their methods, which later inspired his first biographer to fire back in indignation: "He could not have been enthusiastic about their goal of making the Indian children over into industrious obedient little Christians or their attempts to secure economic self-sufficiency for the manual labor school through making them work the land in what amounted to a system of labor peonage."[13] The strongest evidence of all supports this inference: Hunter's own plan for aiding the Quapaws, which was rooted in his admiration for their chief and in his respect for their independence and their fundamental right to their own beliefs. It would have gone against everything he believed in for him to suddenly support a new religious institution that removed Cherokee children from their families, punished them for speaking their language, indoctrinated them in Christianity, and trained them to toil in the fields.[14]

Hunter was not prepared for how dramatically the region had changed in the years that he had been gone. The historian Jeffrey Ostler has documented the "unprecedented population boom" occurring west of the Mississippi, where settlements were expanding, Arkansas was a new federal territory, and Missouri was a new state.[15] The non-Indian population tripled from about 20,000 in 1812 to about 60,000 in 1819, while over 10,000 eastern Indians, the largest groups being Cherokees, Kickapoos, Delawares, and Shawnees, also crossed the Mississippi and eventually settled on Osage lands promised to them by treaties with the United States. (One of the newcomers, John Norton, the mixed-race Mohawk chief who had preceded Hunter in London, had come to live in Arkansas with a group of Cherokees after writing a 1,000-page, unpublished travel narrative about the Cherokees of Tennessee, his father's people.)[16] The influx of new arrivals resulted in fierce conflicts over boundaries, land claims, and resources; vicious cycles of bloodshed and a growing scarcity of game brought hunger and misery and enabled the Americans to seize Native lands with impunity. As white settlers and eastern Indians continued to pour into the region, officials in St. Louis and Washington stubbornly stuck to the same policy dream of Thomas Jefferson: the funneling of eastern Indians off their lands, away from whites, and into the supposedly wide-open western frontier. In a string of treaties in 1824 and 1825, the Osages, Quapaws, Kansas, Iowas, and Caddos had been forced to give up all or most of their land in Arkansas and Missouri for the sake of the policy.

After Hunter left Dwight Mission, his search for the Quapaws took him further upriver to Cantonment Gibson on the western edge of the United States. He crossed paths with a federal surveyor, John Sullivan, dragging his chain over the proposed boundary for a new Indian territory (the future state of Oklahoma). He wrote in his notes that Hunter was headed to the Red River "to locate himself on a farm" with a group of Quapaws.[17] The exodus of the Quapaws from Arkansas did not begin until the following January, when an estimated 455 men, women, and children departed for their treaty land on the Red River, but they had been losing people to migration for several years.[18] Hunter clearly had learned enough by the time he crossed paths with Sullivan to abandon his plan of building a farm on the White River, but we cannot definitively say he intended to put the same plan in motion on the Red River. He perhaps told the surveyor as much, but his objective likely had narrowed to simply finding the people he was searching for.

Six months later, in the fall of 1825, he found them near Nacogdoches, in Mexico's province of Texas, about a two-day walk south from the Red River. This once had been the home of tens of thousands of Kadohadachoes, Hasinais, Natchitoches, Anadarkos, and other Caddoan-speaking peoples, but disease and bloodshed had reduced their population to about 2,000 by the 1820s. The Quapaws were not the only group of immigrant Indians who found a refuge in the rolling hills and pine forests. Several thousand Cherokees, Delawares, Kickapoos, Creeks, and Choctaws had been settling in the region. The Cherokees, who had been given provisional title to their land by the king of Spain, headed a loose alliance among them, and there was hope that they could rebuild their lives here. There was reason for optimism. The new republic of Mexico, badly needing loyalists on the frontier to deter the expansionist ambitions of their sister republic to the north, had made land available for settlement. And the Cherokee chiefs believed John Dunn Hunter would be the ideal emissary to send to Mexico City to appeal for a land grant.

CHAPTER FOURTEEN

Public Enemy

THE YEAR 1825 MARKED a turning point not only in the push for a national policy of Indian removal, which culminated five years later in the Indian Relocation Act, but also for John Dunn Hunter, whose pro-Indian views turned him into a public enemy of the United States. An author in England's *Quarterly Review* had lauded him as a new American voice and used his book to accuse the United States of mistreating Native peoples. British accusations of hypocrisy were guaranteed to strike a nerve with the War of 1812 generation, but the timing of the review in the *Quarterly Review* was the bigger problem. Congress would soon be debating President Monroe's removal plan, which largely amounted to forcing Native peoples to accept one-sided treaties, massive land cessions, and relocation across the Mississippi.[1] While the War Department could count on a high degree of deference on issues related to the Indian tribes, the vote promised to be a close one, and officials did not want to lose control over public opinion. After copies of the *Quarterly Review* reached Washington, Thomas McKenney, the head of the new Bureau of Indian Affairs, published an anonymous rebuttal in the *National Intelligencer* that mocked the British author for being duped by Hunter's falsehoods about Native peoples and life on the western frontier.[2] McKenney accused the British author of repeating an outrageous lie about the savagery of Kentucky militiamen during the last war, which supposedly exceeded the savagery of the Indians themselves. "Ferocity is not, and never has been, a distinguishing trait in the American character," McKenney explained, confident in the goodness of his fellow citizens. "On the contrary, it is remarkable for humanity, and in the midst of the most appalling scenes of bloodshed, the American never loses that sensibility and sympathy, which the scenes of horror around him might be supposed to destroy or deaden."[3] The British author, safely tucked away in his study, had never witnessed, as he had, the gallant Kentuckians fighting for their land. They deserved the nation's thanks.

It was Lewis Cass, governor of Michigan Territory and superintendent of Indian affairs of the Northwest, who took charge of defending US policy and discrediting Hunter and his British supporters. Cass had grown up with the West, first making his name on the Ohio frontier as a charismatic lawyer and as a state representative and then as a general in the War of 1812. He began preparing his rebuttal on a voyage from Detroit to Prairie du Chien on the Mississippi River for a major treaty conference. His convoy of canoes traveled up the shores of Lake Huron to Mackinac Island, where they rendezvoused with the federal Indian agent Henry Rowe Schoolcraft and his contingent of 60 soldiers and officers plus more than 150 Ojibwe warriors and French *voyageurs*. With American flags flapping off the sterns of their canoes, they pushed through the Straits of Mackinac amid cannon salutes and into Lake Michigan. As the Ojibwe crew paddled along the western coast, Cass sat on a trade blanket on the wide bottom of the canoe and read Hunter's book, which Schoolcraft had brought for him. Their route took them into Green Bay and up the Fox River as far as the portage over to the Wisconsin, at which point everyone disembarked and four or five crew members hoisted each of their bark and cedar canoes to their shoulders and trudged along the trail for a few miles. Cass, irritated by what he had

Figure 18 "View of the Great Treaty Held at Prairie du Chien, September 1825." With curious soldiers and warriors watching him work, James Otto Lewis painted this scene of the Treaty at Prairie du Chien in September 1825. The treaty was negotiated between Governor William Clark and Governor Lewis Cass and over 5,000 representatives of the Sioux, Sac, Fox, and Iowa tribes.
Source: Courtesy of Rare Book Division, The New York Public Library. 1836. https://digitalcollections.nypl.org/items/510d47da-d879-a3d9-e040-e00a18064a99

been reading, walked beside Schoolcraft, quoting him aloud the passages from Hunter's book that most offended him. His key objections crystallized in his mind as the Wisconsin carried the convoy into the Mississippi and finally down to the village of Prairie du Chien.[4]

The critique of the treatment of Native peoples in the *Quarterly Review* drew extensively from Hunter's book and another by the Moravian missionary John Heckewelder. Only recently deceased, Heckewelder had lived for over forty years among the Delaware, or Lenni Lenape, and had been an important peacekeeper among the tribes, settlers, and soldiers on the Pennsylvania frontier. He compiled Indian grammars and dictionaries and wrote travel accounts, but the publication of *History, Manners, and Customs of the Indian Nations* at the end of his life confirmed his authority as an unrivaled expert on the eastern tribes. His book is remembered today as James Fenimore Cooper's source for *The Last of the Mohicans*.

Being paired with the venerable Heckewelder in the *Quarterly Review* elevated Hunter's stature. Their books, one focused on the East and the other on the West, were praised by the reviewer for showing the full humanity of Native peoples and the richness and diversity of their cultures, which exposed the shameful assumption driving US Indian policy—namely, that Native peoples lacked the essential traits to become part of American society.[5] Hunter and Heckewelder also laid bare the fatal flaw of American policy: It was toothless without the vigilantism of the white settlers who believed the land was their birthright. The author in the *Quarterly Review* called these settlers the true savages, "a race of men so utterly abandoned to vice and crime" that they thought little of soaking the Indian in whiskey and cheating him out of his land.[6] The pair of books, by two white men with knowledge born from experience in Native communities, had led the reviewer to a damning indictment of the end goal of American policy: "However it may be attempted to preserve appearances by fraudulent and compulsory purchases of Indian lands, and declarations of benevolent intentions towards the injured possessors, it has always been the boast of American policy, that 'the Indians shall be made to vanish before civilization, as the snow melts before the sunbeam.'"[7]

For his part, Lewis Cass spent his mornings in Prairie du Chien writing the treatise that made Hunter a scandal. He rushed a letter to Jared Sparks, the editor of the *North American Review*, telling him it was urgent that he publish Cass's article before Congress debated President Monroe's removal plan, five months from then.[8] When the article appeared in the *North American Review* in January 1826, Hunter's credibility was ruined. Until then, he had been regarded as a principled, honest, and knowledgeable young man from Indian country, but now he had been accused of perpetrating an extravagant hoax. Hiding behind his anonymity, Cass accused Hunter of lying about his childhood, lying about the customs of the Osages, lying about the conduct of settlers and missionaries, lying about his journey to the Pacific Ocean, lying about the ills of the fur trade, lying about Tecumseh visiting his village, lying about his heartache, and lying about so much more. Cass wrote with the courtroom experience he had sharpened as a young lawyer on the Ohio circuit, questioning why Hunter had not provided any corroborating evidence of his years with the Osages. In contrast, Cass had acquired supposedly damning affidavits from the explorer William Clark, currently the Indian superintendent in St. Louis; Pierre Choteau, a fur trader from the same city; Baronet Vásquez, an Indian agent for the Kansas; and a John Dunn from Cape Girardeau, who was supposedly Hunter's namesake. Each man swore that he had never seen nor heard of anyone fitting Hunter's description who had lived with the Osages.

It must be said how expertly Governor Cass used the power of his office to shape public opinion about Native peoples and the issue of Indian removal. The four essays he published in the *North American Review* between 1826 and 1830 painted the image of a great republic in the hands of enlightened officials who had been exceedingly patient in trying to bring the light of civilization to the tribes.[9] Cass's views on Indian removal had changed from a few years earlier, and by the time of his last essay, he was President Jackson's most vocal proponent of a removal policy. He leaned heavily into his experience as a frontier soldier, suggesting that anyone who had not seen firsthand the Indians' cunning and barbaric ways did not really know them at all and thus were susceptible to believing storybook fantasies about them. He purported to know the "real" Indians, a barbarous, degraded, vengeful race of people, inferior in nearly every way to whites. By this stereotype, the man who would implement President Jackson's plan for Indian removal marked an uncrossable boundary between two very different worlds. In the view of historian John Fierst, Cass's "real" Indian was "one who wanted nothing to do with white ways and white improvement and whose hostility and British allegiance presented a serious threat to the United States."[10] The Indians had only themselves to blame for being stuck in their lowly condition. As governor, Cass had learned that tough love was necessary. He lamented that removing the Indian tribes from the graves of their fathers was the only humane solution to the "Indian problem," but he righteously fulfilled his duty on behalf of the American people.

If not for some groundbreaking revelations on Native languages, Cass would not have needed to throw himself into his part, the prosecutor pressing his case against the fraud, with such force. In a collaborative study, Heckewelder and the philologist Peter DuPonceau had collected information on the Lenni Lenape language, conferred with Huron- and Chickasaw speakers, and examined various dictionaries, vocabularies, grammars, and phrase books of different Native languages. Contrary to the consensus view, they concluded that these languages were not fixed, crude, or reflections of an inferior mental aptitude. Their conclusion that Native peoples actually spoke complex languages with copious vocabularies, pleasing sounds, and intricate syntaxes "shocked the public," according to the historian Sean Harvey, and it promised "far reaching implications" for the future of Native peoples.[11] The philologist John Pickering, also writing in the *North American Review*, predicted that the pair's work would move Americans to "feel more kindly towards that unfortunate race." He was not wrong. Former president John Adams, in a remarkable letter to DuPonceau, praised the findings and vowed to overcome "certain prejudices" he had held against Native peoples, which he now saw were irrational and unworthy of a true republican. A minister named Frederick Christian Schaffer, in another letter to DuPonceau, applauded the study for providing a "powerful plea in favour of the claim which the American Indians have to *humane*, to *respectful treatment*, and to all possible justice at the hands of their white countrymen." Heckewelder and DuPonceau had changed the way some people thought about not only Native languages but also the people themselves. Their new revelations, which challenged the very stereotypes and prejudices that made Indian removal seem like a sensible and compassionate policy, challenged government officials to defend their actions.

This backstory explains why Cass was so zealous in attacking Hunter's credibility. Five years earlier, in 1821, Cass had been just as zealous in trying to discredit these heterodox and potentially explosive findings on the complexity of Native languages. With the support of John Calhoun, secretary of war, he devised a questionnaire with 350 inquiries on the languages, mental traits, moral habits, and customs of Native peoples, then distributed it to agents, missionaries, and fur traders throughout the region, along with instructions for conducting interviews in the field. It was the first governmental study of its kind and was marred by problems from the start. The examiners were untrained in linguistics, mostly unacquainted with and confused by the speech and culture of their subjects, and dependent on Native translators, who were understandably evasive and wary under questioning. An ethnographic research project of this scope requires time and loads of expertise. As reports trickled into Detroit over the next several years, Cass struggled to accept any evidence contradicting his belief in the rudimentary languages (and minds) of Native peoples.[12] The most puzzling reports were coming from Sault Ste. Marie, where the US Indian agent, Henry Rowe Schoolcraft, was being taught the Ojibwe language by his wife, Jane Johnston Schoolcraft, the Métis writer. Cass didn't know what to do, so he waited for more questionnaires, and as they trickled in with more contradictions to his theory, he waited for still more questionnaires, putting off submitting his final report to the secretary of war.

The criticism in the *Quarterly Review* provided Cass with a useful distraction from the contradictions of his research study. In his tent at Prairie du Chien, he drafted his argument about the bogus linguistics and the quacks who knew next to nothing about the Indians. He claimed to have more than enough evidence to prove that their languages were deficient in syntax, vocabulary, and order. They were only capable of expressing a limited range of thought with simple ideas and abstractions. They were tarnished by irregularities in tenses and participles, which caused their speakers to quickly forget the past and disregard the future. The poor savages were trapped within their primitive languages and would never be able to articulate and comprehend the concepts and values necessary for living among whites in a Christian, republican society.[13] In defending the consensus, Cass did not allow for any hedging or mention the questionnaires piling up on his desk and disputing his pet theory.

As far as Cass was concerned, Hunter being grouped together with Heckewelder and DuPonceau in the *Quarterly Review* made him guilty by association. Cass accused him of being a charlatan for the same reason he labeled DuPonceau a "quack" and the elderly Heckewelder, who had passed away two years earlier, an "enfeebled" thinker: They challenged the status quo, the intellectual premise of US Indian policy, by emphasizing the intellectual and cultural complexity of Native peoples. Even though his agents in the field were sending back reports that suggested the same, Cass doubled down in his attacks on the purveyors of the new linguistics. He chastised the Frenchman DuPonceau, who had never met a Wyandot in his life, for foolishly praising the melodious quality of the Wyandot language. Cass had sat many times with the Wyandots in their lodges, grimacing at the "harsh, guttural, and undistinguishable" sounds coming out of their mouths.[14] The Wyandot language Cass described and claimed to know so well ultimately turned out to be the forerunner of the grunts of Hollywood's Indians.

Hunter's was only one of the many voices of resistance to the attacks on Native rights and culture during the fateful years between Monroe's removal plan, the election of President Andrew Jackson in 1828, and the lead-up to the Indian Removal Act in 1830. Hunter belongs with the most notable of them. The Cherokee leader Elias Boudinot, on a lecture tour of the East in 1826, defended the rights of the Cherokee, promoted their achievements in farming, education, and trade, and raised money for a printing press and typeset for Sequoyah's syllabary. After returning to Georgia, Boudinot established the *Cherokee Phoenix*, and its many anti-removal voices, in both English and Cherokee, forged Cherokee solidarity against the state of Georgia and generated white support for their cause across the world.[15] Also in 1826, the Tuscarora historian David Cusick, in *Sketches of the Ancient History of the Six Nations*, rejected the core of the removal position by describing the persistence of the Haudenosaunee people in their ancestral home, vigilantly protecting their two-millennia-old sovereignty against waves of invaders and cultivating farms and tidy villages long before the coming of the whites. In 1829, the New England author and reformer Lydia Maria Child protested the push for removal by publishing an alternative account of King Philip's War, the seventeenth-century war between English colonists and New

England Indians.[16] That same year, a missionary named Jeremiah Evarts, under the pseudonym William Penn, published twenty-four essays against the expulsion of Native peoples; the following year, at his urging, people from every corner of the nation flooded Congress with anti-removal petitions.[17] Also in 1829, the Pequot William Apess, in his remarkable autobiography, told the heart-wrenching history of his struggle, and the struggles of other Native peoples in New England, to survive the settler invasion. While these are only some of the authors who spoke out in print, their views echoed the dissident voices of many Native leaders between 1825 and 1830, who repeatedly "stymied efforts to expel their communities," as Claudio Saunt writes, announcing over and over to frustrated officials and supporters alike, and to the world, that "they would not go quietly."[18]

PART IV

Democratic Visionary

CHAPTER FIFTEEN

Promised Land

THOUSANDS OF NATIVE PEOPLES had left the United States for Mexican Texas by the 1820s. Along the upper branches of the Neches, Angelina, and Sabine Rivers north of Nacogdoches, bands and groups from over a dozen Indian tribes, including the Cherokees, Delawares, Shawnees, Quapaws, and Kickapoos, had established a thriving society in what had been Caddo country before epidemics, famines, and wars had drastically reduced their population. The villages of the Indian immigrants were surrounded by farms and pastures. They tilled abandoned Caddo fields, reaped harvests of corn, beans, pumpkins, squash, and melons, and raised cattle and horses. By all accounts, they experienced a better quality of life in Mexican Texas than they had in the United States. There were very few whites around to trouble them. They socialized together and celebrated some of their feast days with each other. They hunted together and married each other. They traded together and learned from each other. This period of relative peace and security probably lasted no more than a decade. It was swiftly coming to an end by the time John Dunn Hunter came to live among them.[1]

Their new lives did not cause them to worry any less about the security of their homes and farms. The Cherokees were slightly more fortunate than the rest because the king of Spain had issued a decree that gave them temporary occupancy rights to their land, but the Mexican Revolution had swept him away and now their fate was as uncertain as that of any of their neighbors. Two important leaders, a venerable chief named Bowles and a younger man of mixed Cherokee and white parentage named Richard Fields, were determined to get a clear answer from the current government about the royal decree, which they kept safe in a tin box. Fields had led a company of Cherokee warriors under General Andrew Jackson during the War of 1812 and later worked as a government interpreter. He was experienced in the nuances of frontier diplomacy. In a petition to the Texas governor, Fields tried to appear compliant and deferential in his broken English: "I wish to fall at your feet and omblay ask you what must be Dun with us pur Indians."[2]

His appeal on behalf of "us poor Indians" hit its mark because Governor José Felix Trespalacios invited Fields and Bowles to meet with him in San Antonio in November 1822. Their large delegation put on a pageant of progress that pleasantly surprised the governor: "They work for their living and dress in cotton cloth of their own manufacture. They raise cattle and horses, and use fire arms. Many of them understand the English Language." While Trespalacios grandfathered in their provisional rights under the royal decree, he stopped short of issuing them title to their land. At least they were not squatters, but neither were they landowners with legal protections. Wanting to help them, the governor provided the chiefs with a travel pass that authorized them to go to Mexico City and plead their case before the emperor of Mexico, Agustín de Iturbide. They arrived in the city at the worst possible time, just as the short-lived emperor was being ousted from power in early 1823, making it impossible for them to drum up support for a permanent land grant. They left with the consolation prize—congressional approval for their agreement with Governor Trespalacios.[3]

The situation was dire when Fields and Bowles arrived back home that summer. Without the military to enforce their agreement, the Cherokees could neither force out the growing number of American settlers who were squatting on their lands nor deter the many others coming into the region down Trammel's Trace. The crisis came to head in early 1825 after the passage of new laws on land concessions, when the state of Coahuila-Texas began issuing grants to seemingly everyone but the Cherokees. Dozens of land speculators from the United States and Europe, who for two years had been "patiently awaiting their opportunity" in the northern capital of Saltillo, swamped the state legislature with grant applications. Fields and Bowles, who had staked their hopes on the new laws, did not even learn about them for months and thus could not promptly apply for a land grant; they were probably intentionally kept in the dark.[4]

To make matters worse, they soon heard that a few thousand Shawnees on the Red River had received a sizable grant. Then there were the dismaying reports of two more grants awarded to two white men who had been around Nacogdoches, Hayden Edwards and his son-in-law Frost Thorn.[5] Thorn, a New Yorker, received a contract to settle 400 American families in the area; Edwards, a Kentuckian, had a contract for 800. To add insult to injury, the land the Cherokees claimed as their own, upon which they had built their homes, farms, and orchards, now fell within the boundaries of the two new grants. They were baffled by this turn of events. They had done everything possible to show that they were civilized and loyal to Mexico. They believed they had met the one essential requirement for a grant: Applicants must pass the government's "good character" test. Were they industrious? Did they have civilized habits and manners? Would they pledge their allegiance to Mexico and its laws? Would they follow Catholicism? In his correspondence with officials, Fields emphasized repeatedly that his people were peaceful, living a happy life as farmers, and always true to their word. They were neither savage raiders like the Comanches nor horse thieves like the white desperados along the border. True, the Cherokees were not Mexican nationals or European Catholics, the government's preferred settlers, but neither were they belligerent Protestants from the United States.

Their predicament did not bode well for the many other Native peoples who were crossing into Texas and settling around Nacogdoches. When the state refused yet again to issue them a grant, Fields called for a council meeting of their Native allies in the region, and rumors immediately spread that they were plotting a rebellion. "Such a notion was ridiculous," concluded Gary Anderson, one of the best historians of early Texas, but the Cherokees were being blamed for a rash of attacks on white farms and settlements, despite all evidence pointing to Comanche and Wichita raiders.[6] In a report to Mexican officials, Stephen Austin, the American whose grant on the Brazos River had nearly 300 families, pointed the finger at the usually diplomatic Fields: He was secretly inciting the raids as a ploy to extort a land grant from the government. The chief's acquaintances thought such behavior was out of character for him, but they chose to believe the alarming rumors anyway. "All apparently misunderstood the motives of Fields and the Cherokees," Everett wrote, "and all assumed the worst."[7]

Stephen Austin, ambitious and cunning, played a major part in escalating the crisis. He was troubled by the presence of Indian immigrants and could not fathom why the government had given land to the Shawnees, the same people, Tecumseh's people, who had waged war against the United States. There was no louder alarm bell in Texas than Austin. He warned about raids by Shawnee warriors and badgered state officials into allowing him to organize militia units to defend his colony against attack. With more armed fighters, he began driving Native people from the valleys of the Colorado and Brazos Rivers, which facilitated the expansion of the cotton frontier into Texas. He was betting that the availability of cheap land would entice farmers who had been priced out of the booming market in the southeastern United States.[8] His rangers took even the most minor affront or threat as a license for aggression, killing hundreds of Native people and terrorizing and displacing many more. Austin did whatever was necessary to strengthen his position in the valley. He had no qualms calling on the military for help or even recruiting Native warriors to his side. Anderson reached a blunt conclusion about his motives: "Austin's geopolitical maneuvering had only one goal: expel the Indians nearest his colony from their lands. If immigrant Indians, or even Mexican troops would help, so much the better. It was classic ethnic cleansing."[9]

Mexican officials could not investigate every conspiracy theory, every raid, but they did try to substantiate some of the more feverish allegations. One time, when rumors of another Cherokee plot reached Saltillo, an agent was dispatched to Nacogdoches to get a sense of the climate. After paying a visit to Fields and touring some Cherokee homes and farms, the agent dismissed the rumors of their "hostile projects" as nothing but the hysteria of white settlers. Fields impressed the agent as a strong leader who wanted peace and whose people were loyal to the government and its laws.

By this time, the spring of 1826, Hunter had made it to Texas and found a home with a group of Quapaws, perhaps the same people he had been searching for. We know this because he reappears in the historical records as the Quapaw envoy to a loose confederacy headed by the Cherokees and including the branches of twenty-three Native nations. As the following events will show, Fields saw in Hunter the makings of an effective diplomat who might tip the balance in their favor. He was familiar with whites and accustomed to dealing with officials, and his international reputation could help in winning support for a land grant. That summer, a proposal was made in council that the confederacy abandon their lands and head somewhere beyond Texas and the reach of white people.[10] It was very likely Fields who convinced the council to defer its decision until they made a final attempt at a land grant. He had Hunter in mind for the mission, and just as well, for the Cherokee chiefs had been prohibited from traveling to Mexico City.

It took Hunter several months to make his way along the rocky paths and dried ruts known as El Camino Real, across the northern deserts and mountains and through the highlands of Guanajuato and Querétaro. In early March, he arrived in a city being overrun by foreigners who were seizing upon the spoils of independence. In a nation desperate for an infusion of capital, the foreigners were establishing banks, buying up land, taking over silver, gold, and copper mines, and building textile mills and cotton plantations. Not to be outdone, American and British diplomats were locked in a struggle for power and influence. On everyone's lips were the sweet words of liberty, equality, and respect for the Mexican people's right to determine the nature of its government. These were President Monroe's words, recently delivered in a speech known today as the statement of the Monroe Doctrine.[11]

Meanwhile, US ambassador Joel Poinsett was doing everything possible to undermine the government, despite his public comments to the contrary. He was covertly working to purge pro-British officials from the cabinet so the government could be more easily influenced by the United States. After forming an opposition party tied to the York Rite Masonic Lodge, his Yorquinos set out to overthrow the government by rigging the election.[12] The silent coup, while still a secret when Hunter was in the capital, was out in the open by 1828. Mexico demanded that the ambassador be recalled, and eventually he was, but not before the pro-American faction won several seats in the elections. During the nineteenth century, *poinsettismo* was the derogatory term for American interference in Mexican affairs.[13]

Texas became a proxy territory in the rivalry between the United States and Great Britain over Mexico. Poinsett's dispatches revealed the full scope of his machinations. In cipher, he described his constant efforts to reassure President Victoria and other leaders, who were very sensitive to foreign meddling, that their sister republic had a sworn aversion to empire and would never invade Texas. His dispatches did the calculus of pure demographics. He outlined for officials in Washington a relatively simple strategy: keep everyone calm, preserve the status quo, and let the growing numbers of American settlers find their way across the Sabine River. At the same time, he understood, like US diplomats before him, how crisis and instability in Texas could convince Mexico to let go of the province.[14] He boasted to his superiors that Mexico would soon have no choice but to make Texas available for sale, as American settlers were already sowing the seeds of liberty there. "We ought to have on the frontier a hardy race of white settlers," Poinsett argued, not remnants of vanquished tribes.[15]

Poinsett was wary of Hunter, especially after he was seen with the British attaché Henry George Ward. Ward was pursuing the opposite strategy in Texas: urging Mexican leaders to redouble their efforts to build a wall of loyal settlers, including Indian immigrants, along the northern border. If they did not act quickly, then they would lose Texas to the Americans. With Ward's help, his countrymen Arthur G. Wavell, a brigadier general in the Mexican army, had received a land grant between the Sabine and Red Rivers, adjacent to lands settled by some of the Indian immigrants. Ward had won this victory in the battle over Texas despite the angry protests of Poinsett. In his dispatch to Foreign Secretary George Canning, Ward

Figure 19 J. R. Poinsett, Secretary of War, 1838. Charles Fenderich, lithographer, and Peter S. Duval. After returning from Mexico, Joel Poinsett was appointed Secretary of War by President Martin Van Buren in 1837. This portrait was painted the following year.
Source: Courtesy of the Library of Congress. https://www.loc.gov/item/2003656274/

explained why Poinsett was so upset: The grant stipulated that General Wavell "was not to admit upon it a single North American colonist."[16]

Ward and Hunter, both in their mid-twenties, and sharing a similar idealistic faith in human progress, were drawn to each other. In his account of those turbulent years after independence, *Mexico in 1827*, Ward provided one of the few, and one of the best, records of Hunter's time in Mexico. Ward knew Hunter's reputation as the white Indian who had taken London by storm a few years earlier, which was why the listless man he first met in his courtyard, slouched in a seat and saying very little, confused him. This was certainly not the vibrant man Ward had imagined. However, as their conversation turned to the future of Native peoples, Ward realized immediately he had misread him. He remembered how a jolt of energy seemed to run through Hunter: "His countenance lighted up at once, his expressions became forcible and picturesque, and where words failed him, (as they sometimes did from his imperfect acquaintance with the English language), the eye, and even the agitation of the man, bespoke the truth of the sentiment, which he was laboring to express."

Ward appreciated the authenticity of Hunter's feelings and convictions. Ward's account was consistent with the near universal view of Hunter's friends and acquaintances, who also described him as being sincere, somber, intensely earnest, and principled. It was often remarked, by people who knew him in the United States, England, and Mexico, how discussions of the struggles of Native peoples quickly overwhelmed him, causing him to speak riotously with his hands because his English words had escaped him. As Ward was writing his Mexico book, he learned of the accusation of imposture against Hunter and then afterward of his assassination in Texas. Ward thought it was a preposterous notion that he could have perpetrated such a hoax and made himself the "hero of a romance of his own creation." It sounded like a smear job to Ward—a conclusion he reached before it was publicly known that Lewis Cass had authored the attack on Hunter in the *North American Review*.[17] Ward never doubted Hunter and believed he was a highly principled and honorable man. It was clear to him that he was being punished for the unpopular stand he had taken in defense of the fundamental rights of Native peoples. "To me," he wrote, "it appears that his crime has been the boldness with which he vindicated the rights of an injured, and persecuted race, to whom he devoted his life, and in whose service he was at last sacrificed."[18]

There is a curious moment in the book where Ward pretends that he doesn't know exactly why Hunter made the arduous journey from Texas to Mexico City. "As far as I could ascertain it," he claims with a straight face, Hunter had come to the capital "to induce the government" to issue a land grant to the Cherokee confederacy. In return, Hunter apparently guaranteed a secure border against the Americans, informing officials that the northern frontier was growing more populated every day. It would soon be filled with "nearly 20,000 Indian warriors, who had been driven from their hunting-lands on the Missouri and the Mississippi, by the rapid spread of the population from the Anglo-American Eastern States." The presence of thousands of warriors on the border would surely "check the tide of emigration," but only if they were fighting to defend the land their government had been wise enough to grant them. Ward, who just so happened to love the idea, blamed Mexican officials for failing to seize a golden opportunity to fortify the remote border. They had dithered for months and finally humiliated Hunter by sending him home empty-handed. What other option did Hunter and the Cherokee confederacy have than to take up arms and defend their land?

Ward could tell only part of the story in his book. Diplomats abroad keep secrets because they must neither provoke the host country nor compromise their own. It would have been scandalous for the British attaché to acknowledge in his book the full extent of the assistance he had given Hunter. He claimed to be in the dark about why Hunter came to the capital, but Ward knew everything about the mission. This hidden part of the story, left out of his book, appeared in Ward's dispatches to the Foreign Office in London. He was delighted to report that the white Indian who had thrilled London was now in Mexico and under his guidance and care. As soon as he caught wind of Hunter's mission, he offered his assistance. Hunter had no friends in Congress, no connections to the president or his cabinet, and no experience with the application process for land grants. He must have been relieved to find a friend in Ward.

In his dispatches, Ward took all the credit for building support in Mexico City for Hunter's mission. It was apparently Ward's idea for Hunter and General Wavell to stroll through the bustling Alameda on Sunday afternoons as if they were old friends. There they were seen by well-connected members of the elite who congregated there and gossiped about the people passing by.[19] The general gave Hunter an important ally with many contacts in the military and the government, none more important than the Saltillo representative, whose endorsement was crucial to winning support for their land grant in the legislature. Wavell made sure to put the proposal for the land grant in his hands.[20] The relationship between Wavell and Hunter also insulated Ward from their lobbying by giving him plausible deniability should anyone accuse him of interfering in Mexico's internal affairs.

Ward's friendship with President Victoria made him confident in his plan. Ward waited patiently for the right moment to casually mention to the president that John Dunn Hunter, the famous white Indian, was in the capital and representing the Indian immigrants up north in their bid for a land grant. When that moment finally came and Ward delivered his pitch, Victoria was intrigued by the idea and asked Ward for his assessment of Hunter and the Cherokees. By Ward's admission, he did his best not to sound too eager or partial. It was risky business because he admired Victoria as a great revolutionary who had led the fight for independence from Spain. Ward had no doubt that he would reject their request in an instant if he discovered that his British friend had an ulterior motive and was pulling the strings behind his back.

The next step for them was to write a petition to President Victoria. Ward, feeling he was more suited to the task, drafted the petition and then gave it to Hunter to copy in his own hand. Since we only have Ward's account to go on, we cannot be certain if there is more to the story. I doubt that Hunter sat in silence, the dutiful scrivener, but more on that in a moment. The petition appealed to Victoria's patriotism and his belief in a Mexican republic that was a haven for all peoples who were fleeing violence and oppression. Hunter, the signatory of the petition, pledged that in exchange for a land grant, the members of the Cherokee confederacy would defend their adopted country, embrace the Catholic religion, and transform the frontier with farms and settlements. "It is thus in Your Excellency's power to confer upon 30,000 souls the inappreciable blessings of civilization and Religion," the petition asserted. If Victoria could possibly make a quick decision, then all the better. For five years the Cherokees had been waiting for legal title to their homes and farms, and while they were waiting patiently, more and more white settlers had crossed the border and encroached on their lands. The petition predicted that Hunter would receive a hero's welcome if he arrived home with the president's gift of a land grant: "I shall be welcomed there on my return as the Bearer of most joyful tidings, and Y[our] E[xcellency]'s name will be blessed by thousands to whom you will have given a home."

Even if Hunter had copied the petition as Ward claimed, there was no denying that the two idealists formed a meaningful partnership during these days. The British attaché, who had no personal experience of the vast frontier to the north, learned more from Hunter about the displacements of the Indian tribes occurring in the United States. Based on the dispatches, Hunter detailed the chaos caused by settler expansion, fraudulent treaties, and Indian refugees. Hunter had told Ward about how private citizens, in one of the many ways they acted as the vanguard of colonization, set up distilleries even before fencing their fields and breeding their livestock. Then they traded the kegs of whiskey to Native peoples in the area for furs, horses, and, after the whiskey had ruined them, parcels of land. Ward believed a catastrophe loomed to the North.

Ward's generation of British diplomats was dedicated to the ideology of progress and freedom in Latin America. The hope was that if they succeeded in their posts, the British Empire would never have to resort to coercion or use its military might. They could quietly expand the "informal empire" through the peaceful arts of diplomacy, investment, and trade.[21] It was why Ward could be so heavily involved with British mining operations but not see himself as perpetuating the Spanish legacy of plundering Mexico's silver and gold. He crisscrossed the country to inspect all seven of the mines because revenue was needed immediately to save the republic from bankruptcy, and British support seemed the only way to make it happen. Nor would it have been difficult for Ward to rationalize his deception of a president he truly admired. Ward was convinced his backing of Hunter advanced Britain's devotion to the spread of humanitarian values in Mexico. He was equally convinced that by concealing his hand in Hunter's mission, he was advancing the greater good in Mexico. A land grant for the Cherokee confederacy would bring thousands of Native people under the protection of the government. Such an act of generosity would win their allegiance and strengthen the republic with a barrier of loyal warriors along the northern border.

Except that is not at all how it worked out. President Victoria did not approve the land grant for reasons not altogether clear, but the opposition of Ambassador Poinsett probably had something to do with it.[22] In a message to Secretary of State Henry Clay, Poinsett portrayed Hunter's application for a land grant as a serious threat to US interests:

> Hunter is certainly a shrewd active man—talking a great deal about the rights of the Indians, and as I believe not very friendly to the interests of the United States. . . . I do not think it would be politic on the part of the United States to suffer the emigration and establishment on the Mexican frontier of so large and powerful a body of Indian warriors, as it is Hunter's desire to move there.[23]

About a year later, after Hunter had returned home without a land grant, reports reached the capital of an insurrection in Texas. Poinsett, feeling good about his early warning, sent off an update to Clay: "A half-breed by the name of Fields, a man by the name of Edwards, to whom the Legislature of Texas granted a large tract of land, and John Hunter of notorious memory, are the ring-leaders."[24] The insurrection threw the capital into a panic. Quickly mobilizing the nation for war, the president ordered 10,000 troops to Texas and authorized the depleted treasury to provision them (these troops ultimately never deployed).

Poinsett was caught off guard by what happened next. There was rampant speculation in Mexico City that Hunter and Fields were secret agents of the United States and the insurrection the beginning of an American invasion. The ambassador had failed to anticipate that the recent history of American adventurers and outlaws crossing into Texas and seizing land and stirring up trouble might implicate him in the insurrection. Much to his shock, Poinsett was shunned in the capital. Unfriendly stares followed him through the Alameda and Plaza Mayor. The few friends who did not desert him had the nerve to question him about his hand in the events. The idea that he would ever tolerate an uprising by savages and half-breeds offended the South Carolinian's sense of honor. His proclivity for scheming and interfering with government, which caused his dismissal from Mexico soon afterward, made his denials of *poinsettismo* very hard to believe.

CHAPTER SIXTEEN

Faithful Friend

IN LONDON, Elias Norgate was worried about his good friend John Dunn Hunter, who had written to him five months earlier from the Ozark Mountains to say he was going in search of the Quapaws. He had not heard anything since and did not know how to reach him, but he was not about to allow the accusations in the *North American Review* to go unanswered. He was concerned that by the time Hunter learned of the attacks against him, it would be too late for him to defend himself and his reputation would be ruined. Upstairs in their old room at Halloway House, Norgate filled his inkstand and rallied to the defense of his friend. After six weeks of furious writing, he finished the pamphlet and gave it the only title that made sense: *Mr. John Dunn Hunter Defended.* He found a publisher in John Miller, who specialized in Americana and Indian history.[1] That spring Miller was bringing out the first English edition of James Fenimore Cooper's *Last of the Mohicans*, a novel about another noteworthy white Indian: Natty Bumppo, like his real-life counterpart John Dunn Hunter, mourns the destruction of Native civilization and chooses exile with his brothers beyond the advancing line of white settlements. With Miller's assurance that the type could be set quickly, Norgate agreed to pay the publishing costs for a pamphlet that hopefully would protect his friend's reputation.

Norgate began his rebuttal by testifying to his friendship with Hunter. They had spent considerable time together during his stay in England. They had lodged in the same room, dined at the same table, explored the city together, attended the same lectures and parties, and taken holidays to the family estate. Norgate thought it was disgraceful that the unnamed writer in the *North American Review*—Lewis Cass's authorship still remained a secret—could hide behind his anonymity and tear down Hunter without one shred of evidence from anyone who had ever met him. By contrast, Norgate knew him personally and had a very clear sense of the man and his values: "If Hunter is an imposter, never can I venture to place confidence in man again; Nature has stamped sincerity and truth upon his very countenance; his thoughts, words, actions—all correspond with this palpable and external impress."[2]

Norgate spoke for the moral character of his friend. Hunter felt a "high calling" to help his Native brethren acquire the "peaceful arts of civilized life" because it was the only way they could stave off annihilation. Norgate recalled how Hunter became depressed about their terrible situation and grew restless to return home as soon as possible. In contrast to the diatribe in the *North American Review,* Norgate drew on Hunter's own words as much as possible so that his feelings, motives, and thoughts would be accurately represented. For instance, to give a sense of his grandiose vision for the Quapaws, Norgate quoted a passage from the pamphlet Hunter had written for the New England Company in London: "The motives are no less than the preservation of a high-minded noble race of the human family, who have been debased, cheated, and slandered, from a destruction which inevitably awaits them, unless some kind arm be interposed to arrest the causes which are rapidly hurrying them to oblivion. The very thought that such a people, inheriting such distinguished gifts from nature, should eventually become extinct, without records even to tell their melancholy fate, must be truly affecting to those who think seriously on the subject."[3]

A man of many achievements, a friend of the aristocracy, Hunter could have looked forward to a comfortable future in England, but he had politely declined the pleas of his friends to stay and build a new life with them. He did not see a need for himself in the capitals of civilization, where so many educated people possessed skills and talents, he said, "in which I am almost a novice." Norgate felt that his friend was devoted to the ideal of service to humanity and ultimately had decided he could make a bigger difference on the western frontier. Hunter was prepared to make every sacrifice to help the Quapaws adapt to modern agriculture and American society. "Is this the language of an imposter?" Norgate asked, marveling at the sheer audacity of Hunter's accuser in the *North American Review*.

Norgate asked his readers not to judge Hunter until he had the chance to answer in his own behalf. Besides, it was the wise thing to do, considering how quickly some of his detractors were suddenly backpedaling and equivocating. There had been the early insinuation that someone else must have secretly written the book for Hunter because he had grown up with Indians in the forests and was so poorly educated, but as the evidence to the contrary mounted, those detractors, oblivious to their hypocrisy, quickly changed their tune. "It is now asserted, not only that he wrote the book, but that he invented the narrative!" Norgate exclaimed, feigning surprise at the new allegation that Hunter had fabricated an Indian tale so fantastical that not even Cooper himself could have pulled it off. "This is, at all events, giving him credit for high poetical and dramatic powers." Norgate conceded that parts of Hunter's amazing story "naturally excited astonishment," but astonishment did not warrant the charge that it was a hoax.[4]

Norgate believed he was the ideal person to dispute what to him was the laughable question of Hunter's authorship. His accuser in the *North American Review* had charged him with concealing the hand of an editor or ghostwriter—but there, glaringly obvious in the first pages of the book, Hunter expressed his gratitude to Edward Clark of Philadelphia for his editorial assistance. Hunter had been slandered as illiterate—but Norgate had watched as Hunter wrote the new chapters for the English edition at a desk in their room. Hunter had been accused of having the rudimentary thinking and writing skills of a child—but Norgate, finding this the most ridiculous of the allegations, had in his possession many wonderful letters from Hunter displaying the powers of his intellect. Norgate reassured readers that they would be impressed by the content of the letters: "A perusal of them would satisfy the most incredulous of his competency to have written the book, of which I firmly belief he was the *real* as well as the *professed* author."[5] (Unfortunately, I could not find these letters. Either they did not survive or are waiting to be discovered.)

Norgate then considered the four letters, or affidavits, at the heart of Cass's case against Hunter. The most damning one came from a man named John Dunn of Cape Girardeau, Missouri, who declared that he had never met his supposed namesake. Norgate felt the timing was suspicious. Why had Dunn waited three years to renounce this abuse of his good name? Hunter was supposed to be a clever swindler, but he had included the names of so many personal references in his book. "He must have a been a very idiot," Norgate drolly concluded, "to have placed in the hands of so many persons the means of exposing an imposture which he might have locked up in his own breast. But the fact is, that Hunter has no disguise about him."[6] There were more people from Cape Girardeau named in Hunter's book, such as the headmaster at his school, the classmates who had harassed him, and George P. Watkins, the trader he had saved from an ambush, and still other people from New Orleans, Mississippi, Missouri, and Kentucky. If his still-anonymous accuser had been interested in finding the truth, he could have done his due diligence and interviewed at least a few of them, but that might have wrecked his entire case. Norgate observed that not one of them had come forward to disavow Hunter.

The affidavit given by the explorer William Clark was flawed for a different reason. He had been governor of Missouri and superintendent of Indian affairs when Hunter was a boy. In a letter to Cass, Clark asserted that never during his visits to any Osage village had he ever seen a white boy: "In answer to your inquiries respecting the man, who calls himself Hunter, I have no hesitation in stating, that he is an imposter. Many of the most important circumstances mentioned by him are, to my certain knowledge, barefaced falsehoods." This statement by the most famous man in the West was supposed to seal Hunter's guilt, but his confident assertion that he knew every child of every Osage family was farcical to Norgate: "General Clark must have known Hunter. Why must General Clark necessarily have known Hunter, more than Hunter must necessarily have known him?"[7] Just as weak, according to Norgate, was the allegation that Hunter blatantly lied about some "important circumstances," which Clark then never specified. No jury on earth, in Norgate's view, would ever impeach a man's character on such vague and empty testimony.[8]

Norgate believed that the other two affidavits were just as thin. One was given by the St. Louis merchant Pierre Choteau, whose family had amassed a fortune trading in furs with the Osages. A year earlier, Choteau and Clark, former partners in the St. Louis Fur Company, had convinced the Osages to accept a treaty that forced them to abandon their homes and hunting grounds and move to land in present-day Kansas.

Chouteau claimed that he had been acquainted with the Osages since 1775, and "during this period there was no white boy ever living, or had been brought up by them." The other affidavit was provided by Baronet Vásquez, formerly the interpreter for Zebulon Pike's exploring expedition, and now the Indian agent for the Kansas, who ran a trading post on the Missouri near the Kansa villages. Vásquez stated that during his nineteen years of doing business with them, he was certain that there had been "no white man prisoner amongst them."

Norgate argued that this was the same flawed logic that had tainted the affidavits of Clark and Dunn. So now Choteau and Vásquez also swore they had never heard of Hunter. What did that prove? Hunter had very likely never heard of them, either. Did that mean Choteau and Vásquez were frauds? Norgate reminded readers that Hunter had been a small child when he was adopted by his Kansa family, which meant he came of age like any other youngster in his village. He had absorbed the mannerisms of his playmates, learned to speak and move like them, and enjoyed the love and attention of his families. He became one of them in every way possible. In short, he had not been "received as a *white* man newly captured," as Choteau and Vásquez seemed to think, "or who had adopted the Indian mode of life at a late period." If someone was looking for an ordinary white boy among the Osages, then they very likely would have had great difficulty identifying him. As Drinnon observed, after two centuries of racial and ethnic mixing in the region, it would have been relatively easy for a fully acculturated Hunter, speaking, moving, and looking like an Indian, to pass as Osage. Even his adopted people might not have considered the boy to be *white*. Norgate remarked that according to custom, Hunter had taken the place of a deceased family member: "He may, therefore, very fairly be presumed to have been accounted amongst both the Kansas and the Osages as one of their *red brethren*."

Norgate, despite being a horticulturalist with no experience in the courtroom, argued his case like a skilled defense attorney. Whether by instinct or design, he pursued a limited strategy of showing the possibility of reasonable doubt. He figuratively put Hunter on the witness stand by quoting passages from his book that testified to his integrity. He probed the relevance of the affidavits and challenged other allegations. He poked holes in the author's reasoning and corrected his exaggerations and insinuations. Norgate had no idea at the time that the author he had locked horns with, Lewis Cass, had once been a prosecutor on the Ohio frontier and had picked up a bag of tricks while riding the circuit between Zanesville and Chillicothe. Cass had learned how to belittle the defendant, exaggerate the evidence, twist the truth, engage in hyperbole, and bluster for effect. He put these skills to work in the *North American Review*, attacking Hunter like the tenacious prosecutor he used to be in Muskingum County. He understood that winning cases meant leaving no room for reasonable doubt.

Norgate proved himself to be a worthy adversary in the court of public opinion. His strongest, most persuasive tactic in *Mr. John Dunn Hunter Defended* was to wonder why Hunter's accuser had failed even to mention the most important piece of evidence: the letter from George P. Watkins. Recall that Hunter's life had changed forever after saving the fur trader from an Osage ambush on the Arkansas. Afterward, unable to return to the Osages, Hunter wandered alone for months through the valley and eventually settled in a hamlet on the White River with some French and American hunters. He picked up some English, became a valuable member of the community, and entered the fur trade as a *freeman*. When he left New Orleans for Philadelphia three years later, without saying farewell to Watkins, the fur trader rushed him an important letter that verified that Hunter had lived with the Osages for years until he was forced to flee that morning of his daring rescue. Watkins instructed him to keep the letter safe. It would be insurance for the inevitable moment when someone questioned the truth of his life story and demanded references. Hunter subsequently heeded this advice by transcribing the letter at the end of his book.

Norgate wondered skeptically why Cass had ignored eyewitness testimony from the only known person who could place Hunter with the Osages. According to Norgate, there were still other omissions that exposed the partisan attack—namely, all possible statements by Hunter's friends and acquaintances. Cass had refused to consider the "host of witnesses" from the United States, including Thomas Jefferson, James Madison, David Hosack, and a "multitude of other gentlemen of high literary character, none of whom have ever breathed a suspicion of his not being what he asserts himself." Cass had made no effort to interview any of them. He had made the "unpardonable suppression of every testimonial in favour of Hunter's veracity," refusing to offer contradictory evidence because it threatened his entire case by raising doubts about the charges. In Norgate's view, the only thing that Cass had proven was that he had brought the charges in "bad spirit" and was utterly incapable of being impartial about Hunter.[9]

Norgate did not rest his defense until he introduced one of these witnesses. It was a shrewd move, intending to highlight the surplus of exculpatory evidence, if one was only diligent and fair-minded enough to look for it. This last witness was Elliot Cresson, a merchant prince from Philadelphia, who considered Hunter a close friend, and held his money for him. They had spent many days together at the Cresson house on Cherry Street. In response to a series of questions from Norgate, Cresson described the accusations of imposture and fraud as far-fetched and obviously intended to slander Hunter. Cresson shared a favorite memory of a dinner party, him mesmerized by Hunter and another guest who had lived among the

Indians, the two of them conversing excitedly "without any signs of embarrassment in the language of (I believe) two distinct nations." It was not a staged performance between two actors. Cresson felt it necessary to clarify that they had been strangers to each other before that evening, so "there had been no opportunity for collusion," and with this last testimonial Norgate concluded *Mr. John Dunn Hunter Defended.*

The scandal over Hunter's identity exploded that July when Norgate's pamphlet was reprinted in Philadelphia's *National Gazette*. The evidence that had been presented in the *North American Review* suddenly seemed full of holes, and his guilt no longer seemed so obvious. Jared Sparks, the owner and editor of the *North American Review*, immediately wrote to Cass, whose authorship remained anonymous. Sparks warned that Hunter had many supporters back East and that he was bound to resurface with his side of the story: "I know several persons who still believe in the truth of Hunter's narrative, and that he will yet come out in self-defense."[10] To prepare for that day, he insisted that Cass initiate a second campaign to firm up the evidence and eliminate support for Hunter once and for all. Having serious doubts that Cass could do it on his own, Sparks instructed him to make better use of Governor William Clark, the legendary explorer, whose affidavit, stating that no white child fitting Hunter's description had been living among the Osages twenty years earlier, was so flimsy and unconvincing as to be unusable. This time the old explorer must be persuaded to read Hunter's book for himself and provide an annotated list of its many mistakes. If he did not have the book, Cass must send him one at once. Sparks surmised that with his long history with the Indian tribes, Clark should be able to complete this task in no time, if Cass would just push him to do it: "A perusal of the book on the spot would suggest many things that otherwise might be passed over."[11]

Sparks could not hide his impatience with Cass, perhaps for a very good reason. In his *North American Review* article, Cass's criticism went beyond Hunter and Heckewelder to question others who professed some knowledge of the Indian tribes in the West. Sparks had written and published in his journal a laudatory review of William H. Keating's *Narrative of an Expedition to the Source of St. Peter's River,* the official account of Major Stephen Long's northern exploratory expedition. Keating's book had inspired Sparks to praise the positive attributes of Native peoples and to express confidence in their ability to climb the ladder of progress, but he had nothing positive to say about frontier Americans, who, he claimed, were exploiting them and treating them unfairly. When Cass disparaged the Long expeditions in his *North American Review* article, he was also disparaging, by extension, Jared Sparks for naively believing what he read and voicing his admiration for a fictitious Indian that did not exist in reality. As he was wont to do, Cass reminded his countrymen, in their comfortable homes far from the frontier, how his knowledge of the tribes came from a lifetime of experience with them.[12] It came as no surprise to him that the inexperienced scientists and scholars on Long's two exploratory expeditions had made mistake after mistake. They were mere travelers through the West without the time for immersion and study. Cass had written with the supreme confidence of a man who was the superintendent of Indian affairs for the Northwest, which probably frustrated Sparks and left him wondering if Cass would follow his instructions to firm up the evidence against Hunter.

So, with his reputation and that of his journal also on the line, Sparks took control of the second campaign to discredit Hunter. He wrote to Clark on the same day, without ever mentioning it to Cass, asking him to find the incriminatory evidence that must be there in Hunter's book:

> I think there can be no just grounds for doubt that Hunter is an imposter yet as many persons are not willing to believe it I hope you will read his narrative over with care and communicate to Governor Cass such observations as occur to you. The accurate knowledge which you possess of all matters pertaining to the Indians during the last twenty-five years will enable you to detect most of his prominent blunders.

Clark would detect the hoax in an instant, according to Sparks. Had he not lived "so near the pretended scene of action" all these years? He should have no problem amending his affidavit with a long list of Hunter's falsehoods. He must also ask the fur traders Choteau and Vásquez to beef up their statements. Sparks implored him to find as much evidence as quickly as possible because his case was at risk of coming apart as soon as Hunter resurfaced in public.

The letter from Sparks was waiting on his desk when Cass returned to Detroit from Fond du Lac on the western shore of Lake Superior. His conference with the Ojibwes had been a personal triumph for him. Along with Thomas McKenney, the head of the new Bureau of Indian Affairs, Cass had negotiated a treaty that gave the United States the eternal rights to mine the rich deposits of copper and other minerals from the land.[13] Cass was irritated that in this proud moment he was being chastised for mishandling the case against the *Quarterly Review* piece and for making Hunter a bigger problem than he would have been if Cass had simply said nothing at all. In an irascible reply, Cass intimated that he could not believe that while he had been hanging presidential medals around the necks of Ojibwe chiefs and bringing them under his jurisdiction, an English companion of Hunter's, who had never set foot on the continent, had impugned his motives and even swayed some of his own countrymen.

The public criticism had wounded the governor's pride, but so too had the private scolding from Sparks. Composing his letter from the safety of his Boston library, Sparks had likened their campaign to war and brazenly assumed he was the general in charge. After admonishing the real general for rushing into combat without having enough facts, Sparks imperiously ordered him back into action with the warning that there could be no more blunders this time. Mistakes in the first article about grammar and syntax in Native languages had recently come to light. As much as the criticism must have irritated him, Cass needed Sparks as much as Sparks needed him. He had little choice but to grudgingly accept the order to work closely with Clark, although he complained the aid was so unnecessary.

Their letters reveal how personally difficult the situation was for Cass. With his own reputation on the line, he did not acknowledge any mistakes but rather insisted repeatedly that he was right about Hunter and that Sparks should trust him. He claimed to be in the possession of more than enough facts to take down Hunter: "I can [attest?] a thousand circumstances within my own knowledge, which will prove his [Hunter's] imposture." One of those thousand circumstances apparently was an incredible discovery that he had been waiting to share with Sparks. Cass said that he had traveled back to St. Louis with Clark after the treaty conference at Prairie du Chien to investigate a hunch about Hunter. In the *North American Review*, Cass had asserted that Hunter's journey to the Pacific with an Osage and Kansa hunting party was a sham. Now he could conclusively prove it never happened. Sparks would be pleased to learn that he had discovered the exact spot on the banks of the Mississippi where Hunter had supposedly ended his return journey—"and I know he was never there," declared Cass.[14]

This statement alone should be proof enough to question his motives in attacking Hunter. It was a ludicrous claim, to say the least. Hunter had never disclosed anything about the location. There were no landmarks or other clues in his book that could have led Cass to the supposed mystery spot on the Mississippi. Besides, Cass had already excoriated Hunter for fabricating his account of traveling to the Pacific. Cass would have Sparks believe that he had found an eyewitness who could confidently prove the negative: Ten or maybe eleven years earlier, the witness had *never* seen an anonymous and nondescript group of Native men, with an equally anonymous and nondescript Hunter among them, pull their canoes ashore on the banks of the Mississippi.

I suppose Cass might have believed what his sources were telling him. I doubt it, though. It seems more likely that he made up the story to boost his flagging authority with Sparks and his circle. But whatever the truth of the matter, Cass returned to Detroit that fall without any solid evidence to discredit Hunter or undermine the support for him generated by *Mr. John Dunn Hunter Defended.* As the second campaign unfolded from St. Louis, outside of his control, Cass groused again about Norgate's pamphlet in a November letter to Sparks: "The London pamphlet about Hunter is not worth notice." Here were the less appealing traits of the governor's character: When backed into a corner, he overestimated his capabilities and his knowledge of the facts and bluffed and blustered his way through any opposition. He also blamed the doubters for being gullible and not trusting him, as politicians are wont to do in a self-inflicted crisis. "I know that every important particular mentioned by me is literally true," he insisted to Sparks. "If the publick are not prepared for such disclosures, but to choose to go on believing the garrulous tales of credulous men, so let it be."

Suffice to say, the second campaign against Hunter did not go smoothly. It hinged on William Clark's willingness to lead the effort, but he never provided Sparks with the annotated accounting of all the mistakes Hunter had supposedly made in his book. He never wrote the second affidavit nor another word ever again about Hunter. His reasons for staying silent are unclear, but he had more pressing business at hand. After completing seventeen treaties the year before, he was overseeing the taking possession of an estimated 300 million acres of land from Native peoples. He was preparing the people for removal, marshaling supplies, and managing his agents and subagents in the field. There were the white squatters who refused to leave the ceded lands and had to be dealt with. There were the depredation claims for stolen or destroyed property that piled high on his desk and the boundary disputes that were his duty to resolve.[15] In short, he was struggling to keep the lid on a tinderbox west of the Mississippi.

Clark was also responsible for the welfare of the eastern Indians passing through Missouri on their way to their new treaty lands. In the council hall inside his brick manor on the corner of Main and Vine, he presided over welcoming ceremonies for the Native peoples arriving in his jurisdiction. The hall was adorned with many of the artifacts and novelties collected on his expedition with Meriwether Lewis.[16] Displayed on the walls and in cabinets were feathered headdresses, treaty pipes, beaded clothing, buffalo robes, tomahawks, battleaxes, jewelry, pipes, cradles, and cookware. Hanging from the rafters were canoes, animal skins, and snowshoes. A recent addition were portraits of the chiefs who had signed treaties with Clark. The hall was described as a museum by his contemporaries, who were permitted to visit on off days.

The logbook he kept for the Indian Office in the War Department is a telling artifact of that era. Spare notations document a humanitarian catastrophe. In September alone, the same month he had been told to focus on discrediting Hunter's book, there were thirteen days of ceremonies for separate groups of Potawatomies, Kickapoos, Shawnees, Delawares,

Osages, Peorias, and Piankashaws. In addition to heading the ceremonies, Clark provisioned them for the next leg of their western exodus. He supplied food and clothing, provided medical care, and set up campsites on the outskirts of town.[17] On top of all his regular duties, Clark also traveled downriver in October with the aim of convincing the Chickasaws and Choctaws to move west across the Mississippi (which he ultimately failed to do). Searching for evidence against Hunter was not a high priority at the time.

Instead, Clark assigned the task of investigating Hunter to the paymaster for the army at St. Louis, Major Thomas Biddle.[18] From a prominent family in Philadelphia, Biddle had come west as an artilleryman during the War of 1812 and joined Stephen Long aboard the *Western Engineer* on his exploring expedition up the Missouri in 1820. Biddle married the daughter of a St. Louis millionaire, founded a bank, and built an opulent manor house. He purchased six enslaved persons to do the domestic work, farm the land, and serve his guests at his renowned parties. He is remembered, if he is remembered at all, for dying in an 1831 duel with the Missouri congressman Spencer Pettis. As army paymaster, Biddle maintained the ledgers, paid soldiers, distributed clothing, and purchased supplies. He confided in friends that the worst part of his accounting job was traveling to Native villages to make annuity payments.

The paymaster wrapped up his investigation of Hunter in less than two weeks. The evidence he brought forth was deeply flawed and woefully incomplete. His primary piece of evidence was a questionnaire he had prepared and given to a delegation of Osage leaders in Clark's council room. Biddle recited each of the four questions to one of the chiefs, Sans-Nerf, who read them aloud in Osage to Mad Buffalo, Old Corn, La Montre, and Noel Maugrain. Then Sans-Nerf translated their answers for Biddle:

1. *Question:* Was there a white man, who lived a number of years in your nation, who from his skills in hunting was called the Hunter and who left your nation about 10 years ago?

   Answer: All say they never heard of such a person, that if a man of that kind lived among them, it was improbable but that some of them should have remembered him. Noel Maugrain, a white man, has lived with the Osage 20 years and never heard of such a man.

2. *Question:* Was there ever a white man came to your nation who had been a prisoner among the Kansas?

   Answer: All say they never heard of such a circumstance.

3. *Question:* Did any of your nation go to the Pacific Ocean?

   Answer: Never. We have heard talk of the great Salt Lake beyond the mountains, but none of our people have ever been there. The further they have ever gone was the foot of the side of the mountains.

4. *Question:* Did Tecumthe ever visit your nation?

   Answer: Never. We have heard of Tecumthe as we have heard of the Devil, but he was never at our nation.

Biddle's questionnaire was devised with a single purpose in mind: to confirm Hunter was an imposter. The Osage delegation claimed that a white man with the name Hunter had never lived among them, that their people had never heard of the Pacific or crossed the Rockies, and that Tecumseh had never visited their nation. This was meant to be convincing evidence, but his questionnaire obviously does not meet any reasonable standard of reliability or accuracy. Its questions and answers were unsound for many reasons, not the least of which were Biddle's prejudice against Hunter and a sampling bias of using only five respondents. The last answer is the only one that can be substantiated, and not to Biddle's advantage. As we know from an earlier chapter, Tecumseh's travels had taken him across the Mississippi, and historians now believe that he very likely visited the Osages, just as Hunter claimed.

The caricature of the Indian may be the most egregious mistake in the questionnaire. The Osages speak and think in precisely the manner of the literary Indians of the day, exactly as a white man imagines they would. Their reply to question number three is meant to prove that Hunter had lied about his journey to Pacific, but the transcription cannot be trusted. It further defies reason that the Osages, a people known for traveling great distances, had never ventured beyond the eastern face of the Rockies or learned about the existence of the Pacific.[19] Biddle's Indians are simple reflections of the popular savage stereotype.

Along with the questionnaire, Biddle included three affidavits that provided nothing concrete or substantial about Hunter. The surveyor John C. Sullivan, who had met Hunter on the western border of Arkansas, refused to believe Hunter had spent most of his life among Native peoples. According to Sullivan, who seemed to have no experience to base his conclusion on, Hunter did not exhibit the "manners of a man raised among them, or those of man raised to the hunting life." Pierre Menard, former lieutenant governor of Illinois, friend of the late Manuel Lisa, and once a partner of Clark and Choteau in the St. Louis Fur Company, attempted to discredit both Hunter and the most important eyewitness, claiming he had "never heard of a trader of the name of Colonel Watkins among the Osages, or of John D. Hunter."[20] Menard also stated that Hunter lied about Tecumseh: The Shawnee warrior could not have "visited and made a speech to the Osage without the circumstances having come to my knowledge," he wrote, using the same faulty logic as Cass and Clark. The third witness, Major William Davenport, the commander at Cantonment Gibson in Arkansas, had questioned Hunter during his stop at the fort in April 1825. In contrast to the surveyor, the commander believed Hunter undoubtedly had the "rough and unpolished" deportment of someone raised by Indians, but he did not believe he had lived among the Osages. Davenport included information given to him by Captain Nathaniel Pryor, a veteran of the Lewis and Clark expedition, who had queried some of the Osages at his trading post on the fork of the Arkansas and Verdigris Rivers. Pryor stated that none of them remembered any man matching Hunter's description.

Biddle wanted to raise doubts about whether Hunter even knew how to speak the Osage language. He had solicited from Major Davenport a dubious confession from Hunter, who supposedly told him that "he had been but a short time with them [the Osages]; and the little he had learn[ed] he had forgotten."[21] From the surveyor, Biddle received the same information: "I understood that he did not or would not speak the Osage language." Questioning whether a person is fluent in the language has long been a favorite way to challenge a person's authenticity or, in extreme cases, to expose them as a fraud. However, these claims revealed the spidering cracks in the case against Hunter.

This line of attack rested on the linguistic expertise of Peter Stephen DuPonceau, who knew next to nothing about Osage or other languages west of the Mississippi. He and Hunter had met at David Hosack's famous gatherings in New York City. After having the opportunity to question Hunter in Philadelphia and finding fault with his translations of Osage words and grammar, the Frenchman determined that Hunter must be a fraud. However, he kept his conclusion to himself until the scandal over Hunter blew up. Even though Sullivan and Davenport condemned Hunter, they did not go as far as his other accusers. They seemed to think that Hunter had some level of fluency and experience with the Osages. Whoever he might be—and who could really say for sure?—he probably had come from somewhere west of the Mississippi.

CHAPTER SEVENTEEN

Rebellion

AFTER WINNING its independence in 1821, Mexico began giving away vast tracts of Texas land to empresarios, or contractors, in exchange for bringing in settlers and establishing farms and towns. While none of the Cherokee chiefs had been named empresarios, they had been making a parallel argument for why the government should give them permanent rights to their land near Nacogdoches. In Mexico City, John Dunn Hunter envisioned a future where tens of thousands of Indian settlers, displaced from the United States, called Texas their home, cultivated the land, and protected the northern border. It was not a pipe dream for the Cherokees and the other members of their confederacy. As Hunter was lobbying in the capital, Richard Fields was recruiting Native peoples from across the border to settle in the region. Government records estimate that a few thousand of them moved to eastern Texas during these years; while we don't know what percentage of them responded to Fields's call, an increase in the population of peaceable and industrious Native peoples was a boon for all, since it further proved their competence and usefulness to the government. Fields and the other chiefs were fully aware that their recruiting efforts could be misunderstood as a threat to Mexico, and so they tried to be as transparent as possible. They informed officials like Samuel Norris, the alcalde of Nacogdoches, that several thousand Shawnees had settled recently near Pecan Point and that "twelve tribes, four of them large ones, were about to emigrate to Texas."[1] They assured Norris the newcomers had come in peace and were civilized.

Unrest in Texas doomed their strategy from the start. From the arid plains to the west of them, in a region known as Comanchería, the Comanches and their allies had intensified their raids on Mexican settlements and ranches and pushed the northern frontier to the brink of war.[2] The crisis cast suspicion on every group of Native peoples, turning them into potential threats against Mexico and civilization itself. The empresario Benjamin Milam reported that the families on his land grant were "greatly frightened by the immigration of a considerable number of Northern Indians." Insinuating a sinister motive at play, he later added that "their numbers are increasing daily from some unknown cause."[3] Provincial officials, sharing the same worry, were convinced some "bad men" would use the newcomers as their proxy army in a scheme to overthrow the government. They implored their superiors to dispatch troops at once to defend Nacogdoches and San Antonio.

If war was coming, then it was vital that the Cherokee confederacy prove its allegiance and usefulness to Mexico. Fields proposed to the government that his warriors be given the duty of patrolling against raiding parties from Comanchería, and officials were intrigued by the idea of a Cherokee-led defense force. An agent sent among them to quietly investigate the situation came away confident that Fields and the chiefs were true to their word and loyal to Mexico. When war preparations began the following month, in April 1826, the empresario Stephen Austin wanted the Cherokees on his side against the Comanches and Wichitas who were attacking his people. Even though Fields had come up with the idea, Austin assumed he was reluctant to join the war effort and cajoled him to consent to the plan. Austin argued that this was the best way, perhaps the only way, for the Cherokees to demonstrate "to their new friends the Mexicans how useful they could be," which might ultimately earn them the land grant.[4] The Cherokees finally had some leverage, but it quickly vanished in the face of Lieutenant Colonel Mateo Ahumada's fears of an intertribal war destroying the frontier settlements. He abruptly canceled plans for the offensive before May was out.[5]

Around this time Hunter returned from Mexico City without having acquired the land grant. Somewhere along the way he gave up his dream of a peaceful revolution and decided the time had come to fight, a feeling shared by others in the Cherokee confederacy. At a council meeting late that summer, Hunter denounced Mexico for refusing to make their land rights permanent and told his comrades that they had run out of diplomatic options. Their only choice now was either to return to the United States or defend their homes. His fiery speech was described fifteen years later in Henry Stuart Foote's history of Texas: Hunter "pictured in strong and glowing language the gloomy alternative, now plainly presented to the Indians, of abandoning their present abodes and returning within the limits of the United States—or preparing to defend themselves against the whole power of the Mexican Government by force of arms."[6]

In Foote's version of events, what happened next startled Hunter. A faction of warriors rose and shouted their intention to attack the Americans who had settled in the area, on the land grant of empresario Hayden Edwards. Surprised by the power of his words, Hunter tried to tamp down the anger of his comrades:

> At this crisis the attitude of Hunter became one of great and painful responsibility: if he ventured to dissuade his tawny associates from this terrible project before their ardour had a little moderated, it was obvious that he must, in a great degree, forfeit their confidence, if he did not

> draw down their vengeance upon himself; if he coincided in the plan of attack suggested, he must soon witness scenes of devastation and bloodshed, which would fill his soul with horror, and render him for ever miserable. Under such circumstances, he adopted a middle course, acquiescing in the proposition of war, but urging the expediency of suspending hostile movements for a week or two, until he could have an opportunity of visiting Nacogdoches, and ascertaining the exact condition of the colony.

Whoever it was who narrated this incident for Foote remembered Hunter as the hero of the moment, pulling his comrades back from the brink of war and advocating for a measured response. While this version of events is definitely biased in Hunter's favor, Fields and the other chiefs also supported a "middle course," which the council ultimately adopted. They had maintained peace for over a decade with whoever was in power—king of Spain, emperor of Mexico, or president of the Republic. They had worked hard proving their usefulness and loyalty to Mexico, and they did not want to act rashly and thus validate any suspicions about them. The middle course amounted to delaying any hostile action until they could gain more information about the simmering tensions in Nacogdoches. There were rumors of a revolt there, which Hunter and Fields soon discovered to be true.

The Mexican policy of using land grants to settle and stabilize the frontier had finally split wide open. In contrast to Stephen Austin in the south, Hayden Edwards, a speculator from Bourbon County, Kentucky, and the son of a US senator, did not appear at all interested in obeying the government and enforcing the law. He seemed to be from the same mold as Aaron Burr, Philip Nolan, James Wilkinson, William Shaler, Augustus Magee, Samuel Kemper, Reuben Ross, Henry Perry, and the other schemers and filibusterers who had attempted to seize parts of Texas over the years.[7] There were alarming reports about Edwards's authoritarian behavior, specifically his mistreatment of the Creole families whose tenure on the land predated his grant. He refused to recognize their rights as Mexican citizens and threatened eviction if they did not provide him with proof of their land deeds, which he had no authority to do. Then, in a reckless show of power aimed at the government itself, he meddled in the election for alcalde in Nacogdoches. That was the last straw. The state legislature revoked his grant and ordered him arrested, but by then he had already returned to the United States to recruit settlers. He would soon be back.[8]

His brother Benjamin Edwards had stayed behind to oversee the settlement, but he was also organizing the resistance to the government. When Hayden Edwards returned from Kentucky that fall, he found his settlers "in an intensely aggravated state" and promptly set the coup in motion.[9] On November 22, 1826, a force of forty men, led by Martin Parmer, the notorious "Ring-Tailed Panther" from Missouri, marched into Nacogdoches, and the residents scrambled for cover. Parmer and his men detained Samuel Norris, several of his councilmen, and the captain of the civil militia.[10] In a ploy to insulate Hayden Edwards from the coup, Parmer later pretended to arrest him, as if it wasn't clear to all that the empresario was the leader, and then released him. The others were put in irons, tried in a kangaroo court, and pronounced guilty of corruption.[11] The coup had begun.

The Cherokees and their allies, having heard the rumblings for weeks, were not caught completely off guard. Fields and Hunter, along with Chiefs Nekolake, Cuktokeh, and John Bags, were sent by the council to Nacogdoches to sit down with Edwards and the rebel faction. Both sides, over three days of talks at the stone fort, found common ground in their grievances against Mexico. In a letter to Stephen Austin, Peter Ellis Bean,

Mexico's Indian agent, provided a remarkable account of a speech by Fields that described his position on the origins of the conflict. Diplomatic efforts by the Cherokees had failed repeatedly to obtain legal possession of the land, and to fight was the only honorable option left:

> In my old days I travelled 2000 miles to the City of Mexico to beg some lands to settle a poor orphan tribe of Red People that looked up to me for Protection. I was Promised lands for them after staying one year in Mexico and spending all I had I then came to my People and waited two years and then sent Mr. Hunter again after selling my stock to Provide him money for his expenses when he got there he stated his mission to government they said that they knew nothing of this Richard Fields and treated him with contempt—I am a Red man and a man of honor and cant be imposed on this way we will lift up our tomahauks and fight for land with all those friendly tribes that wishes land also If I am Beaton I then will Resign to fate and if not I will hold lands By the forse of my Red Warriors.[12]

Fields, Hunter, and the rest of their delegation had been sent to Nacogdoches to talk with the Americans, but they went against their orders by forming an alliance with them. It was a mistake that ultimately cost them their lives. On December 21, both sides signed a treaty proclaiming the independence of the Fredonian Republic, announcing that the territory would be divided into a northern section for "red people" and a southern section for "white people." Both groups, they declared, would be united in a single nation founded on the ideals of universal equality and freedom.

According to the treaty articles, all roads and rivers would be freely used by everyone, trade would flow across open borders, property rights would be sacrosanct, and their combined forces would defend both territories against aggressors. They made their case for independence in the language of revolutionary republicanism. They courageously faced the "dreadful alternative of either submitting their free-born necks to the yoke of the imbecile, unfaithful, and despotic government, miscalled a Republic, or of taking up arms in defense of their inalienable rights and asserting their independence." The Fredonian flag, lined with bars of red and white to symbolize their union, and emblazoned with "Independence, Liberty, and Justice," was raised above the fort.[13]

Fields, Hunter, and the four chiefs were under intense pressure to explain themselves to the council. They had agreed to a treaty despite not being given that authority. They must have been persuasive, according to a historian of the Texas Cherokees, because after Fields and Hunter addressed the council, they were allowed to go seek the consent of the other members of their confederacy. They crisscrossed the region between the Red River and Nacogdoches, stopping at each village and camp to make their case for joining forces with the whites and fighting for their land. There was no time to waste; the government was mobilizing troops and would soon be marching to Nacogdoches. But even if the treaty had been an easy sell, and it was certainly not, the process of ratification was not built for speed. It required time for ceremony, for days of debating, feasting, socializing, and acquiring feedback from family members. At least the Kickapoos, who were said to loathe any interaction with the Americans, gave a quick and resounding refusal. Bad timing also made a bad situation even worse, as some of the men were still out on their fall hunting expeditions. A collective decision on whether to go to war had to wait until they returned home to speak on the proposed war movement.

Their enemies were able to move much quicker. Within days of learning about the coup, they were moving against the rebel faction. Political chief Jose Antonio Saucedo offered amnesty to anyone who surrendered and pledged their allegiance to Mexico. Colonel Ahumada left San Antonio with a company of infantrymen and dragoons. Stephen Austin readied his militia and demanded obedience from his people, threatening them with revenge if they threw their lot in with "a small party of infatuated madmen."[14] They would lose their land, their homes, their crops, their cattle, their dreams. Austin's opposition killed any chance the rebel faction had of recruiting fighters from the land grants and border towns.

In a flurry of letters to Hunter, Fields, and other chiefs, Austin attempted to turn the Cherokees against the rebel faction. He flattered Hunter—so wise and honorable was he—and feigned disbelief that Hunter would join a rebellion against the government. It was not too late for peace, though, perhaps even for title to their land, which Austin would gladly explain to the chiefs, if Hunter would just escort them to San Antonio for a conference. "If you are the man of talents I believe you to be and actuated by the benevolent feelings toward the Cherokees which you profess," Austin wrote to Hunter, "you will see that the favorable moment in the tide of affairs has arrived and you will embrace it."[15] If Hunter was not wise enough to grab hold of the olive branch, then blood would be on his hands. The government had been more than patient, but Austin warned him that once they drew their sword against traitors and savages, "nothing short of extermination or expulsion of that nation will satisfy them." He waited, but when Hunter failed to appear with the chiefs, Austin sent an urgent missive to them: "My brothers, I fear you have been deceived by bad men who wish to make use of you to fight their battles. They will ruin you and your people if you follow their council."

Meanwhile, Indian agent Peter Ellis Bean was playing a major role in undermining support for the rebellion. He was an American adventurer, a veteran of the Mexican War of Independence, and an infamous schemer.[16] He and his best men fanned out to the Indian villages and cast doubts on the motives of white rebels. In a letter to Fields, Bean argued that Hunter had only himself to blame for his failure to bring home a land grant from the capital. If Hunter had not lacked the proper credentials of a Cherokee envoy, then officials would have made time for him and looked favorably upon his appeal for a land grant. Bean said that the rebellion was still in its early days, but he headed a company eagerly waiting to deploy and he begged Fields not to make him give the order. They could end it now, quietly, if only Fields agreed to a conference with him, Saucedo, and Austin on the banks of the Trinity River. "I dare say that you would not be displeased with the results," Bean wrote to Fields, hinting about the gifts he would bring the chief.[17]

More than anyone else, Bean had the important duty of keeping the Cherokee chief Duwali loyal to Mexico. Also known as Bowl and Bowles, Duwali apparently did not require much convincing because he was angry with Fields for his affair with the chief's niece, Laulerac.[18] With Duwali and his warriors sidelined, Bean then made sure that the other members of the confederacy rejected the alliance. While Bean gave their leaders gifts and promised them permanent rights to their land, they had already decided to follow Duwali and Gatunwali, or Big Mush, another important Cherokee chief. They had good reasons for not placing their faith in the American faction, according to the historian Gary Anderson: "Many of them had little in common with Americans like Edwards to begin with; they saw such men as manipulative, land-hungry speculators of the sort that had forced Indian removal in the East."[19]

The Cherokee confederacy's withdrawal of support ended the Fredonian Rebellion before the first shot was even fired. With a few dozen men, Hunter and Parmer had achieved an improbable victory against the deposed alcalde Samuel Norris and about eighty men, who had marched into Nacogdoches not expecting to meet resistance. But three days later, on January 28, lines of soldiers stretching as far as the eye could see were reported only hours away and there were no signs of the hundreds of warriors coming to join the fight, so Hunter, Fields, and their comrades fled the fort and scattered through the warren of trails running between Texas and Louisiana. Bean and his mostly American militiamen chased them toward the settlement at Ayish Bayou, capturing nine of them, but Hayden and Benjamin Edwards escaped across the Sabine on the Gaines Ferry. The coup was over.

In the aftermath, the confederated tribes were expected to demonstrate their loyalty to Mexico.[20] Their mutinous alliance with Edwards could not be ignored or attributed to a few bad apples. Three weeks later in Nacogdoches, Colonel Ahumada, flanked by 300 soldiers, with the Mexican flag flying overhead once again, would preside over a procession of reconciliation. After each of the Indian delegations stopped before Colonel Ahumada to declare their allegiance to Mexico, Duwali and Gatunwali and their warriors filed down the main street. Many of them had just returned from a successful mission, given to them by the government, to assassinate Hunter and Fields. Held high above their heads, Hunter's rifles and the red and white striped Fredonian flag—taken from Fields's house—declared their allegiance to Mexico.[21]

CHAPTER EIGHTEEN

Outlaw

DIED

Near Natchitoches, Mr. John D Hunter, author of the "Narrative" the correctness of which has been so much disputed. He was assassinated by an Indian. (*Portsmouth Journal*, May 26, 1827)

DEATHS

Near Nacogdoches, Mr. John Dunn Hunter, author of "Hunter's Narrative," published a few years ago. He belonged to the party, which lately attempted a revolution in Texas, and after the failure of the attempt, he was killed by one of the Indians whom he had induced to join in the revolt. (*New Hampshire State Gazette*, May 28, 1827)

JOHN D. HUNTER

This individual, who rendered himself so well known in Europe and America, by the publication of his singular book, and by the imputations which were thrown upon him by several gentleman of the first respectability, of being an impostor, and of having deceived the English public by a relation of the adventures, which he never experienced, was lately cut off by two Indian assassins not far from Nacogdoches, in the province of Texas. (*Richmond Enquirer*, June 8, 1827)

Reports of Hunter's death made their way across the country during the spring and summer of 1827 and were published in dozens of newspapers and journals.[1] The mystery of his identity had become even more mystifying after his death in an Indian uprising. The man who had risen to fame as the newest version of the Daniel Boone myth had come crashing back to reality, largely because he had violated the most sacred of all Boone's mythical virtues. Of all of them—his sense of freedom, his special kinship with Native peoples, his feeling at home in the wilderness—it was his whiteness, above all else, that made Boone an icon of national greatness during this age of Jacksonian expansionism. His most famous descendant in popular culture was Natty Bumppo from the Leatherstocking Tales novels, who moved, dressed, and looked so much like his Delaware companions that he was constantly being mistaken for one of them. In those moments, Bumppo was quick to announce, lest there by any confusion about the purity of his white ancestry, that he was a "man without a cross," meaning a native-born white man, not a product of miscegenation.[2]

For an amazing few years, Hunter had burst onto the scene and given new form to the Boone myth until committing the unpardonable sin of turning traitor and leading his Indian comrades in revolt. It was as if Natty Bumppo had suddenly switched sides in *Last of the Mohicans* and joined Magua's rampage against the English. There was always the fear of the white Indian abandoning civilized society and returning to his savage state.[3] The fear was so deeply ingrained in the American and British consciousness that poets had been prophesying Hunter's doom even before he left London for the West. Recall how Felicia Dorothea Heman, in "The Child of the Forests," urged Hunter to resist the "wild voices" calling him back to the wilderness, and how the unknown poet in *The Atlantic* lamented how Hunter brushed off the sweet melodies and etiquette lessons of his mistress and bolted for the wilderness.

In the wake of the Fredonian Rebellion, these prophecies of Hunter's fall from grace, of savagery triumphing over civilization, had seemingly come true.[4]

Nobody did more than the American novelist John Neal to mold this image of Hunter. Neal had moved to London in 1824 and made a reputation as an entertaining new voice on American matters. Fortunately for him, he also boarded at Mrs. Halloway's house, in the room below Hunter's, so he took breakfast and tea for most of five months with one of the main American attractions in London up until the day Hunter left for home. It also so happened that Neal had published a novel four years earlier, *Logan: A Family History*, whose protagonist was not only of mixed Native and white ancestry but also an ardent reformer who comes to London to raise money for a Native settlement he dreams of building on the American frontier. The resemblances between his protagonist and Hunter were uncanny. "When Neal encounters Hunter in England," Jonathan Elmer remarks, "he must have felt like he had just walked into his own novel."[5]

The revelations in the *North American Review* that his former housemate was an imposter and his life story a hoax put Neal in an embarrassing position in London. He was supposed to be an expert on all things American, but if it was true that Hunter was an imposter, then how had Neal failed to notice the ruse? He decided to exact his revenge in the best way he knew how, in print, mocking Hunter in the papers: "I profess to believe the man was a thorough-bred imposter, (made so by accident, however); his book a forgery, (though true in part, perhaps—true in part of somebody or other, I dare say)." His ridicule contained an important truth for Neal. He did not believe Hunter was a complete fake. Hunter was impressive on any subject related to Native peoples and could speak what sounded like some Indian language. Neal admitted that Hunter was an "honest fellow, at bottom," but thought that his ambition to grow rich and famous had led him to embellish his life story. Neal had no doubt that he had grown up somewhere on the frontier, but he did not believe he had been taken captive and then adopted into an Indian tribe. Neal left it unsaid that Hunter was probably the racially mixed child of an Indian woman and a white trader, insinuating that Hunter may have invented the story of his captivity because it was less humiliating, and more exciting, than the truth that he was the "half-breed" son of a squaw.

Neal was a literary brawler who did not let the lack of evidence quiet his pen. He had come to London with the aim of showing he was the best American writer of his time, better than even James Fenimore Cooper and Washington Irving, and it must have been a blow to his ego when he arrived at his boardinghouse in Charing Cross and discovered that he was not even the most celebrated American author in the parlor. Perhaps envy motivated his attacks on Hunter, as Drinnon suggests, but the enterprising Neal also saw opportunity in the scandal.[6] By playing the jester and taunting the British for being so easily fooled by a pretend Indian, Neal made himself an important arbiter on American matters, and his contributions to the *Monthly Magazine* and *Blackwood's* became must-reads.

His tour de force on Hunter was a tale called "The Adventurer," which appeared in a collection of stories in 1831.[7] In the mischievous preface to the tale, the volume editor, Samuel Goodrich, pretends to be confused by the real identity of the author. The manuscript seemed to be "a genuine piece of autobiography from the pen of John Dunn HUNTER himself," but the editor assured readers that "it came to us in a handwriting much resembling that of our friend, J. NEAL." The eponymous narrator in "The Adventurer" is a mysterious young man who returns to his New England village after years away. Not even his family knew about his secret identity. Nobody in the village suspected something amiss with the affable lad "with his shirt-sleeves rolled up, hammering away at a tin comb, or a pewter gunlock" in his father's shop. Little did they know he had published a scandalous hoax under the name of John Dunn Hunter.

The conceit of Neal's story is that "Hunter" finally gets the chance to tell his "true story" to the world. As a boy, he had fished the Connecticut River from a boulder on the boundary line of Massachusetts, New Hampshire, and Vermont. "That single fact made me an adventurer and a dreamer," he reminisces, his reveries stimulated by reading *Robinson Crusoe* and Hubbard's *Indian Wars*. He skipped the tedium of school and chores to roam through the woods and let his imagination run wild. He began apprenticing in his father's tin workshop, but he daydreamed and cared little for learning the craftsmanship of his father's "soft soder." When his father tried to teach him the technique with cryptic platitudes about patience, diligence, and thrift, the boy thought he was being slyly trained how to cut corners and turn a bigger profit. He was soon turning out more pint dippers, ladles, dredgers, pepperboxes, graters, skimmers, foot stoves, and milkpans, at less expense of wire and labor, than any hand in the shop. Unfortunately, the quality of the products was exceptionally bad and ruined the business. "My soft soder had spoilt the trade of my father in tin ware—the noses and the bottoms of our coffee pots dropped off at a touch." This misfortune did not stop him from arrogantly demanding higher wages, which his broken father could not pay, so the ungrateful "Hunter" struck off for the western lands in search of opportunity.

He practiced his kind of "soft soder" for a stretch in Pittsburgh, tried his hand as an herbalist, and bounced around to several other trades. His attempts at honest work left him penniless and mixed up with the wrong people, whereas grifting put money in his pocket and a pint in his hand. He was drowning his sorrows in drink one day, as he was in the habit of doing, when he heard booming drums; his window suddenly darkened with a magnificent American flag, and then he saw a battalion of "cheerful-looking, proudly stepping men" marching up the street. With a knock on his door, a recruitment officer announced that his country needed him to help win the war against the British and their savage allies. Sensing a chance for a fresh start and perhaps a measure of glory, he enlisted on the spot for five years.

He was marched off to Fort Osage in Missouri, where troops nearly died every day from boredom and were too scared of venturing outside the walls and being scalped by savages. After a sickly Indian nearly dropped dead at the main gate, "Hunter" brought him back to life with a "tumbler of wormwood tea" and thereafter, just like the real Hunter, he was respected as a healer. He grew jaded with military life until he could take no more and deserted his post to live with the Kansa further west. By his own account, he "flourished as a regular professor of the black art," and he might have lived comfortably among them for years if war had not broken out with the Osages. Rather than fighting with the Kansa, he saved his own skin and left in the dead of night to join their more powerful enemy. The next two years were prosperous and happy ones, but his treachery had not been forgotten by the Kansas. He had the feeling for a while that evil spirits were lurking in the woods, but one day he realized the spirits were Kansa "spies out to kill him." In the pitch black, he slipped a raft into the river and escaped to New Orleans.

When he landed on the levee 500 miles later, he was penniless and hungry, but when he finally told his story in the hopes of gaining a sympathetic ear, he was given a meal and a bed for the night. A storyteller was born. He began telling his story on the levee, in the French Quarter, and in the fashionable districts; the hat full of money he received in return for the entertainment never ceased to surprise him. He confessed that his "imagination was better than his memory," and he learned quickly how to invent details and bits of dialogue, how to solder them in here and there to make the tale flow and heighten the dramatic effect. He used his earnings a few months later to book passage to New York City, where the tale of his harrowing escape from the Indians preceded him down the gangplank, amply providing for his room and board during his stay in the city.

A seasoned storyteller now, he liked to see the looks on the faces of his audience as he planted a few Kickapoo words into the description of the scene or sprinkled in esoteric references to the Great Spirit. He had become so good that he almost believed he had lived the life he had invented for his audiences. In a matter of weeks, he says, "my story was in everybody's mouth," but it had become so altered from the original version that "I hardly knew it for my own."[8] With the seeds he had sprinkled in the public imagination, the good people of New York, "the believers, the proselytes, the professors, and the critics," had picked up his narrative and unwittingly added their own embellishments. "They contrived the story for me," he says, "they put it together." Sure, he invented John Dunn Hunter, "but what of that? The stories I told were substantially true."[9]

He claims he was too bashful to put a stop to the story. Had not his well-to-do friends furnished him with glowing letters of reference and dispatched him to Philadelphia to find a publisher, he might have found the courage to confess that he had lost control of the story. But how could he disappoint them? He could not well turn back after Thomas Jefferson and James Madison had served him tea, listened to his story, and afterward added their own impressions and fancies to the narrative. And it was even harder to turn back after his book wowed even the stingiest of scholars and made him famous in England, after he "grew to be the lion of fashionable society" and lords and ladies of the first rank fought for his attendance at their dinners and parties. He dined every week at Kensington Palace with the Duke of Sussex, and who could forget how he was "bagged, powdered, and ruffled" and "set face to face with the Majesty of Great Britain, by the American Ambassador"?

"Need I go further?" he asks. He fell in love with this version of himself and was not about to throw it away for nothing. He packed up his belongings, secreted away the donations given to him by his wealthy benefactors, and sailed for America. Every word he had to say about civilizing the Indians was taken as gospel in New York, Philadelphia, and Baltimore. He was "gathering contributions by the cartload," money and supplies but also a pleasing amount of "wonder and admiration." In the marvelous closing paragraph, "Hunter" distinctly remembered feeling the world was his oyster. He had a difficult decision to make:

> Whether I should cut a canal from the Atlantic to the Pacific, revolutionize Texas, or bring about a confederation of the tribes mentioned above—an event which the philanthropists and philosophers of England had begun to calculate on from my operations, as a check for the incredible growth of the United States, and a proper balance of power in the New World; how, after a variety of adventures, among which a second visit to Mr. Jefferson ought to be remembered, I got back among the natives that wear feathers and scalps? Or would you have me relate, how, after a world of expostulation, I got four chiefs of some notoriety to sign a paper which I prepared for them, according to my best knowledge of what a proclamation would be; or how we kicked up a little revolutionary dust, which ended in my being taken prisoner by the government of Mexico, and put to death? I shall do no such thing. All these details may be found in the newspapers of the

> day. And here I throw aside the pen forever—appealing once more from the unjust and cruel judgement of this age, to that of posterity.
>
> J.D.H.

By the last passage, we are no closer to understanding the mystery of John Dunn Hunter. The narrator had promised to "undeceive the world about my Narrative," but the boundary between truth and fiction was now even murkier. Neal constructed the fiction from what he believed were the raw facts of the real Hunter's past: his upbringing out west, his knowledge of Native life, his rise to fame as an author in England, his philanthropic mission, and his death in the Fredonian Rebellion. In Neal's imagination, Hunter experienced an epiphany after receiving his first full hat after telling his story on the levee in New Orleans. He instantly grasped that his persona as the white Indian was a lucrative asset, so he leaned into the craftsmanship and eventually mastered the "soft soder" of his life story. However, he should not be made to shoulder all the blame for the fictionalizing. He had handed his story over to gullible listeners who were only too eager to project themselves into the mythic world of the white Indian.

Whether clairvoyant or not, Neal portrayed John Dunn Hunter, whoever he may be in the story, as an antihero of American democracy. In rebellion against his father, the workshop, the military, and society at large, "Hunter" is reborn in the wilderness as a free man, like the American nation itself, without any values or loyalties that cannot be easily sacrificed to his own ambitions and desires. He was even ready to betray his countrymen, his *race*, by kicking up a rebellion among the Texas Indians. He is not the virtuous Boone with his family in tow to tame the Kentucky wilderness and expand the empire of liberty. In this era of visionaries, confidence men, and charlatans, Neal's "Hunter" was an ingenious trickster who over time entered the history books as a proxy for the real person.

Neal's should not be the last words from someone who knew the real Hunter. Herman Mayo, the editor of the *Natchitoches Courier* and fellow signatory of the Fredonian treaty, broke the news of Hunter's assassination and provided a testimonial of his life. The little information we have about the months leading up to his death comes from Mayo's pen. He described how Hunter was dismayed by, and ultimately could not accept, the decision by the Cherokee council to remain loyal to Mexico and thus withdraw their support of the rebel faction. After agreeing to the treaty with Fields and the four other chiefs, Hunter felt honor bound at that moment to "go and share the fate of his American friends in Nacogdoches," and he headed to the stone fort with a few Native comrades who he felt were of the same mind. But when they stopped at a creek to let their horses drink, one of his "savage companions" according to Mayo, a false friend as it turned out, unsheathed his rifle and shot Hunter in the shoulder. "His horse started and he fell into the creek," suddenly realizing the betrayal. "The monster raised another fatal weapon, and while the unfortunate Hunter implored him not to fire, for it was hard, he said, to die by the hands of his friends,—sent this extraordinary spirit to appear before an unerring tribunal."[10]

A great admirer of Hunter, Mayo portrayed him as generous, selfless, and compassionate, grave, thoughtful, and intelligent on every subject.[11] Mayo appreciated a unique part of his personality noted by other close acquaintances, from Ward to Owen to Norgate to Coke: "Any discussion relative to the situation and character of the Indians would rouse the level calm of his ordinary manner into a storm that agitated his entire soul."[12] Once unleashed, the storm of feelings and ideas would often cause him to lose "all command over words," and he would resort to speaking in the language of signs used by the

Plains Indians. Mayo painted a memorable picture of Hunter—face animated, hands signaling, arms flowing—"eloquent in gesticulation." Mayo was shocked by the accusations against his friend, not because they were credible but because they were based "upon evidence most uncertain" and swallowed whole by the public. None of his accusers had observed him, as Mayo had observed him, talking, eating, socializing, and playing games with his Indian comrades in Texas. "Can it be that this man was an imposter?" he asks incredulously. "I for one will not believe it."[13]

He was certain Hunter had spent many years living with Native peoples. As verification, Mayo shared a telling anecdote about this man the world "once delighted to honor" to refute the bogus nature of the charges against him. "I went with him last summer to the Cherokee village," Mayo related, "and while there, was informed, by some of that tribe, of a Nottoway Chief who well knew Hunter in his early life, when he lived with that or some neighboring tribes, and whose account, as far as I learned it, and as my memory now serves, corroborates his own narrative."[14] Mayo had been aware of the scandal over Hunter prior to unexpectedly meeting him "in the wilds of Texas," but he confessed that he never told him his name was being dragged through the mud back east. Mayo did not want to embarrass Hunter by telling him, and even though he "died profoundly ignorant that any stain rested upon his reputation," Mayo regretted not doing the honorable thing of telling him. To make amends, Mayo publicly paid tribute to Hunter as an honest man and visionary philanthropist, whose "imagination burned with the distant prospect of the civilization and happiness of the persecuted Indians."[15] He had been destined to change their world before being shot dead in the creek.

Epilogue

THE FINAL CHAPTER in Hunter's life brings to light a poorly understood history of Indigenous resistance in North America. Marked as a precursor to the Texas independence movement, the Fredonian Rebellion has always been viewed as an episode of white settler history in which only the only motives, concerns, and actions that mattered were those of the white participants. If the members of the Cherokee confederacy are given their rightful place in this history, the Fredonian Rebellion can no longer be mistaken for an all-white affair that precipitated the fight for Texas independence.

As a result, our attention necessarily shifts toward previously overlooked turning points: the expulsion and displacement of Native peoples from their lands in the United States and their settlement in the region between the Red River and Nacogdoches; the provisional land rights granted to the Cherokees by the king of Spain and subsequently affirmed by the governor of Texas; the formation of a confederacy headed by the Cherokees; the two failed missions to the capital, the first by Fields and the second by Hunter, to secure a land grant; the treaty agreed to by Hunter and Fields and four other chiefs for the creation of a nation equally divided between "red" and "white" people; the council's rejection of the treaty and its resolution to make peace with Mexico by killing Hunter and

Fields. These are the turning points in a very different history of the event known as the Fredonian Rebellion. It gives a disaffected group of white settlers a smaller, more appropriately sized part in the larger struggle for land and power in the US-Mexico borderland.

As we track Hunter into Texas and Mexico, we come to learn of the motives, concerns, and actions of the members of the Cherokee confederacy. They were not mercenaries who fought for pay or revenge or pleasure, as the history books made them out to be. They were fighting for their survival, for their land, for their homes and their children. Far from being unique, their movement was only latest effort by Native peoples across North America to survive colonialism by selectively adapting to the demands of settler states and societies. Like the Five Civilized Tribes, the Choctaws, Chickasaws, Creeks, Cherokees, and Seminoles, or the six tribes of the Iroquois Confederacy, the Mohawks, Oneidas, Onondagas, Cayugas, Senecas, and Tuscaroras, the members of the Cherokee confederacy had been patiently proving their competence as settled farmers and making their case for a land grant; however, their patience was wearing thin as their formal appeals went nowhere at the same time the Mexican government was giving vast tracts of land to increasing numbers of white settlers who now surrounded them.

Perhaps it should not come as a surprise that Robert Owen appeared in Mexico City at this time, just after his New Harmony experiment failed. His interest in the land rush had been piqued by Benjamin Milan, a business partner with fellow empresario General Arthur Wavell of the Mexican army, who, you may recall, used to accompany John Dunn Hunter on walks through the Alameda in the hopes of raising Hunter's political profile and facilitating approval of his land grant application. In Owen's published proposal, he did not ask for just a piece of Texas; he asked for all of it! His failure at New Harmony had clarified for him that his new community must be located on an even more remote frontier, where there would be fewer obstacles to implementing his vision of a society free of war, poverty, ignorance, prejudice, and religious conflict. Over nine days at the start of 1828, Owen met with various Mexican officials, including President Victoria, but he spent much of his time with the US ambassador, Joel Poinsett, and they seemed to bond over Owen's plans for Texas. It seems not to have occurred to Owen that he was confiding in an "experienced intriguer" whose name was a byword for American meddling and who was conspiring to acquire Texas for the United States; or that Poinsett would have been suspicious of him because he knew all about his public relationship with Hunter; or that it had been Poinsett who had personally undermined Hunter's efforts to obtain a land grant; or that Poinsett himself was also angling for a land grant in Texas.[1] While no surviving document proves Poinsett was also undermining Owen's venture, the circumstantial evidence appears overwhelming. José María Herrera concludes after examining the available evidence: "Whatever slim chance Owen's project had of being implemented died the moment he placed his confidence in Poinsett."[2]

Also at this time, Cherokee leaders were growing frustrated by the government dragging its heels to reward them with the land grant promised to them in exchange for killing Hunter and Fields. Provincial officials were stalling, passing all inquiries to their superiors in Saltillo and Mexico City, and as the crisis passed and the frontier was relatively calm again, the Cherokee confederacy lost the little leverage they had over the government. Even objections by Colonel Ahumada, who was desperate to keep the Cherokee confederacy as an ally, were ignored. In one dispatch, he pleaded with General Bustamante to fulfill the deal they had made with Chiefs Gatunwali and Duwali:

> Justice obliges me to inform you that Mohs ["Big Mush" or Gatunwali] and Buls ["Bowl" or Duwali]—civil and military chiefs of the Cherokees—agreed to and gave orders to kill Hunter and Fields, recovering the papers and flag mentioned, and giving me proof of loyalty to and love for our government, from which they hope for a grant of some land in the district for the settlement of their tribe, which solicitation I commend to your Excellency very particularly. I beg you will take it into consideration in order that the reward may be granted them which they have earned by the valuable services they have rendered.

In Ahumada's assessment, giving the Cherokees title to their land was not only the ethical thing to do but also a strategic necessity. The members of the confederacy, from over twenty different tribes, had seriously contemplated going to war against Mexico, which would have added to the turmoil on the northern frontier. The rebellion might have succeeded if only the chiefs had backed Hunter and Fields and the Fredonian agreement and deployed their warriors against an outnumbered enemy who had to wait for reinforcements from the south. Fortunately for Mexico, the chiefs stayed true to their word and carried out the "valuable services" of assassinating Fields and Hunter and stamping out the resistance. Ahumada suggests that a republic worth its name should honor its debt to the Cherokees.

In the end, suspicion and fear mongering won out over the agreement with the Cherokee confederacy. The loudest voice was Stephen Austin's, decrying the weakness of the government, complaining about the tolerance for Indian settlers, and always threatening to move his people back to the United States if his demands were not taken seriously. It just so happened that a new federal law against slavery left him and his people feeling betrayed and worried about the future of their cotton plantations. Austin argued that Mexico should amend the law and not force them to leave their new country, especially since they were the right sort of settlers, a civilized and Christian people who had driven out the "savages" and made farming profitable. When Mexico's Congress convened again, a law was passed exempting Texas cotton farmers from the federal law against slavery.[3]

A decade later, Mexico was failing to slow down a secessionist movement in Texas. By 1836, two years after Antonio López de Santa Anna had seized power in the capital, fifty-eight Texans convened near the Brazos River and declared their independence from Mexico. Rumors of the Cherokees and their allies joining the fight on the Mexican side raised the ghosts of the Fredonian Rebellion. Sam Houston, the new president of Texas, took an old page from the Mexican government's book: He secured the allegiance of the Cherokees with the promise of legal title to their land. However, this hopeful moment did not last the year. The new congress refused to ratify the treaty, which divided the Cherokee confederacy, pushing many of its warriors to join the opposition. Duwali and Gatunwali tried a different tack by claiming neutrality in the conflict between Mexico and Texas, but the number of Americans flocking to the region doomed their strategy. The Texans had issued the Americans over 300 land titles, many for parcels already occupied by Cherokee families, with nary a word about the latter's languishing claims.[4]

The Texans, like the Mexicans before them, questioned repeatedly whether the Cherokees had ever received permission from Spain or Mexico to occupy their land. In 1839, Mirabeau Lamar, President Houston's successor, contemplated the question for a moment and decided they had not. Schooled in Indian affairs in the cauldron of his native Georgia, Lamar reneged on all prior agreements and ordered the "immediate removal of the Cherokee Indians, and the ultimate removal of all other emigrant tribes now residing in Texas."[5] The Texans had initially planned to follow diplomatic custom and give the Cherokees several weeks to discuss the decree, but the council had barely begun to deliberate when a battalion appeared at Council Creek, near Duwali's village, and a contingent of officers, under the pretext of a security threat, dictated the terms of removal and demanded a quick response from the council. Per the proposed terms of the order, the Cherokees would be fairly compensated for their houses, farms, barns, crops, cattle, orchards, and any other improvements they had made to the land. The military would safely escort them to the border. Money, provisions, and other supplies would be distributed along the evacuation route. They would be required to disarm by removing the gunlocks from their rifles and pistols. Pressed for signatures of approval, Duwali and Gatunwali pleaded for more time to mollify several of their fellow chiefs, who were angry with the humiliating clause stipulating they be disarmed and marched out of Texas like a conquered people.

On the third day of deliberations, which seemed like an eternity to the Texans, the soldiers were ordered to march on the village in the first action of what is commonly called the Cherokee War. When they got there, they found it deserted and went in pursuit of the people. Early that evening, on July 15, they clashed on the Neches River, resulting in eighteen Native people and two Texans dead. The Cherokees, along with groups of Delawares, Shawnees, and Kickapoos, fled under the cover of night as the Texans chased them to the upper reaches of the river. The next day the Texans, whose Pennsylvania long rifles had a range of 200 yards, went on the offensive, slaughtering over 100 warriors. Gatunwali was among those killed in the assault; Duwali was critically wounded, then shot by a soldier in an apparent mercy killing. After more than twenty years of appeasing Mexico and establishing themselves as reliable allies, the longtime friends had confronted an enemy in the Texans who only wanted them gone. With no more diplomatic solutions on the table, the chiefs had belatedly come to the same realization as Hunter and Fields, their former comrades, and decided to fight.

The survivors disappeared into the forests, bayous, and swamps. They wandered and scavenged for food. Some eventually made their way back to their villages only to find them razed and their crops burned in the fields. Some started over on the upper Brazos among contingents of Caddos, Shawnees, and Delawares. Some escaped to Mexico and volunteered for the fight in Texas. Most of them, perhaps as many as 1,500 or 2,000, escaped across the border to the newly created Indian Territory in what became Oklahoma, where they joined several thousand Arkansas Cherokees who had recently moved there.[6] Also arriving in 1839 and 1840 were many of the 18,000 Cherokees who had been forced west on the "Trail of Tears."[7] The Cherokees were fast becoming a traveling, diasporic people during these years, according to the historian Gregory Smithers. They persevered in the face of displacement, violence, poverty, starvation, disease, and factionalism; adapted to their new surroundings; and reinvented themselves under extreme duress. In the ensuing years, they overcame cultural differences, developed new social and political structures, and maintained many of their traditions.

That future for the greater Cherokee Nation was still to come. Throughout 1839 and 1840, many of the Texas Cherokees, refusing to surrender their land, waged a guerilla war from bases in Indian Territory and the bayous and forests across the border.[8] They raided settlements and ranches, stole horses and livestock, and harassed traders and travelers. Here is the legacy of Hunter, Fields, and their Indigenous comrades: Their resistance became part of an insurgency, a longer Fredonian Rebellion, which never ended for the Cherokees. Edwards and his American faction may have surrendered in 1827, and

Hunter and Fields may have been sacrificed for the sake of peace and land never granted, but the Cherokees had never stopped protesting for their land rights. The tragic irony twelve years later was that Duwali and Gatunwali, after seeing all of Mexico's promises of land come to naught, and then having the Texas Republic also betray them, had decided that armed resistance was the only option for their people's survival.

Hunter's legacy in this resistance movement has never been acknowledged until now, but it is clearly visible in the long struggle of the Cherokees for reparations for their lost land. Of course, his legacy has never been his alone. He was just one of the leaders in a resistance movement spanning many generations. In the 1850s, the Cherokee Nation petitioned to sue Texas for the return of the land they had been evicted from, 1.5 million acres north of Nacogdoches; the state countered with an offer of 14 million acres in the Texas Panhandle, but the Cherokees rejected it. In the 1870s, the suit was reactivated by a group including a descendant of Chief Fields, a man also named Richard Fields, but their effort failed as well. In 1921, the suit was tried again by George Fields, also a relative, who represented 900 "heirs of Texas Cherokees" in a $100 million action against Texas for the land taken from their ancestors, but the U.S. Supreme Court avoided the issue by ruling the Cherokees did not have standing under the law.[9] In 1948, the Cherokees made a claim against the United States for $5 million in compensation, but the Indian Claims Commission ruled against them.

By the 1960s, tribal attorney Earl Boyd Pierce had researched and established the legitimacy of their claims. After investigating documents dating back to the Spanish period, from official correspondence and legal rulings to oral narratives and testimonials, Pierce presented his findings to the Texas court in 1963. He knew full well the state would never entertain the idea of giving the land back to the Cherokees, but he instead proposed a unique settlement: Texas would be allowed to keep the land in exchange for financial reparations. These would take the form of college scholarships for 1,000 Cherokees over a twenty-five-year period; the measure would be funded by a cash settlement of $1 dollar per acre for the land taken from them a century earlier. Pierce ultimately convinced the commission of the Cherokee Nation's fundamental argument: The Cherokees were once the lawful occupants of 1,640,000 acres in eastern Texas. And yet, in the legal world, the acknowledgment of a basic truth did not mean the state was responsible in any way for the lost property. With a fiduciary stratagem left to play, the attorney general ruled that the state of Texas was exempt and no longer liable for any losses caused by the defunct Republic of Texas.[10]

I see parallels between Hunter and another white man, also maligned as a race traitor, who died in a rebellion for freedom, the abolitionist John Brown, whose 1859 raid on Harper's Ferry was supposed to ignite a slave insurrection across the South. Perhaps if Hunter had been found guilty in a polarizing national trial and died bravely at the gallows like Brown, he might also have been mourned by Henry David Thoreau as a "crucified hero," held up ever after (at least in the North) as a martyr for freedom and equality, and be the subject of numerous books, songs, and films about his life. I wish it were otherwise, but this counterfactual history of Hunter seems implausible for one main reason: Americans were deeply divided over slavery, but they were truly unified in their belief that Native peoples had no place in the nation and were racing toward extinction. In contrast to Brown, Hunter could not easily be cast as part of America's redemption story. The inescapable truth remains that American solidarity, the nation's democratic institutions, and its mythologies of freedom and rugged individualism were achieved in no small measure through the removal of Native peoples from their homelands. The belief that ultimately unified white Americans during and after these turbulent decades before the Civil War was that the nation was destined to inherit the continent from a rapidly disappearing race of people whose claims, petitions, and treaties could be easily ignored because they were disappearing and not long for this world.

And yet Native peoples have resisted settler colonialism and whites-only democracy for over four centuries. The US Census of 1900 counted 237,000 American Indians; today there are more than 3 million, and over 570 federally recognized Indian tribes. These numbers do not include the more than 200 tribes and several thousand people who are not recognized by the federal government. Native peoples today have survived displacement and genocide. They have persevered in the teeth of relentless opposition to their presence. They have practiced selective assimilation. They have maintained their traditions, beliefs, and languages. And they are to be reckoned with. There are countless examples today of their movements for justice. Their ongoing efforts to defend their land and their civil rights have resulted in significant legal victories and large settlements from the federal government for breaches of treaties and mishandled annuities. Even when they have been defeated in the courts, or in the political arena, public opinion, or school curriculums, the legacies of the past are a haunting precedent. Hunter's ghost, among many other ghosts from that bygone era, is alive and well and reminding us about our nation's unfinished business.

ACKNOWLEDGMENTS

I AM INDEBTED to the librarians and archivists at the National Archives and Records Administration in Chicago, the Beinecke Library of Yale University, the Newberry Library of Chicago, the Library Company of Philadelphia, the University of Washington Special Collections, and the University of Kentucky Special Collections. They aided my research and answered my many questions about their collections. The University of Kentucky's Office of the Provost and the College of Arts & Sciences supported my archival research through financial grants.

This book began as a series of papers at various conferences and meetings. I am thankful for the insightful feedback I received from my colleagues at the Modern Language Association Conference (2016), the CUNY Graduate Center's symposium "Rethinking Region in Early America" (2016), the Society of Early Americanists Conference (2017), the Charles Brockden Brown Society Conference (2017), and the Society of Nineteenth-Century Americanists Conference (2018). I leaned on my friends in the Charles Brockden Brown Society, who have been a constant source of support, erudition, and camaraderie throughout my career.

I was honored when Rodrigo Lazo and Kirsten Silva Gruesz included my essay on Hunter in a special issue of *Early American Literature*, which gave me the opportunity to share his story with a broader audience. I am also grateful to Robert Allen Warrior for meeting with me to talk about Hunter at a time when I was still unsure if I could do justice to a biography of him.

I owe many thanks to my agent, Don Fehr, for his insightful feedback and encouragement during the writing process. He inspired me and helped this book live up to my vision for it.

Thanks to my editor, Laura Davulis, and the editorial production staff at Johns Hopkins University Press for their care and attention to detail at every stage of publication. They were a pleasure to work with. I am especially grateful to Michelle Scott for her help in navigating the editing process. A special word of thanks must also go to Dave Jones for his assistance with the artwork.

My sincere appreciation goes to the anonymous reviewers whose observations and suggestions were crucial in shaping the final draft of this book.

I cannot imagine having written this book without the guidance and friendship of David Correia, whose influence is knotted into these pages.

At every stage of the journey, I benefitted from the encouragement and generosity of my parents, Carl and Mary Doolen.

Finally, I am deeply grateful to Alice Turkington for her love and support and invaluable help in brainstorming about this book and to our amazing children, Mary and Ellis, who have grown up hearing my stories about Hunter.

NOTES

Prologue

1. Jefferson described Hunter's visit to James Madison in a letter. I return to this scene later in the book. Jefferson to Madison, November 22, 1822, *The Papers of James Madison*, Retirement Series, vol. 2, *1 February 1820–26 February 1823*, ed. David B. Mattern, J. C. A. Stagg, Mary Parke Johnson, and Anne Mandeville Colony (Charlottesville: University of Virginia Press, 2013), 603–4.
2. I am drawing on a number of historical accounts of Indian removal, including Brian W. Dippie, *The Vanishing American: White Attitudes and U.S. Indian Policy* (Middletown, CT: Wesleyan University Press, 1982); Ned Blackhawk, *Violence over the Land: Indians and Empires in the Early American West* (Cambridge, MA: Harvard University Press, 2006); Gregory Evans Dowd, *A Spirited Resistance: The North American Indian Struggle for Unity, 1745–1815* (Baltimore: Johns Hopkins University Press, 1992); Kathleen DuVal, *The Native Ground: Indians and Colonists in the Heart of the Continent* (Philadelphia: University of Pennsylvania Press, 2006); Reginald Horsman, *Race and Manifest Destiny: The Origins of American Racial Anglo-Saxonism* (Cambridge, MA: Harvard University Press, 1981); Anne Farrar Hyde, *Empires, Nations, and Families: A History of the North American West, 1800–1860* (Lincoln: University of Nebraska Press, 2011); D. W. Meinig, *The Shaping of America: A Geographical Perspective on 500 Years of History*, vol. 2, *Continental America, 1800–1867* (New Haven, CT: Yale University Press, 1993); Jeffrey Ostler, *Surviving Genocide: Native Nations and the United States from the American Revolution to Bleeding Kansas* (New Haven, CT: Yale University Press, 2019); Patricia Nelson Limerick, *The Legacy of Conquest: The Unbroken*

Past of the American West (New York: Norton, 1987); Claudio Saunt, *Unworthy Republic: The Dispossession of Native Americans and the Road to Indian Territory* (New York: Norton, 2021); Bernard W. Sheehan, *Seeds of Extinction: Jeffersonian Philanthropy and the American Indian* (Chapel Hill, NC: Institute of Early American History and Culture at Williamsburg, 1973); Gregory D. Smithers, *The Cherokee Diaspora: An Indigenous History of Migration, Resettlement, and Identity* (New Haven, CT: Yale University Press, 2015); Frederick E. Hoxie, "Retrieving the Red Continent: Settler Colonialism and the History of American Indians in the US," *Ethnic and Racial Studies* 31, no. 6 (2008): 1153–67.

3. Malcolm J. Rohrbough, *The Trans-Appalachian Frontier: People, Societies, and Institutions, 1775–1850* (Belmont, CA: Wadsworth 1990); Daniel Walker Howe, *What Hath God Wrought: The Transformation of America, 1815–1848* (New York: Oxford University Press, 2007); Meinig, *Shaping of America*, vol. 2.
4. Richard Drinnon, *White Savage: The Case of John Dunn Hunter* (New York: Schocken Books, 1972). I am deeply indebted to Drinnon for his spirited effort to vindicate Hunter and to incorporate him into a more complex historical narrative about American life. While he could not singlehandedly rescue Hunter from obscurity and misinformation, he provided an opening for future scholars to investigate the full scope of Hunter's life story. I think Drinnon's book was ahead of its time. From the 1970s onward, historians began looking beyond the achievements of "great men" at the top of American society and paying more attention to the lives and experiences of so-called ordinary people like Hunter, who were important historical actors in their time but then often forgotten afterward.
5. Many scholars have explored how the cultural realm facilitates both the erasure of Native peoples and the formation of settler ideology, consciousness, and identity, including Philip Joseph Deloria, *Playing Indian* (New Haven, CT: Yale University Press, 1998); Joshua David Bellin, *The Demon of the Continent: Indians and the Shaping of American Literature* (Philadelphia: University of Pennsylvania Press, 2012); Robert F. Berkhofer, *The White Man's Indian: Images of the American Indian from Columbus to the Present* (New York: Vintage, 1979); Jill Lepore, *The Name of War: King Philip's War and the Origins of American Identity* (New York: Knopf, 1998);

Laura L. Mielke, *Moving Encounters: Sympathy and the Indian Question in Antebellum Literature* (Amherst: University of Massachusetts Press, 2008); Richard Slotkin, *Regeneration Through Violence: The Mythology of the American Frontier, 1600–1860* (Middletown, CT: Wesleyan University Press, 1973); Susan Scheckel, *The Insistence of the Indian: Race and Nationalism in Nineteenth-Century American Culture* (Princeton, NJ: Princeton University Press, 1998).

6. Dippie, *The Vanishing American*, 15.
7. Colin G. Calloway, "Neither White nor Red: White Renegades on the American Indian Frontier," *Western Historical Quarterly* 17, no. 1 (1986): 44.
8. Lewis Cass, "Indians of North America," *North American Review* 22, no. 50 (1826): 53–119.
9. On the history of the Texas Cherokees, see Dianna Everett, *The Texas Cherokees: A People Between Two Fires, 1819–1840* (Norman: University of Oklahoma Press, 1990).
10. For the best recent study of the Fredonian Rebellion, see Gary Clayton Anderson, *The Conquest of Texas: Ethnic Cleansing in the Promised Land, 1820–1875* (Norman: University of Oklahoma Press, 2019).
11. This problem of representation is fully examined in Hilary E. Wyss, "Captivity and Conversion: William Apess, Mary Jemison, and Narratives of Racial Identity," *American Indian Quarterly* 23, nos. 3–4 (1999): 63–82.
12. I am in dialogue here with Hilary Wyss (on Jemison), Gordon Sayre (on Tanner), Susan Walsh (on Jemison), and Kathleen Sands ("cross-cultural autobiographical texts"). See Wyss, "Captivity and Conversion"; Gordon M. Sayre, "Abridging Between Two Worlds: John Tanner as American Indian Autobiographer," *American Literary History* 11, no. 3 (1999): 480–99; Kathleen M. Sands, "Narrative Resistance: Native American Collaborative Autobiography," *Studies in American Indian Literatures* (ser. 2) 10, no. 1 (1998): 1–18. For an analysis of Jemison and the experience of white captivity more generally, see June Namias, *White Captives: Gender and Ethnicity on the American Frontier* (Chapel Hill: University of North Carolina Press, 1993). On white captivity during the colonial period, see James Axtell, "The White Indians of Colonial America," *William and Mary Quarterly* 32, no. 1 (1975): 55–88.
13. William Apess, *On Our Own Ground: The Complete Writings of William Apess, a Pequot*, ed. Barry O'Connell (Amherst: University of

Massachusetts Press, 1992); Black Hawk, *Life of Black Hawk, or Ma-ka-tai-me-she-kia-kiak*, ed. J. Gerald Kennedy (New York: Penguin, 2008); Samson Occom, *The Collected Writings of Samson Occom, Mohegan*, ed. Joanna Brooks (New York: Oxford University Press, 2006); George Copway, *Life, Letters and Speeches*, ed. Donald B. Smith and A. Lavonne Brown Ruoff (Lincoln: University of Nebraska Press, 2006); John Norton, *The Journal of Major John Norton, 1816*, ed. Carl F. Klinck and James J. Talman (Toronto: Champlain Society, 1970).

14. This is fundamental to scholarship on Native American autobiography. See H. David Brumble, *American Indian Autobiography* (Lincoln: University of Nebraska Press, 1988); Lisa Brooks, *The Common Pot: The Recovery of Native Space in the Northeast* (Minneapolis: University of Minnesota Press, 2008); Arnold Krupat, *The Voice in the Margin: Native American Literature and the Canon* (Berkeley: University of California Press, 1989); Robert Allen Warrior, *The People and the Word: Reading Native Nonfiction* (Minneapolis: University of Minnesota Press, 2005); Hertha Dawn Wong, *Sending My Heart Back Across the Years: Tradition and Innovation in Native American Autobiography* (New York: Oxford University Press, 1992).
15. John Dunn Hunter, *Memoirs of a Captivity Among the Indians of North America: From Childhood to the Age of Nineteen: With Anecdotes Descriptive of Their Manners and Customs*, ed. Richard Drinnon (1824; repr., New York: Schocken Books, 1973), 26. In her analysis of Mary Jemison's personal narrative, Wyss observes that Jemison's "mixed" identity is more intelligible if understood inside an indigenous context of identity formation characterized by fluid definitions of racial and cultural belonging ("Captivity and Conversion," 65).
16. William Owen, *Diary of William Owen from November 10, 1824 to April 20, 1825*, ed. Joel W. Hiatt (Indianapolis: Bobbs-Merrill, 1906); Donald Macdonald, *The Diaries of Donald Macdonald, 1824–1826* (Indianapolis: Indiana Historical Society, 1942).

Chapter One: First Years with the Kickapoos

1. Hunter, *Memoirs of a Captivity*, 6.
2. Hunter, *Memoirs of a Captivity*, 5.
3. Hunter, *Memoirs of a Captivity*, 7.

4. Richard White, *The Middle Ground: Indians, Empires, and Republics in the Great Lakes Region, 1650–1815* (Cambridge: Cambridge University Press, 1991), 261.
5. Hunter, *Memoirs of a Captivity*, 10.
6. On the history of the Kickapoos, see Arrell M. Gibson, *Kickapoos: Lords of the Middle Border* (Norman: University of Oklahoma Press, 1975); George R. Nielsen, *The Kickapoo People* (Phoenix: Indian Tribal Series, 1975); Joseph B. Herring, *Kenekuk the Kickapoo Prophet* (Lawrence: University Press of Kansas, 1988).
7. Gibson, *Kickapoos*, 5.
8. Gibson, *Kickapoos*, 45. The Kickapoos attacked French missions and outposts, disrupted the fur supply lines, and generally refused to surrender or get in line with imperial policies. Their fighting ability was legendary. See Herring, *Kenekuk the Kickapoo Prophet*, 10–11.
9. On Harrison's crucial role in formulating US Indian policy, see Robert M. Owens, *Mr. Jefferson's Hammer: William Henry Harrison and the Origins of American Indian Policy* (Norman: University of Oklahoma Press, 2007).
10. On the history of US treaty-making, see Ronald N. Satz, *American Indian Policy in the Jacksonian Era* (Lincoln: University of Nebraska Press, 1974); Vine Deloria and Raymond J. DeMallie, *Documents of American Indian Diplomacy: Treaties, Agreements, and Conventions, 1775–1979*, vol. 1 (Norman: University of Oklahoma Press, 1999); Colin G. Calloway, *Pen and Ink Witchcraft: Treaties and Treaty Making in American Indian History* (Oxford: Oxford University Press, 2013).
11. Black Hawk, *Life of Black Hawk*, 19.
12. Quoted in R. David Edmunds, *The Shawnee Prophet* (Lincoln: University of Nebraska Press, 1985), 49.
13. Quoted in Gibson, *Kickapoos*, 53–54.
14. Quoted in Gibson, *Kickapoos*, 53.
15. White, *The Middle Ground*, 512.
16. Hunter, *Memoirs of a Captivity*, 11.
17. An early account of the Kickapoos and maple sugar is William H. Keating, *Narrative of an Expedition to the Source of St. Peter's River, Lake Winnepeek, Lake of the Woods, & C., Performed in the Year 1823*, vol. 2 (London: G. B. Whittaker, 1825), 116–17. See also Henry Wetherbee Henshaw, "Indian Origin of Maple Sugar," *American Anthropologist* 3, no. 4 (1890): 344.

18. Hunter, *Memoirs of a Captivity*, 8.
19. For a cogent analysis of this dynamic in a settler nation, see Adam Dahl, *Empire of the People: Settler Colonialism and the Foundations of Modern Democratic Thought* (Lawrence: University Press of Kansas, 2018).
20. Hunter, *Memoirs of a Captivity*, 9.
21. I use the term *settler colonialism* throughout this book to refer to the practices, laws, and ideas by which the United States and its citizens oppressed Native peoples, displaced them from their homes, and confiscated their lands. I have been influenced by several excellent studies of the subject, including Hoxie, "Retrieving the Red Continent"; Walter Hixson, *American Settler Colonialism: A History* (New York: Springer, 2013); Dahl, *Empire of the People*; Alyosha Goldstein, *Formations of United States Colonialism* (Durham, NC: Duke University Press, 2014); Roxanne Dunbar-Ortiz, *Not "a Nation of Immigrants": Settler Colonialism, White Supremacy, and a History of Erasure and Exclusion* (Boston: Beacon Press, 2021); Jodi A. Byrd, *The Transit of Empire: Indigenous Critiques of Colonialism* (Minneapolis: University of Minnesota Press, 2011); Patrick Wolfe, "Settler Colonialism and the Elimination of the Native," *Journal of Genocide Research* 8, no. 4 (2006): 387–409.
22. Hunter, *Memoirs of a Captivity*, 12. On the history of Rogerstown, see Stephen Warren, *The Shawnees and Their Neighbors, 1795–1870* (Urbana: University of Illinois Press, 2005), 78.
23. Stephen Aron, *Peace and Friendship: An Alternative History of the American West* (Oxford: Oxford University Press, 2022), 56–60.
24. John Mack Faragher, *Daniel Boone: The Life and Legend of an American Pioneer* (New York: Henry Holt, 1993), 313.
25. Hunter, *Memoirs of a Captivity*, 12.
26. Aron, *Peace and Friendship*, 67.
27. Hunter, *Memoirs of a Captivity*, 13.

Chapter Two: Growing Up Among the Osages and Kansas

1. Before I get any deeper into Hunter's childhood, I should explain why I am using the name Kansa. Their real name—what they called themselves in their own language before the Europeans and Americans tried one translation after another—remains unknown. The Spanish wrote down many variations, names such as *Kansa*

and *Cansa* and *Caw*, and the French altered some of them, adding *Konza* and *Kanza* and *Kaw*. American missionaries and traders compiled several tribal vocabularies during the nineteenth century, but they merely repeated the tribal designations that were already in use. In 1907, the ethnologist George Morehouse pledged to settle the nomenclature question once and for all, but his quest to find the origin of the tribal name resulted in a surprising discovery. He unearthed in the archives more than 125 different variations of the tribal name. It has been the common practice among scholars and members of the Kansa nation to use either *Kansa* or *Kaw*, or sometimes both interchangeably.

2. William E. Unrau, *The Kansa Indians: A History of the Wind People, 1673–1873* (Norman: University of Oklahoma Press, 1986), 25.
3. On the history of the Kansa, see Unrau, *The Kansa Indians*; Joseph B. Herring, *The Enduring Indians of Kansas: A Century and a Half of Acculturation* (Lawrence: University Press of Kansas, 1990); Benjamin Y. Dixon, "Furthering Their Own Demise: How Kansa Indian Death Customs Accelerated Their Depopulation," *Ethnohistory* 54, no. 3 (2007): 473–508; Ronald D. Parks, *The Darkest Period: The Kanza Indians and Their Last Homeland, 1846–1873* (Norman: University of Oklahoma Press, 2014). On the Missouria people, see Michael Dickey, *The People of the River's Mouth: In Search of the Missouria Indians* (Columbia: University of Missouri Press, 2011).
4. Hunter, *Memoirs of a Captivity*, 15.
5. In her analysis of captivity and masculinity, Namias notes that "Hunter, like all captive boys, was required to learn the meaning of manhood in the Indian context." Namias, *White Captives*, 75.
6. Hunter, *Memoirs of a Captivity*, 16.
7. Hunter, *Memoirs of a Captivity*, 18.
8. Dunbar-Ortiz and Gilio-Whitaker discuss the historical persistence of this damaging stereotype. Roxanne Dunbar-Ortiz and Dina Gilio-Whitaker, *"All the Real Indians Died Off": And 20 Other Myths About Native Americans* (Boston: Beacon Press, 2016).
9. Hunter and John Tanner have much in common. Both were adopted to replace a dead son; both their Native mothers were caregivers and teachers and were central to their respective stories; both boys navigated a rite of passage based in succeeding as hunters and warriors. For more on this point, see Namias, *White Captives*.

10. Hunter, *Memoirs of a Captivity*, 18–19.
11. Hunter, *Memoirs of a Captivity*, 16.
12. Unrau, *The Kansa Indians: A History of the Wind People, 1673–1873*, 46.
13. Hunter, *Memoirs of a Captivity*, 17.
14. For a more balanced account of the Pawnees, see George E. Hyde, *The Pawnee Indians* (Norman: University of Oklahoma Press, 1988).
15. Hunter, *Memoirs of a Captivity*, 20.
16. Hunter, *Memoirs of a Captivity*, 19.
17. Hunter, *Memoirs of a Captivity*, 21.
18. This description is based on my reading of John Joseph Matthews, *The Osages: Children of the Middle Waters* (Norman: University of Oklahoma Press, 1961). The phrase "reliable allies in a crisis" is on page 87 and "rivals but not blood enemies" on page 90.
19. Hunter, *Memoirs of a Captivity*, 23.
20. In addition to Matthews's *The Osages*, my understanding of Osage history and culture has been shaped by Louis F. Burns, *A History of the Osage People* (Tuscaloosa: University of Alabama Press, 2004); Jean Dennison, *Colonial Entanglement: Constituting a Twenty-First-Century Osage Nation* (Chapel Hill: University of North Carolina Press, 2012); Willard H. Rollings, *The Osage: An Ethnohistorical Study of Hegemony on the Prairie-Plains* (Columbia: University of Missouri Press, 1995); Francis La Flesche, *The Osage and the Invisible World: From the Works of Francis La Flesche* (Norman: University of Oklahoma Press, 1995).
21. Hunter, *Memoirs of a Captivity*, 23.
22. Zebulon Montgomery Pike, *Journals, with Letters and Related Documents*, 2 vols., ed. Donald Jackson (Norman: University of Oklahoma Press, 1966).
23. Matthews provided a similar account of the destructive effects of the fur trade. Matthews, *The Osages*, 438.
24. Hunter, *Memoirs of a Captivity*, 25.
25. Hunter, *Memoirs of a Captivity*, 26.
26. Hunter, *Memoirs of a Captivity*, 27.
27. On the history of Osage resistance to Catholic and Protestant missionaries, see Willard H. Rollings, *Unaffected by the Gospel: Osage Resistance to the Christian Invasion (1673–1906): A Cultural Victory* (Albuquerque: University of New Mexico Press, 2004).
28. George E. Tinker, *Missionary Conquest: The Gospel and Native American Cultural Genocide* (Minneapolis: Fortress Press, 1993), 10.

Chapter Three: Western Odyssey

1. Hunter, *Memoirs of a Captivity*, 32.
2. Hunter, *Memoirs of a Captivity*, 33.
3. Matthews, *The Osages*, 594–95.
4. Hunter, *Memoirs of a Captivity*, 36.
5. Pike, *Journals*.
6. Hunter, *Memoirs of a Captivity*, 36. They "would be sacrificed to requite such treachery."
7. Hunter, *Memoirs of a Captivity*, 39.
8. I am elaborating on Drinnon's gem of a footnote to Hunter's narrative. Hunter, *Memoirs of a Captivity*, 235.
9. Frederick Webb Hodge, *Handbook of American Indians North of Mexico*, vol. 2 (Washington, DC: Government Printing Office, 1910), 632.
10. Warhus also informs this discussion of Native cartography. Mark Warhus, *Another America: Native American Maps and the History of Our Land* (New York: St. Martin's Griffin, 1998), 1–57.
11. In her study of European and Native cartographies, Barbara Belyea demonstrates how "the assumptions and standards of European cartography," which were taken as "universal measures of accuracy," defined Native mapmaking as a crude and inferior spatial practice. Barbara Belyea, "Amerindian Maps: The Explorer as Translator," *Journal of Historical Geography* 18, no. 3 (1992): 267.
12. Hunter, *Memoirs of a Captivity*, 39.
13. Hunter, *Memoirs of a Captivity*, 39.
14. Hunter, *Memoirs of a Captivity*, 42–43.
15. Hunter, *Memoirs of a Captivity*, 43.
16. Quoted in Drinnon, *White Savage*, 75.
17. There are various and slightly different versions of the Osage creation story. This description comes from Tai Edwards, *Osage Women and Empire: Gender and Power* (Lawrence: University Press of Kansas, 2018), 15.
18. Drinnon, *White Savage*, 76.
19. Gordon M. Sayre, "A Native American Scoops Lewis and Clark: The Voyage of Moncacht-Apé," *Common-place* 5, no. 4 (2005).
20. Meinig, *The Shaping of America*, 2; William H. Goetzmann, *Exploration and Empire: The Explorer and the Scientist in the Winning of the American West* (New York: History Book Club, 1966).
21. For an overview of the Indigenous world of the Pacific Northwest, see Robert H. Ruby and John Arthur Brown, *Indians of the Pacific*

Northwest: A History (Norman: University of Oklahoma Press, 1988).

22. There were certainly more overt political uses of the trope of nature in Indian country, as Maureen Konkle shows in her cogent reading of William Apess's "Eulogy of King Philip." By taking up the trope of nature to argue for the "natural rights" of Native peoples, Apess subverted and redefined the stereotype that they belong to a pre-political state of nature. Even if Hunter's argument is not as direct, his trope of nature also invested Native peoples with the inalienable rights that no Western state was supposed to supersede. Maureen Konkle, *Writing Indian Nations: Native Intellectuals and the Politics of Historiography, 1827–1863* (Chapel Hill: University of North Carolina Press, 2004), 97–160.
23. Hunter, *Memoirs of a Captivity*, 238.
24. Hunter wanted his readers to understand its significance. He explained that for Native peoples west of the Mississippi, the ceremony was as sacred as a Christian liturgy, in a place as sacred as any cathedral, for it elicited their most soulful devotions to the Great Creator.
25. Drinnon makes this observation about the South Pass in his editorial commentary on Hunter's narrative. Hunter, *Memoirs of a Captivity*, 238.
26. Hunter, *Memoirs of a Captivity*, 48.
27. Hunter, *Memoirs of a Captivity*, 51.
28. Richard Edward Oglesby, *Manuel Lisa and the Opening of the Missouri Fur Trade* (Norman: University of Oklahoma Press, 1963).
29. When some chiefs refused to attend the conference, Clark coerced them into coming by taking some of their people as hostages. (He never did compel Black Hawk to submit.) Clark's tactics were effective. As a biographer of Clark notes, he ultimately "divested Indians of more land than any other American" and signed more treaties than any US official in history. Jay H. Buckley, *William Clark: Indian Diplomat* (Norman: University of Oklahoma Press, 2008), xiii.
30. Hunter, *Memoirs of a Captivity*, 51.
31. Hunter, *Memoirs of a Captivity*, 52.
32. Hunter, *Memoirs of a Captivity*, 52.
33. Hunter, *Memoirs of a Captivity*, 52–53.
34. Hunter, *Memoirs of a Captivity*, 53.

35. Oglesby, *Manuel Lisa and the Opening of the Missouri Fur Trade*, 78.
36. Oglesby, *Manuel Lisa and the Opening of the Missouri Fur Trade*, 158–61; Hiram Martin Chittenden, *The American Fur Trade of the Far West* (New York: Press of the Pioneers, 1935), 128.
37. Oglesby, *Manuel Lisa and the Opening of the Missouri Fur Trade*, 160–61.
38. Oglesby, *Manuel Lisa and the Opening of the Missouri Fur Trade*, 160. This important discovery has gone unnoticed for years, probably because it does not appear in *White Savage*—it appears in Drinnon's editorial commentary to Hunter's *Memoirs of a Captivity*, published the following year. See Hunter, *Memoirs of a Captivity*, 238–39.

Chapter Four: Sugar Moon

1. Hunter, *Memoirs of a Captivity*, 54.
2. Hunter, *Memoirs of a Captivity*, 54.
3. I discuss the impact of Pike's journal in chapter 2 of Doolen, *Territories of Empire*. Leo Oliva offers this summary: "It is safe to declare that everyone who ventured forth from the United States to establish contact with northern Mexico after 1811 benefitted either directly or indirectly from Pike's expedition and journal." Leo E. Oliva, "Enemies and Friends: Zebulon Montgomery Pike and Facundo Melgares in the Competition for the Great Plains, 1806–1807," *Kansas History* 29, no. 1 (2006): 36.
4. On the history of the Mandans, see Elizabeth A. Fenn, *Encounters at the Heart of the World: A History of the Mandan People* (New York: Macmillan, 2014).
5. Like other agriculturalists on the Great Plains, they used fire to prevent forests from invading the grasslands, to create new grazing land for buffalo, elk, and antelope, and to secure the perimeter of their villages.
6. Hunter, *Memoirs of a Captivity*, 55.
7. For insight into how Indigenous peoples navigated and oriented themselves in space, see Claudio Aporta, "Inuit Orienting: Travelling Along Familiar Horizons," *Sensory Studies*, 2020.
8. David Treuer, *The Heartbeat of Wounded Knee: Native America from 1890 to the Present* (New York: Riverhead Books, 2019), 185; Anton Treuer, *Ojibwe in Minnesota* (St. Paul: Minnesota Historical Society, 2010).
9. Hunter, *Memoirs of a Captivity*, 56.
10. Hunter, *Memoirs of a Captivity*, 56.

11. Hunter, *Memoirs of a Captivity*, 56.
12. Hunter, *Memoirs of a Captivity*, 57.
13. Hunter, *Memoirs of a Captivity*, 57.
14. Hunter, *Memoirs of a Captivity*, 57.
15. Hunter, *Memoirs of a Captivity*, 58.
16. Hunter, *Memoirs of a Captivity*, 58.
17. Hunter, *Memoirs of a Captivity*, 59.
18. Hunter, *Memoirs of a Captivity*, 59.
19. Hunter, *Memoirs of a Captivity*, 59.
20. On the creation of the Osages, see section 1 of Matthews, *The Osages*.
21. Hunter, *Memoirs of a Captivity*, 59.
22. Hunter, *Memoirs of a Captivity*, 60.
23. Hunter, *Memoirs of a Captivity*, 60–61. Hunter remarked that "Nee-he-gah, or the Rocky Hills, a chief of considerable note, received us in the most hospitable manner, supplied all our wants, and, as is customary among them in regard to those they esteem real friends, offered us the attendance of their women," who he believed were the most beautiful Native women he had ever seen. Even so, Hunter stated that everyone in his party, "to a man, declined the acceptance of their services."
24. Hunter, *Memoirs of a Captivity*, 61.
25. Kathleen DuVal, "Debating Identity, Sovereignty, and Civilization: The Arkansas Valley After the Louisiana Purchase," *Journal of the Early Republic* 26, no. 1 (2006): 47.
26. In 1808, the treaty commissioners were the explorers Meriwether Lewis and William Clark, now respectively the governor of Missouri and the superintendent of Indian affairs in the West, and Pierre Choteau, US agent to the Osages. Their treaty drew a north-south boundary that commenced near Fire Prairie on the Missouri and ran due south to the Arkansas, then southeasterly along that river to its confluence with the Mississippi. In exchange for the land, the Osages expected to receive a stronger alliance with the United States, annuities payable in merchandise, a blacksmith, farming implements, a water mill, and inviolable boundaries.
27. DuVal, "Debating Identity, Sovereignty, and Civilization," 33.
28. Hunter, *Memoirs of a Captivity*, 61.
29. Hunter, *Memoirs of a Captivity*, 62.

Chapter Five: Sanctuary

1. Hunter, *Memoirs of a Captivity*, 66.
2. Hunter, *Memoirs of a Captivity*, 66.
3. William Cronon, "The Trouble with Wilderness: or, Getting Back to the Wrong Nature," *Environmental History* 1, no. 1 (1996): 10. Thoreau was so enthralled by Hunter's descriptions of nature that he copied pages into his "Indian Notebooks."
4. Hunter, *Memoirs of a Captivity*, 69.
5. Hunter, *Memoirs of a Captivity*, 69.
6. Hyde, *Empires, Nations, and Families*, 4–5.
7. Quoted in Hyde, *Empires, Nations, and Families*, 270.
8. I wrote about Timothy Flint in a previous book, Andy Doolen, *Territories of Empire: U.S. Writing from the Louisiana Purchase to Mexican Independence* (New York: Oxford University Press, 2014). See also Keri Holt, "Double-Crossings: The Trans-American Patriotism of Francis Berrian," *Western American Literature* 44, no. 4 (2010): 312–41; Andrea Tinnemeyer, "Enlightenment Ideology and the Crisis of Whiteness in *Francis Berrian* and *Caballero*," *Western American Literature* 35, no. 1 (2000): 21–32; Edward Watts, *An American Colony: Regionalism and the Roots of Midwestern Culture* (Athens: Ohio University Press, 2002).
9. Samuel Brown, *The Western Gazetteer; Or Emigrant's Directory* (Auburn, NY: H. C. Southwick., 1817), 193.
10. Hunter, *Memoirs of a Captivity*, 182.
11. Virgil J. Vogel, *American Indian Medicine* (Norman: University of Oklahoma Press, 2013), 14.
12. Vogel, *American Indian Medicine*, 107.
13. Horsman, *Race and Manifest Destiny*, 98. Horsman notes: "There is considerable evidence that by the end of the colonial era the Enlightenment view of innate human equality was being challenged on a practical level in the American colonies. Whites, by the very laws they passed and the attitudes they assumed, placed blacks on a different human level" (100).
14. Drew R. McCoy, *The Elusive Republic: Political Economy in Jeffersonian America* (Chapel Hill: University of North Carolina Press, 1980).
15. The details in this scene are taken from Chittenden's exhaustive history of the American fur trade. Chittenden, *The American Fur Trade of the Far West*, 32–33.
16. Hunter, *Memoirs of a Captivity*, 70.

17. Hunter, *Memoirs of a Captivity*, 72.
18. Hunter, *Memoirs of a Captivity*, 73. Years later, in Texas, Stephen Austin would make the same threat to Hunter.

Chapter Six: Freeman

1. Hunter, *Memoirs of a Captivity*, 74.
2. According to John Cawelti, stories of the self-made man in American culture have always been useful in assuaging public concerns about the capabilities of certain peoples to improve themselves. John G. Cawelti, *The Six-Gun Mystique Sequel* (Bowling Green, OH: Popular Press, 1999).
3. Quoted in Adam Rothman, *Slave Country: American Expansion and the Origins of the Deep South* (Cambridge, MA: Harvard University Press, 2005), 218. According to Rothman, "few nineteenth-century travelers" failed to remark on the "astonishing diversity" in their travelogues (224).
4. Walter Johnson, *River of Dark Dreams* (Cambridge, MA: Harvard University Press, 2013), 81. These numbers included enslaved persons and free Blacks. A widely read travel guide, Robert Baird's *View of the Valley of the Mississippi*, had this to say: "If he passes through the market, he will see such a scene as he never before witnessed. Babel itself could not have exceeded it. He will hear French, Spanish, English, and sometimes German languages spoken by Negroes, mulattoes, and *quartre unes*, and whites" (quoted in Johnson, *River of Dark Dreams*, 81).
5. Leland D. Baldwin, *The Keelboat Age on Western Waters* (Pittsburgh: University of Pittsburgh Press, 1941), 104. Three years later, Timothy Flint, the author and minister from Cincinnati, commented on New Orleans: "Much has been said about the profligacy of manners and morals here; and this place has more than once been called the modern Sodom. Amidst such a multitude, composed in a great measure of the low people of all nations, there must of course be much debauchery, and low vice." However, Flint, like Hunter, wanted his readers to know that not all of New Orleans was lost in sin and vice: "There are many excellent people here, many people who mourn over the prevailing degeneracy." Timothy Flint, *Recollections of the Last Ten Years in the Valley of the Mississippi*, ed. George R. Brooks (1826; repr., Carbondale: Southern Illinois University Press, 1968), 223–24.

6. Rollings, *The Osage*, 35.
7. In his attack on Hunter, Lewis Cass included an affidavit from a John Dunn who denied ever meeting anyone matching Hunter's description. Nearly a century and a half passed before Drinnon questioned this evidence by pointing out that more than a few people named John Dunn resided in Missouri, and it remains unclear which one provided the affidavit.
8. Johnson, *River of Dark Dreams*, 80. Timothy Flint offered a vivid tableau of commerce moving downriver in *Recollections of the Last Ten Years in the Valley of the Mississippi*, 76–77.
9. Allen observes that "in an increasingly complicated era, the rugged boatmen stood apart: independent, uncomplicated, and unconquerable." Michael R. Allen, *Western Rivermen, 1763–1861: Ohio and Mississippi Boatmen and the Myth of the Alligator Horse* (Baton Rouge: Louisiana State University Press, 1994), 25.
10. Doyce B. Nunis, "The Sublettes of Kentucky: Their Early Contribution to the Opening of the West," *Register of the Kentucky Historical Society* 57, no. 1 (1959): 20–34.
11. Howe, *What Hath God Wrought*, 423.
12. Apess, *On Our Own Ground*; Drew Lopenzina, *Through an Indian's Looking-Glass: A Cultural Biography of William Apess, Pequot* (Amherst: University of Massachusetts Press, 2018); Philip F. Gura, *The Life of William Apess, Pequot* (Chapel Hill: University of North Carolina Press, 2015).
13. Victor Francis O'Daniel, *A Light of the Church in Kentucky: Or the Life, Labors, and Character of the Very Rev. Samuel Thomas Wilson, OP, STM, Pioneer Educator and the First Provincial of a Religious Order in the United States* (Washington, DC: The Dominicana, 1932). I have not located the student records from this period, and they probably did not survive. As I looked for clues on how Hunter may have found his way to the school, I discovered in this biography of Wilson that they shared a connection with the Boone family. After arriving in Kentucky, Wilson was injured in a wagon accident, and he recuperated at the home of Henry Boone.
14. Hunter, *Memoirs of a Captivity*, 78.
15. Shawneetown and Washington, DC, share the distinction of being the only towns platted and chartered by the US government. A special act of Congress established the land office. The first bank in Illinois was chartered there in 1816. The first wave of settlers came

mainly from the southern states of Kentucky, Virginia, Tennessee, Georgia, and Alabama. They purchased their lots at the land office, built their cabins, cleared their fields, and planted their crops.

16. Hunter, *Memoirs of a Captivity*, 78.
17. Hunter, *Memoirs of a Captivity*, 79.

Chapter 7: White Indian

1. Jefferson to Madison, November 22, 1822, *The Papers of James Madison*, Retirement Series, vol. 2, *1 February 1820–26 February 1823*, ed. David B. Mattern, J. C. A. Stagg, Mary Parke Johnson, and Anne Mandeville Colony (Charlottesville: University of Virginia Press, 2013), 603–4.
2. Calloway, "Neither White nor Red," 44.
3. Berkhofer, *The White Man's Indian*, 94.
4. Richard Slotkin demonstrated in his classic study the many ways in which this new identity was based in the selective appropriation of Native traditions, customs, and teachings. Slotkin, *Regeneration Through Violence*.
5. This is his son Alexander's recollection. Alexander Eddy Hosack, *A Memoir of the Late David Hosack* (Philadelphia: Lindsay & Blakiston, 1861), 337.
6. See the outstanding biography of Hosack by Victoria Johnson, *American Eden: David Hosack, Botany, and Medicine in the Garden of the Early Republic* (New York: Liveright, 2018), 3.
7. Johnson, *American Eden*, 98.
8. Joshua David Bellin, *Medicine Bundle: Indian Sacred Performance and American Literature, 1824–1932* (Philadelphia: University of Pennsylvania Press, 2008), 28. See also Jack Weatherford, *Indian Givers: How the Indians of the Americas Transformed the World* (New York: Ballantine Books, 2010).
9. The Confederate Army, always short of quinine, adopted it as an alternative treatment for the disease. Guy R. Hasegawa, "Quinine Substitutes in the Confederate Army," *Military Medicine* 172, no. 6 (2007): 650–55.
10. Hunter, *Memoirs of a Captivity*, 202.
11. Hunter, *Memoirs of a Captivity*, 246–47.
12. Robert Gunn uncovered Akerly's lecture in the 1824 edition of the *American Journal of Science and Arts*. Robert Lawrence Gunn, *Ethnology and Empire: Languages, Literature, and the Making of the North*

American Borderlands (New York: New York University Press, 2015). For the lecture: Samuel Akerly, "Observations on the Language of Signs, Read Before the New-York Lyceum of Natural History, on the 23d June, 1823," *American Journal of Science and Arts* 8, no. 2 (1824).

13. Gunn, *Ethnology and Empire*, 75. Thomas Gallaudet, the cofounder of the first American school for the deaf, in Hartford, also recognized the significance of Long's glossary. He spent the remainder of his life investigating the connections between the two languages. He published his thoughts in the inaugural issue of the *Annals of the Deaf and Dumb*. See Jeffrey Davis, "A Historical Linguistic Account of Sign Language Among North American Indian Groups," in *Multilingualism and Sign Languages: From the Great Plains to Australia*, Sociolinguistics of the Deaf Community, ed. Ceil Lucas, 3–35 (Washington, DC: Gallaudet University Press, 2006); Ted Supalla, Fanny Limousin, and Betsy Hicks McDonald, "Historical Change in American Sign Language," *Handbook of Historical Linguistics* 2 (2020): 423–46.
14. Edwin James, *Account of an Expedition from Pittsburgh to the Rocky Mountains, Performed in the Years 1819 and '20* (Carey, 1823).
15. Gunn, *Ethnology and Empire*, 92.
16. Hunter, *Memoirs of a Captivity*, 39.
17. Hunter, *Memoirs of a Captivity*, 54.
18. Hunter, *Memoirs of a Captivity*, 64.
19. Hunter, *Memoirs of a Captivity*, 30–31.
20. Hunter, *Memoirs of a Captivity*, 28.
21. On Tecumseh's travels, see Dowd, *A Spirited Resistance*. Tecumseh's position was that the land was the common property of Native peoples and could not be parceled off and sold without their unanimous consent. By rejecting the legitimacy of the treaty process, Tecumseh turned himself into an archenemy of the United States. William Henry Harrison, the governor of Indiana Territory at the time, respected him and speculated that if history had been different and the United States had not expanded across the continent, then the Shawnee warrior might have established an empire that rivaled Mexico or Peru.
22. Cass, "Indians of North America," 102.
23. During the 1960s and 1970s, scholars began challenging the official accounts of American progress and expansion. They were researching

and writing anticolonial histories of the lives of Indian leaders, such as Tecumseh, Red Cloud, Geronimo, Crazy Horse, and Sitting Bull.

24. John Sugden, *Tecumseh: A Life* (New York: Henry Holt, 1998).

Chapter Eight: Celebrity

1. John Thomas Scharf and Thompson Westcott, *History of Philadelphia, 1609–1884*, vol. 1 (Philadelphia: L. H. Everts, 1884), 577.
2. Edward Clark, *Description of a Plan for Navigating the Rapids in Rivers: With an Account of Some Experiments Instituted to Establish Its Practicability* (Philadelphia: William Brown, 1823).
3. *The Port Folio*, vol. XVIII (1824): 350.
4. Drinnon, *White Savage*, 111.
5. A writer in the *Cincinnati Literary Gazette* expressed the same view, observing how Hunter's "feelings, views and affections are completely identified with theirs [Native peoples]."
6. *The Eclectic Review*, July–December 1823, 173–74.
7. *The British Critic*, January 1823, 622.
8. *The Quarterly Review*, December 1824–March 1825, 81.
9. *The Monthly Review*, vol. CII (November 1823): 243–44.
10. *The Literary Gazette*, April 19, 1823, 242–44.
11. I am citing this review as it appeared in the *New England Galaxy and United States Literary Advertiser*, where it was reprinted from the *National Gazette*. See *New England Galaxy and United States Literary Advertiser*, April 11, 1823.
12. *The Quarterly Review*, December 1824–March 1825, 80.
13. *The Cincinnati Literary Gazette*, vol. 1 (January 1824): 1.
14. Mary Louise Pratt, *Imperial Eyes: Travel Writing and Transculturation* (London: Routledge, 1992), 7.
15. I am using Pratt's key insight about ongoing colonialism in contact zones to redefine Krupat's formulation of Native American autobiography as the "textual equivalent of the frontier" (*Those Who Come After*, 33). Christopher Taylor's contact zone model is also useful for locating these borders texts at the many *intersections* between Native American and settler cultures. See Christopher Taylor, "North America as Contact Zone: Native American Literary Nationalism and the Cross-Cultural Dilemma," *Studies in American Indian Literatures* 22, no. 3 (2010): 26–44.
16. *Missouri Gazette*, May 26, 1819.
17. *The Monthly Review*, vol. CII (November 1823): 247.

18. *The Monthly Review*, vol. CII (November 1823): 247.
19. Alden T. Vaughan, *Transatlantic Encounters: American Indians in Britain, 1500–1776* (Cambridge: Cambridge University Press, 2006); Timothy John Shannon, *Iroquois Diplomacy on the Early American Frontier* (New York: Penguin, 2008).
20. Tim Fulford, *Romantic Indians: Native Americans, British Literature, and Transatlantic Culture, 1756–1830* (Oxford: Oxford University Press, 2006), 5.
21. Fulford provides a vivid account of Hunter's fame in England. Fulford, *Romantic Indians*.
22. Drinnon, *White Savage*, 26–27.
23. "Viator," *Natchitoches Courier*, March 20, 1827. According to Drinnon, this visit took place in January 1824.
24. Drinnon, *White Savage*, 28.
25. Chester Harding, *My Egotistigraphy* (Cambridge: John Wilson & Son, 1866), 64–65.
26. Drinnon, *White Savage*, 33.

Chapter Nine: Dreamers

1. In Fulford's view, "What most recommended Hunter was his project to save the Indians. The plan was to turn Indians from hunters to farmers, on the best new British principles." Fulford, *Romantic Indians*, 238.
2. Hunter, *Memoirs of a Captivity*, 225.
3. Ostler, *Surviving Genocide*, 230. I'm also drawing on W. David Baird, *The Quapaw Indians: A History of the Downstream People* (Norman: University of Oklahoma Press, 1980); S. Charles Bolton, *Arkansas, 1800–1860: Remote and Restless* (Fayetteville: University of Arkansas Press, 2014); Joseph Patrick Key, "'Outcasts upon the world': The Louisiana Purchase and the Quapaws," *The Arkansas Historical Quarterly* 62, no. 3 (2003): 272–288.
4. Quoted in George Sabo and James P. Harcourt, *Human Adaptation in the Ozark and Ouachita Mountains* (Fayetteville: Arkansas Archeological Survey, 1990), 124. In a frequently quoted description, the botanist Thomas Nuttal documented their achievements as he traveled up the Arkansas in 1819: "Both banks of the river, as we proceeded, were lined with the houses and farms of the Cherokees, and though their dress was a mixture of indigenous and European taste, yet in their houses, which are decently furnished, and in

their farms, which were well fenced and stocked with cattle, we perceive a happy approach towards civilization. Their numerous families, also well fed and clothed, argue a propitious progress in their population. Their superior industry, either as hunters or farmers, proves the value of property among them, and they are no longer strangers to avarice, and the distinctions created by wealth; some of them are possessed of property to the amount of many thousands of dollars, have houses handsomely and conveniently furnished, and their tables spread with our dainties and luxuries." Thomas Nuttall, *A Journal of Travels into the Arkansas Territory During the Year 1819*, ed. Savoie Lottinville (Fayetteville: University of Arkansas Press, 1999), 136.

5. Henry Harvey was the man's name. Quoted in Calloway, "Neither White nor Red," 122.
6. Calloway, "Neither White nor Red," 125.
7. Fulford, *Romantic Indians*, 217.
8. Chris Jennings, *Paradise Now: The Story of American Utopianism* (New York: Random House, 2016); John F. C. Harrison, *Quest for the New Moral World: Robert Owen and the Owenities in Britain and America* (New York: Scribner, 1969); Chris Williams and Noel Thompson, *Robert Owen and His Legacy* (Cardiff: University of Wales Press, 2011); Sidney Pollard and John Salt, *Robert Owen, Prophet of the Poor: Essays in Honour of the Two Hundredth Anniversary of His Birth* (Lewisburg, PA: Bucknell University Press, 1971).
9. Carl Guarneri, *The Utopian Alternative: Fourierism in Nineteenth-Century America* (Ithaca, NY: Cornell University Press, 1991). Guarneri calculates that "between 1825 and 1860 thousands of Americans formed almost a hundred new utopias or joined colonies established earlier by millennial religious sects" (7).
10. Smith to Owen, June 30, 1823, Robert Owen Collection, National Co-operative Archive, GB 1499 ROC/18/48/1. Drinnon uncovered the letter, but he didn't realize that Smith was John Adams Smith (44). Smith's grandmother Abigail Adams had secured him the position.
11. Drinnon drew the reasonable conclusion that Owen introduced Hunter to them. Owen and Hunter, in addition to John Adams Smith, shared another friend in common, John Smith in the House of Commons.

12. Hunter, *Memoirs of a Captivity*, 217.
13. Hunter, *Memoirs of a Captivity*, 224.
14. Hunter, *Memoirs of a Captivity*, 227.
15. Drinnon, *White Savage*, 49.
16. Drinnon, *White Savage*, 50.
17. Drinnon, *White Savage*, 45.
18. Quoted in Drinnon, *White Savage*, 21.
19. Anna Maria W. Stirling, *Coke of Norfolk and His Friends: The Life of Thomas William Coke, First Earl of Leicester of Holkham* (London: Lane, 1908), 319.
20. Quoted in Drinnon, *White Savage*, 21.
21. This description of the Holkham grounds is based on Richard Bacon's 1821 report. Richard N. Bacon, *A Report of the Transactions at the Holkham Sheep-Shearing, on Monday, Tuesday, Wednesday, and Thursday, July 2, 3, 4, and 5: Being the Forty-Third Anniversary of That Meeting* (n.p.: n.p., 1821), 49.
22. Stirling, *Coke of Norfolk and His Friends*, 488.
23. Bacon reported on Coke's speech in his account of the sheep-shearing festival. Stirling, *Coke of Norfolk and His Friends*.
24. Lipton came to this conclusion after searching the estate records. Leah Lipton, *A Truthful Likeness: Chester Harding and His Portraits* (Washington, DC: National Portrait Gallery, Smithsonian Institution, 1985), 67.

Chapter Ten: Forest Shadows

1. Nancy Moore Goslee, "Heman's 'Red Indians,'" in *Romanticism, Race, and Imperial Culture, 1780–1834*, ed. A. T. Richardson et al. (Bloomington: Indiana University Press, 1996).
2. *The New Monthly Magazine*, vol. 10 (January 1824): 282.
3. *The New Monthly Magazine*, vol. 8 (July–December 1824): 278.
4. Several notable works have informed my understanding of this historical moment, including Howe, *What Hath God Wrought*; Johnson, *River of Dark Dreams*; Thomas R. Hietala, *Manifest Design: Anxious Aggrandizement in Late Jacksonian America* (Ithaca, NY: Cornell University Press, 1985); Meinig, *The Shaping of America*, 2; Saunt, *Unworthy Republic*.
5. Elizabeth Linn Brown was the widow of the novelist Charles Brockden Brown.

6. Auguste Levasseur and John D. Godman, *Lafayette in America in 1824 and 1825: Or, Journal of a Voyage to the United States* (Philadelphia: Carey and Lea, 1829), 141–43.
7. "To James Madison from John Dunn Hunter, 15 October 1824," *Founders Online*, National Archives, https://founders.archives.gov/documents/Madison/04-03-02-0404.
8. In Drinnon's view, "This rather banal, pleasant exchange is comment enough on the charges that Hunter lied about or exploited his acquaintance with two of America's founding fathers." Drinnon, *White Savage*, 159.
9. Sara Day, "'With Peace and Freedom Blest!': Woman as Symbol in America, 1590–1800," American Women: Topical Essays, Library of Congress, accessed May 20, 2024, https://guides.loc.gov/american-women-essays/woman-as-symbol. See also Pamela Scott, *Temple of Liberty: Building the Capitol for a New Nation* (New York: Oxford University Press, 1995).
10. Macdonald wrote: "He received two letters from Hunter the American Indian, stating that he was confined at Philadelphia by ill health, and was longing to see him." Macdonald, *Diaries*, 177.
11. According to Macdonald, Hosack's son told William Owen that "on Hunter's return from Europe, he was not so much at ease in society as before he crossed the Atlantic. He had the peculiar habit of the Indians of never keeping his eyes fixed, but wandering with them from object to object." Macdonald, *Diaries*, 184.
12. William wrote that they went "to shake Hunter by the hand before heading to the hotel." Owen, *Diary*, 28.
13. Clark was impressed and "wished him every success, and added that he would himself be an active co-operator." Macdonald, *Diaries*, 208.
14. This group was the famous "boatload of knowledge," which Pitzer called one of the biggest intellectual migrations in American history. Donald E. Pitzer, "The Original Boatload of Knowledge down the Ohio River: William Maclure's and Robert Owen's transfer of Science and Education to the Midwest, 1825–1826," *Ohio Journal of Science* 89, no. 5 (December 1989): 128–42.

Chapter Eleven: "Singing the Corn Songs"

1. This information comes from the diaries of Macdonald and William Owen.

2. Henry Hope Reed, *The United States Capitol: Its Architecture and Decoration* (New York: Norton, 2005).
3. Macdonald, *Diaries*, 215. They were mounted in the Rotunda in 1826. We know that the two paintings they had seen, *Declaration of Independence* and *Surrender of Lord Cornwallis*, had been on display in various rooms at the Capitol for a few years. The architect was waiting for Trumbull to complete the last painting, *General George Washington Resigning His Commission*, which he did in April 1824, but then he took it on a tour of eastern cities. He probably delivered the painting to the Capitol later that year or early the next.
4. On the interplay between these works and Indian removal policy, see Vivien Green Fryd, *Art and Empire: The Politics of Ethnicity in the United States Capitol, 1815–1860* (New Haven, CT: Yale University Press, 1992).
5. Macdonald, *Diaries*, 215.
6. He was twice the official architect of the Capitol (1803–11 and 1815–17). For a recent study of his life, see Jean H. Baker, *Building America: The Life of Benjamin Henry Latrobe* (New York: Oxford University Press, 2020).
7. The Pilgrim leader William Bradford documented the establishment of Plymouth Colony. William Bradford, *Of Plymouth Plantation, 1620–1647* (New Brunswick, NJ: Rutgers University Press, 1952).
8. I am suggesting here parallels with the impact of oil on political development. See Timothy Mitchell, "Carbon Democracy," *Economy and Society* 38, no. 3 (2009): 399–432. For an old but engaging and detailed account of the impact of corn on territorial expansion, see Eugene C. Brooks, *The Story of Corn and the Westward Migration* (Chicago: Rand, McNally, 1916).
9. Hunter, *Memoirs of a Captivity*, 135.
10. Hunter, *Memoirs of a Captivity*, 134. On the corn ceremony, see Louis F. Burns, *Osage Indian Customs and Myths* (Fayetteville: University of Alabama Press, 2005).
11. Hunter, *Memoirs of a Captivity*, 135.
12. Paula Gunn Allen, *The Sacred Hoop: Recovering the Feminine in American Indian Traditions* (Boston, MA: Beacon Press, 1986), 13–29.
13. Deloria is the definitive voice on the cultural construction of this settler identity. Deloria, *Playing Indian*.
14. On hospitality rituals, see David A. Nichols, *Red Gentlemen and White Savages: Indians, Federalists, and the Search for Order on the*

American Frontier (Charlottesville: University of Virginia Press, 2008), 11.

15. Owen, *Diary*, 43.
16. Owen, *Diary*, 43.
17. According to Debo, "The War of 1812 thus demonstrated that the Choctaw people had definitely joined their future with that of the growing American Republic" (41). Angie Debo, *The Rise and Fall of the Choctaw Republic* (Norman: University of Oklahoma Press, 1961).
18. As Deloria memorably put it about the real-world resistance to settler colonialism across the nineteenth century, "Real Indian people continued to challenge American expansion and steadfastly refused to vanish." Deloria, *Playing Indian*, 69.
19. On the situation across the southern United States, see Grant Foreman, *Indian Removal: The Emigration of the Five Civilized Tribes of Indians* (Norman: University of Oklahoma Press, 1953).
20. Mielke's introduction to the following collection of essays informed my thinking about the Choctaw performance. Joshua David Bellin and Laura L. Mielke, *Native Acts: Indian Performance, 1603–1832* (Lincoln: University of Nebraska Press, 2011).
21. Macdonald, *Diaries*, 218.
22. Macdonald, *Diaries*, 218.
23. Macdonald, *Diaries*, 215.
24. George Catlin, *Letters and Notes on the Manners, Customs, and Condition of the North American Indians* (New York: Wiley & Putnam, 1844), 196.
25. Quoted in Brian W. Dippie, *Catlin and His Contemporaries: The Politics of Patronage* (Lincoln: University of Nebraska Press, 1990), 63.
26. Benita Eisler, *The Red Man's Bones: George Catlin, Artist and Showman* (New York: Norton, 2013), 106. For a synopsis of these racist caricatures, see Eric Foner, *Forever Free: The Story of Emancipation and Reconstruction* (New York: Knopf, 2013), 38.
27. Dunbar-Ortiz and Gilio-Whitaker, *"All the Real Indians Died Off": And 20 Other Myths About Native Americans*, 130.
28. Total expenses amounted to $5,662.99, which I have calculated to be approximately $152,700 in today's dollars. Debo, *The Rise and Fall of the Choctaw Republic*, 50.
29. Richard White, *The Roots of Dependency: Subsistence, Environment, and Social Change Among the Choctaws, Pawnees, and Navajos* (Lincoln: University of Nebraska Press, 1988), 122.
30. Macdonald, *Diaries*, 218.

31. According to Debo, the deal stipulated $6,000 a year for sixteen years and a permanent annuity of $6,320. Debo, *The Rise and Fall of the Choctaw Republic*, 50.

Chapter Twelve: Overland and Downriver

1. John D. Sutton, *History of Braxton County and Central West Virginia* (n.p.: n.p., 1919). Later that year, Braddock and 1,500 troops, including Colonel Washington, marched over the upgraded road with heavy artillery and straight into a disastrous defeat at Fort Duquesne (Pittsburgh). Five hundred British were killed, including Braddock, and 450 more were wounded; the general's men buried his body in the middle of the unfinished road.
2. Mary Helen Dunlop, *Sixty Miles from Contentment: Traveling the Nineteenth-Century American Interior* (New York: Routledge, 2019), 125.
3. Karl B. Raitz, George F. Thompson, and Charles Walters, *A Guide to the National Road* (Baltimore: Johns Hopkins University Press, 1996), 92. I would like to thank Karl Raitz for generously sharing his deep expertise in the field and for communicating with me about the travel routes across America in the early nineteenth century.
4. Macdonald, *Diaries*, 224.
5. Quoted in Richard C. Wade, *The Urban Frontier: The Rise of Western Cities, 1790–1830* (Cambridge, MA: Harvard University Press, 1959), 181.
6. Quoted in Zadoc Cramer's popular travel guide from the period, which provides a basis for the travel narrative in this chapter. Zadoc Cramer, *The Navigator: Containing Directions for Navigating the Monongahela, Allegheny, Ohio and Mississippi Rivers; with an Ample Account of These Much Admired Waters, from the Head of the Former to the Mouth of the Latter; and a Concise Description of Their Towns, Villages, Harbors, Settlements, &c. with Maps of the Ohio and Mississippi; to Which Is Added an Appendix, Containing an Account of Louisiana, and of the Missouri and Columbia Rivers, as Discovered by the Voyage Under Capts. Lewis and Clark* (Pittsburgh: Cramer & Spear, 1821), 57.
7. Jennings, *Paradise Now*. Jennings refers to them as "European visionaries" (5).
8. Macdonald, *Diaries*, 228.

9. Silvia Rode, "Johann Georg Rapp (1757–1847)," *Immigrant Entrepreneurship: German-American Business Biographies, 1720–Present*, accessed May 21, 2024, http://www.immigrantentrepreneurship.org/entries/johann-georg-rapp/.
10. Owen, *Diary*, 53.
11. Raitz, Thompson, and Walters, *A Guide to the National Road*, 119.
12. Macdonald, *Diaries*, 234.
13. Owen, *Diary*, 62.
14. Daniel Drake, *Natural and Statistical View; Or Picture of Cincinnati and the Miami Country, Illustrated by Maps: With an Appendix, Containing Observations on the Late Earthquakes, the Aurora Borealis, and the South-west Wind* (Cincinnati, OH: Looker and Wallace, 1815).
15. Drinnon, *White Savage*, 166.
16. Calloway makes this point about the white Indian. Calloway, "Neither White nor Red," 46.
17. Owen, *Diary*, 68–69. The punishment in Kentucky is referenced in Charles Humphreys, *A Compendium of the Common Law in Force in Kentucky: To Which Is Prefixed a Brief Summary of the Laws of the United States* (Lexington, KY: William Gibbes Hunt, 1822).

Chapter Thirteen: Exodus

1. These descriptions are quoted in Dunlop, *Sixty Miles from Contentment*, 77.
2. Hunter wrote to Robert Owen on January 2, 1825. Quoted in Drinnon, *White Savage*, 167.
3. Bessy Walker to John Neal, April 10, 1825, in Irving T. Richards, "The Life and Works of John Neal" (unpublished Ph.D. dissertation, Harvard University, 1932), IV.
4. Offering regular service from New Orleans, the *Eagle* and the *Florence* made the nearly 900-mile trip in anywhere between ten and twenty days, water permitting. Grant Foreman, "River Navigation in the Early Southwest," *Mississippi Valley Historical Review* 15, no. 1 (1928): 40.
5. Baird, *The Quapaws*; DuVal, *The Native Ground*.
6. Quoted in Baird, *The Quapaws*, 61.
7. These "friendly hosts [were] recast as enemies to progress" during the period. As DuVal writes, "The Quapaw had built their art of negotiation around avoiding violence," which became increasingly

difficult as white and Native settlers began flooding into the valley. DuVal, *The Native Ground*, 244.

8. Baird, *The Quapaws*, 65.
9. DuVal argues that the governor of Arkansas Territory, Robert Crittenden, "strong armed" the Quapaws into the treaty. The treaties were printed in the *Arkansas Gazette* twice, on July 13 and November 23. Baird calls the 1824 treaty one of the "most ignominious" in US history (69–69).
10. Drinnon wrote down the wrong date for Hunter's arrival at the mission—he arrived on January 28, not February 28, according to the missionaries' report published in the *New York Religious Chronicle* (August 6, 1825). Drinnon also incorrectly placed Hunter at the Dwight Mission on the Neosho River near the Three Forks. Dwight Mission did not move to that site until 1830, after the United States had forced the Cherokees out of Arkansas; Drinnon, *White Savage*, 173.
11. Robert F. Berkhofer, "Model Zions for the American Indian," *American Quarterly* 15, no. 2 (1963): 176–90.
12. Nuttall, *A Journal of Travels into the Arkansas Territory During the Year 1819*, 174.
13. Drinnon, *White Savage*, 173.
14. The missionaries had no intention of transforming these children into scholars. Their report to the American Board stated that the children received a basic education "suited to the condition of the Indians." The curriculum was designed to make them useful and to "prepare their minds gradually to be pleased with industrious habits." *The Missionary Herald* (United States: Board, 1822), 107–8.
15. Ostler, *Surviving Genocide*, 224.
16. Fulford, *Romantic Indians*, 219. Norton's journal sat on the shelf in the library of an English duke until being published more than 150 years later: Norton, *The Journal of Major John Norton, 1816*, ed. Carl F. Klinck and James J. Talman (Toronto: Champlain Society, 1970).
17. Drinnon, *White Savage*, 174. Ten years later, the nation's westernmost military outpost, renamed Fort Gibson, was the terminus on the "Trail of Tears" for the Creeks, Chickasaws, Cherokees, Seminoles, and Choctaws.
18. Baird, *The Quapaws*, 69.

Chapter Fourteen: Public Enemy

1. As Berkhofer notes, a removal policy took shape after President Monroe sent his "Plan for Removing . . . Tribes West of the Mississippi River" to Congress in January. Berkhofer, *The White Man's Indian*, 158–60.
2. Secretary of War Calhoun established the Bureau of Indian Affairs in 1824 and appointed McKenney as director. On the growing bureaucracy required for the implementation of a national policy of Indian removal, see Stephen J. Rockwell, *Indian Affairs and the Administrative State in the Nineteenth Century* (Cambridge: Cambridge University Press, 2010).
3. Quoted in Drinnon, *White Savage*, 65.
4. The details from this opening scene come from Schoolcraft's recollections. Henry Rowe Schoolcraft, *Personal Memoirs of a Residence of Thirty Years with the Indian Tribes on the American Frontiers: With Brief Notices of Passing Events, Facts, and Opinions, A.D. 1812 to A.D. 1842* (Philadelphia: Lippincott, Grambo, 1851), 217.
5. Sean P. Harvey, "'Must Not Their Languages Be Savage and Barbarous Like Them?' Philology, Indian Removal, and Race Science," *Journal of the Early Republic* 30, no. 4 (2010): 519.
6. *The Quarterly Review*, December 1824–March 1825, 94.
7. *The Quarterly Review*, December 1824–March 1825, 108–9.
8. Cass to Sparks, July 30, 1825, Jared Sparks Manuscripts, Houghton Library, Harvard University.
9. Fierst's analysis of the four essays is the place to begin for anyone who wishes to understand Cass during this period. John T. Fierst, "Rationalizing Removal: Anti-Indianism in Lewis Cass's North American Review Essays," *Michigan Historical Review* 36, no. 2 (2010): 15.
10. Fierst, "Rationalizing Removal," 16.
11. Harvey, "'Must Not Their Languages Be Savage and Barbarous Like Them,'" 514. My discussion is based in Harvey's excellent account.
12. Harvey, "'Must Not Their Languages Be Savage and Barbarous Like Them,'" 520.
13. Harvey, "'Must Not Their Languages Be Savage and Barbarous Like Them,'" 507.
14. Fierst, "Rationalizing Removal," 21.
15. Saunt, *Unworthy Republic*, 54.
16. Lepore, *The Name of War*, 205.

17. Saunt, *Unworthy Republic*, 65.
18. Saunt, *Unworthy Republic*, 47. On the Cherokees and the anti-removal movement, see Ostler, *Surviving Genocide*, 183–214.

Chapter Fifteen: Promised Land

1. This historical account is based on Everett, *The Texas Cherokees;* Ernest William Winkler, "The Cherokee Indians in Texas," *Quarterly of the Texas State Historical Association* 7, no. 2 (1903): 95–165; Henderson King Yoakum, *History of Texas from Its First Settlement in 1685 to Its Annexation to the United States in 1846*, 2 vols. (New York: Redfield, 1855); Henry Stuart Foote, *Texas and the Texans: Or, Advance of the Anglo-Americans to the South-west; Including a History of Leading Events in Mexico, from the Conquest by Fernando Cortes to the Termination of the Texan Revolution*, 2 vols. (Philadelphia: Thomas, Cowperthwait, 1841); Drinnon, *White Savage*; Anderson, *The Conquest of Texas*.
2. Quoted in Anderson, *The Conquest of Texas*, 51.
3. Everett describes Fields's mission to Mexico City. Everett, *The Texas Cherokees*, 28. Officials wanted to wait to decide on the grant until a new law on land concessions was on the books. On Mexico during the era of revolution and independence, see Timothy E. Anna, *The Mexican Empire of Iturbide* (Lincoln: University of Nebraska Press, 1990); Stanley C. Green, *The Mexican Republic: The First Decade, 1823–1832* (Pittsburgh: University of Pittsburgh Press, 1987); Eric Van Young, *The Other Rebellion: Popular Violence, Ideology, and the Mexican Struggle for Independence, 1810–1821* (Stanford, CA: Stanford University Press, 2001).
4. Everett, *The Texas Cherokees*, 32.
5. Drinnon, *White Savage*, 181.
6. Anderson, *The Conquest of Texas*, 55.
7. Everett, *The Texas Cherokees*, 37.
8. Andrew J. Torget, *Seeds of Empire: Cotton, Slavery, and the Transformation of the Texas Borderlands, 1800–1850* (Chapel Hill: University of North Carolina Press, 2015), 51.
9. Anderson, *The Conquest of Texas*, 57.
10. Hunter later informed Henry George Ward, the British envoy in Mexico City, that a resolution for leaving Texas and heading someplace beyond the reach of whites had garnered support from several representatives.

11. A number of studies have shaped my understanding of the relationship between the United States and Mexico during these years, including James E. Lewis, *The American Union and the Problem of Neighborhood: The United States and the Collapse of the Spanish Empire, 1783–1829* (Chapel Hill: University of North Carolina Press, 1998); Edward H. Moseley, "The United States and Mexico, 1810–1850," in *United States–Latin American Relations, 1800–1850: The Formative Generations*, ed. Thomas Ray Shurbutt (Tuscaloosa: University of Alabama Press, 1991), 122–96; Gene M. Brack, *Mexico Views Manifest Destiny, 1821–1846: An Essay on the Origins of the Mexican War* (Albuquerque: University of New Mexico Press, 1975); Harris Gaylord Warren, *The Sword Was Their Passport: A History of American Filibustering in the Mexican Revolution* (Baton Rouge: Louisiana State University Press, 1943); Arthur Preston Whitaker, *The United States and the Independence of Latin America, 1800–1830* (Baltimore: Johns Hopkins University Press, 1941); Francisco Valdés-Ugalde, "Janus and the Northern Colossus: Perceptions of the United States in the Building of the Mexican Nation," *Journal of American History* 86, no. 2 (1999): 568–600; David J. Weber, *The Mexican Frontier, 1821–1846: The American Southwest Under Mexico* (Albuquerque: University of New Mexico Press, 1982).
12. James F. Rippy, *Joel R. Poinsett, Versatile American* (New York: Greenwood Press, 1968), 131; John J. Carter, *Covert Operations as a Tool of Presidential Foreign Policy in American History from 1800 to 1920: Foreign Policy in the Shadows* (Lewiston, NY: Edwin Mellen Press, 2000), 50. On Poinsett's time in Mexico, see Green, *The Mexican Republic*.
13. Ernest E. Rossi and Jack C. Plano, *Latin America: A Political Dictionary* (Santa Barbara, CA: ABC-CLIO, 1992), 216.
14. David Weber examines this expansionist tactic by which a supposedly neutral United States exploited instability, tolerated and encouraged filibustering expeditions, and pressed its advantages in Florida, Louisiana, and Texas. David J. Weber, *The Spanish Frontier in North America* (New Haven, CT: Yale University Press, 1992), 299.
15. See the chapter "Texas and the Boundary Issue" in William Ray Manning, *Early Diplomatic Relations Between the United States and Mexico* (Baltimore: Johns Hopkins University Press, 1916). Poinsett's remark on the "hardy race of white settlers" is on page 294.
16. Quoted in Drinnon, *White Savage*, 184.

17. Henry George Ward, *Mexico in 1827*, vol. 2 (London: H. Colburn, 1828), 587.
18. Ward, *Mexico in 1827*, 2:587.
19. Drinnon found a letter from James Kerr, an Austin agent, to the empresario. Kerr writes, "It is a well known fact that waval [Wavell] and Hunter were together in Mexico last winter and that Hunter said he was treated with more than ordinary politeness by said waval, and other Englishmen in Mexico." Drinnon, *White Savage*, 194.
20. Drinnon has Wavell forwarding his application to a "Doctor Cervallos," a state representative from Coahuila-Texas, but the name appears to be misspelled (Drinnon, *White Savage*, 185). There was a Senator Manuel Ceballos who was involved in the land business, as Jack Jackson notes in his biography of Peter Ellis Bean. Jack Jackson, *Indian Agent: Peter Ellis Bean in Mexican Texas* (College Station: Texas A&M University Press, 2005), 46.
21. Matthew Brown, *Informal Empire in Latin America: Culture, Commerce and Capital* (Chichester, UK: Wiley, 2009). Later in the century, in the Middle East, it would be called "humanitarian diplomacy."
22. For Drinnon, it was "most probable" that it did. Drinnon, *White Savage*, 191.
23. Poinsett to Clay, April 30, 1826, "Despatches from US Ministers to Mexico, 1823–1860," M97, R2, National Archives.
24. Poinsett to Clay, February 21, 1827, "Despatches from US Ministers to Mexico, 1823–1860," M97, R3, National Archives.

Chapter Sixteen: Faithful Friend

1. Catherine Seville, *The Internationalisation of Copyright Law: Books, Buccaneers and the Black Flag in the Nineteenth Century* (Cambridge: Cambridge University Press, 2006), 156.
2. Elias Norgate, *Mr. John Dunn Hunter Defended: Or, Some Remarks on an Article in the North American Review, in which that Gentleman is Branded as an Imposter* (London: John Miller, 1826), 4.
3. Norgate, *Mr. John Dunn Hunter Defended*, 5–6.
4. Norgate, *Mr. John Dunn Hunter Defended*, 9.
5. Norgate, *Mr. John Dunn Hunter Defended*, 10.
6. Norgate, *Mr. John Dunn Hunter Defended*, 37.
7. Norgate, *Mr. John Dunn Hunter Defended*, 22.
8. Norgate, *Mr. John Dunn Hunter Defended*, 24.

9. Norgate, *Mr. John Dunn Hunter Defended*, 34.
10. Sparks to Cass, July 26, 1826, Sparks Manuscripts, Houghton Library, Harvard University.
11. Sparks to Cass, September 11, 1826, Sparks Manuscripts, Houghton Library, Harvard University.
12. Fierst, "Rationalizing Removal," 16.
13. Ronald N. Satz and Laura Apfelbeck, *Chippewa Treaty Rights: The Reserved Rights of Wisconsin's Chippewa Indians in Historical Perspective* (Madison: University of Wisconsin Press, 1996), 8–9.
14. Cass to Sparks, September 21, 1826, Sparks Manuscripts, Houghton Library, Harvard University.
15. Jay H. Buckley, *William Clark: Indian Diplomat* (Norman: University of Oklahoma Press, 2008), 201.
16. Castle McLaughlin and Hillel S. Burger, *Arts of Diplomacy: Lewis and Clark's Indian Collection* (Cambridge, MA: Peabody Museum of Archaeology and Ethnology, Harvard University, 2003), 130–31.
17. An account book shows a $50 payment to his wife, Harriet, for making shirts. Landon Y. Jones, *William Clark and the Shaping of the West* (New York: Farrar, Straus and Giroux, 2005), 293.
18. Nicholas B. Wainwright, "The Life and Death of Major Thomas Biddle," *Pennsylvania Magazine of History and Biography* 104, no. 3 (1980): 326–44.
19. We will never know what the Osage respondents were truly saying or thinking. They may have been reluctant to answer truthfully, or they may have wanted to tell Biddle what he wanted to hear.
20. Recall from an earlier chapter that Hunter's first trading expedition had been under Lisa, and it ended abruptly after Hunter and the Osage and Kansa crew walked away from the expedition and a belligerent Captain Lisa.
21. Quoted in Drinnon, *White Savage*, 87.

Chapter Seventeen: Rebellion

1. Winkler, "The Cherokee Indians in Texas," 131.
2. For the definitive study of the Comanchería, see Pekka Hämäläinen, *The Comanche Empire* (New Haven, CT: Yale University Press, 2008).
3. Winkler, "The Cherokee Indians in Texas," 131.
4. Everett, *The Texas Cherokees*, 41.

5. On his fears of an intertribal conflict, see Everett, *The Texas Cherokees*, 41.
6. Laura Lyons McLemore, *Inventing Texas: Early Historians of the Lone Star State* (College Station: Texas A&M University Press, 2004), 48–49.
7. On the illegal incursions known as filibustering, see Frank Lawrence Owsley and Gene A. Smith, *Filibusters and Expansionists: Jeffersonian Manifest Destiny, 1800–1821* (Tuscaloosa: University of Alabama Press, 1997); Amy S. Greenberg, *Manifest Manhood and the Antebellum American Empire* (Cambridge: Cambridge University Press, 2005); Robert E. May, *Manifest Destiny's Underworld: Filibustering in Antebellum America* (Chapel Hill: University of North Carolina Press, 2002); Andy Doolen, *Fugitive Empire: Locating Early American Imperialism* (Minneapolis: University of Minnesota Press, 2005).
8. Everett, *The Texas Cherokees*, 43.
9. Everett, *The Texas Cherokees*, 44.
10. Anderson, *The Conquest of Texas*, 63.
11. The description of a "kangaroo court" comes from Jackson, *Indian Agent*, 63.
12. Peter Ellis Bean to Stephen F. Austin, December 31, 1826, Barker, *Austin Papers*, vol.1, pt.2, 1554. The letter is also quoted in Drinnon, *White Savage*, 183; Everett, *The Texas Cherokees*, 45; and Jackson, *Indian Agent*, 64-65.
13. Everett, *The Texas Cherokees*, 44. See also Mary Whatley Clarke, *Chief Bowles and the Texas Cherokees*, Civilization of the American Indian Series, vol. 113 (Norman: University of Oklahoma Press, 2003), 41.
14. Quoted in Jackson, *Indian Agent*, 65.
15. Austin to Hunter, *Austin Papers*, II:1565. Also, Clarke, *Chief Bowles and the Texas Cherokees*, 45–46.
16. On the life of Peter Ellis Bean, see Jackson, *Indian Agent*; Bennett Lay, *The Lives of Ellis P. Bean* (Austin: University of Texas Press, 1960).
17. Jackson, *Indian Agent*, 74.
18. Anderson, *The Conquest of Texas*, 63.
19. Anderson, *The Conquest of Texas*, 64.
20. Everett, *The Texas Cherokees*, 46.
21. Everett, *The Texas Cherokees*, 47; Anderson, *The Conquest of Texas*, 64–65.

Chapter Eighteen: Outlaw

1. Some of these include the *Arkansas Gazette*, May 20, 1827; *Eastern Argus* (Portland, ME), May 25, 1827; *New Bedford Mercury*, May 25, 1827; *Rhode Island American*, May 25, 1827; *Haverhill Gazette* (Haverhill, MA), May 26, 1827; *Newport Mercury*, May 26, 1827; *New Hampshire Patriot & State Gazette*, May 28, 1827; *Norwich Courier*, May 30, 1827; *Christian Register*, May 26, 1827; *Connecticut Mirror*, July 1827; and *Ohio State Journal*, June 21, 1827.
2. According to literary historian Eric Sundquist, Boone was depicted in the period's histories, novels, poems, plays, folktales, and songs as "a hero destined by Providence and by the laws of nature to journey through a dark wilderness and lead his people into a promised land of rich, pristine territory. A true Enlightenment hero, Boone is tempted by the forces of primitivism but remains a harbinger of progress, in particular the agricultural regeneration of the wilderness." Eric J. Sundquist, "The Frontier and American Indians," in *The Cambridge History of American Literature: Volume 2, Prose Writing 1820–1865*, ed. Sacvan Bercovitch (Cambridge: Cambridge University Press, 1994), 226. In his biography of Boone, Faragher writes that "it was as a providential pathfinder for civilization that Boone was most celebrated by his contemporaries." Faragher, *Daniel Boone*, 322.
3. Slotkin makes this point in his classic study of the American frontier. Slotkin, *Regeneration Through Violence*, 98.
4. O'Toole makes a similar point about William Johnson, a white Indian from the eighteenth century. Fintan O'Toole, *White Savage: William Johnson and the Invention of America* (New York: Macmillan, 2005), 339.
5. Jonathan Elmer, "John Neal and John Dunn Hunter," in *John Neal and Nineteenth-Century American Literature and Culture*, ed. Edward Watts and David J. Carlson (Lewisburg, PA: Bucknell University Press, 2012), 150. This is an excellent collection of essays on Neal. On his life and career, see Benjamin Lease, *That Wild Fellow John Neal and the American Literary Revolution* (Chicago: University of Chicago Press, 1973). See also Ulrich Halfmann, "In Search of the 'Real North American Story': John Neal's Short Stories 'Otter-Bag' and 'David Whicher,'" *New England Quarterly* 63, no. 3 (1990): 429–45; Paul Gilmore, "John Neal, American Romance, and International Romanticism," *American Literature* 84, no. 3 (2012): 477–504.

6. Drinnon believed that Neal was as reckless as Cass with these accusations: "The truth was that Neal had no evidence whatever. His technique was to scatter charges with a generous hand and hope that some doubts would take root"; his slanderous words were the "froth of his ill-will." Drinnon, *White Savage*, 118–19.
7. John Neal, "The Adventurer," in *The Token: A Christmas and New Year's Present*, ed. Samuel G. Goodrich (Boston: Gray and Bowen, 1831), 189–212.
8. Neal, "The Adventurer," 204.
9. Neal, "The Adventurer," 206.
10. Quoted in Foote, *Texas and the Texans*, 280.
11. Mayo's eulogy on Hunter's life and character was one of two substantial testimonials to appear in print at the time. The other, by an anonymous author, was published in the *New York Times* and reprinted in the *New-York Spectator*.
12. Foote, *Texas and the Texans*, 245.
13. Foote, *Texas and the Texans*, 246.
14. Foote, *Texas and the Texans*, 246. The Nottoway, also known as the Cheroenhaka, are a southern Iroquois people from present-day Virginia. As Americans encroached on their reservation during the 1800s, many of them headed west.
15. Foote, *Texas and the Texans*, 246.

Epilogue

1. I am relying here on Herrera's examination of Owen's Texas venture. José María Herrera, "Vision of a Utopian Texas: Robert Owen's Colonization Scheme," *Southwestern Historical Quarterly* 116, no. 4 (2013): 342–56. Owen's proposal, which was originally published in Philadelphia, is reprinted in Wilbert H. Timmons, "Robert Owen's Texas Project," *Southwestern Historical Quarterly* 52, no. 3 (1949): 286–93. Owen's biographers offer little or no commentary on his Texas proposal.
2. Herrera, "Vision of a Utopian Texas," 356.
3. Anderson, *The Conquest of Texas*, 64.
4. In Everett's analysis, "a total of 101 titles had been issued within the borders of land claimed by the Cherokees" by Mexico in 1835. After the land office was reopened two years later, "several hundred more titles were registered." Everett, *The Texas Cherokees*, 88.
5. Everett, *The Texas Cherokees*, 104.

6. Everett, *The Texas Cherokees*, 109.
7. Smithers, *The Cherokee Diaspora*, 104.
8. Everett, *The Texas Cherokees*, 113–14.
9. George W. Fields, *Texas Cherokees, 1820–1839: A Document for Litigation, 1921*, ed. Jeff Bowen (Baltimore: Clearfield, 2012).
10. Richard S. Crump, "Twentieth Century Cherokee Property Claims: A Study Based on the Case Files of Earl Boyd Pierce," *American Indian Law Review* 19, no. 2 (1994): 507–41. See also Everett's conclusion to her history of the Texas Cherokees (*The Texas Cherokees*, 120–21).

BIBLIOGRAPHY

Akerly, Samuel. "Observations on the Language of Signs, Read Before the New-York Lyceum of Natural History, on the 23d June, 1823." *American Journal of Science and Arts* 8, no. 2 (1824).

Allen, Michael R. *Western Rivermen, 1763–1861: Ohio and Mississippi Boatmen and the Myth of the Alligator Horse.* Baton Rouge: Louisiana State University Press, 1994.

Anderson, Gary Clayton. *The Conquest of Texas: Ethnic Cleansing in the Promised Land, 1820–1875.* Norman: University of Oklahoma Press, 2019.

Anna, Timothy E. *The Mexican Empire of Iturbide.* Lincoln: University of Nebraska Press, 1990.

Apess, William, and Barry O'Connell. *On Our Own Ground: The Complete Writings of William Apess, a Pequot.* Amherst: University of Massachusetts Press, 1992.

Aporta, Claudio. "Inuit Orienting: Travelling Along Familiar Horizons." *Sensory Studies* (2020).

Aron, Stephen. *Peace and Friendship: An Alternative History of the American West.* Oxford: Oxford University Press, 2022.

Axtell, James. "The White Indians of Colonial America." *William and Mary Quarterly: A Magazine of Early American History* 32, no. 1 (1975): 55–88.

Bacon, Richard N. *A Report of the Transactions at the Holkham Sheep-Shearing, on Monday, Tuesday, Wednesday, and Thursday, July 2, 3, 4, and 5: Being the Forty-Third Anniversary of That Meeting.* N.p.: n.p., 1821.

Baird, W. David. *The Quapaw Indians: A History of the Downstream People.* Norman: University of Oklahoma Press, 1980.

Baker, Jean H. *Building America: The Life of Benjamin Henry Latrobe.* New York: Oxford University Press, 2020.

Baldwin, Leland D. *The Keelboat Age on Western Waters*. Pittsburgh: University of Pittsburgh Press, 1941.

Barker, Eugene C. *The Austin Papers*. 2 vols. Washington, DC: US Government Printing Office, 1928.

Bellin, Joshua David. *The Demon of the Continent: Indians and the Shaping of American Literature*. Philadelphia: University of Pennsylvania Press, 2012.

Bellin, Joshua David. *Medicine Bundle: Indian Sacred Performance and American Literature, 1824–1932*. Philadelphia: University of Pennsylvania Press, 2008.

Bellin, Joshua David, and Laura L. Mielke. *Native Acts: Indian Performance, 1603–1832*. Lincoln: University of Nebraska Press, 2011.

Belyea, Barbara. "Amerindian Maps: The Explorer as Translator." *Journal of Historical Geography* 18, no. 3 (1992): 267–77.

Berkhofer, Robert F. "Model Zions for the American Indian." *American Quarterly* 15, no. 2 (1963): 176–90.

Berkhofer, Robert F. *The White Man's Indian: Images of the American Indian from Columbus to the Present*. New York: Vintage, 1979.

Black Hawk. *Life of Black Hawk, or Ma-Ka-Tai-Me-She-Kia-Kiak*. Edited by J. Gerald Kennedy. New York: Penguin, 2008.

Blackhawk, Ned. *Violence over the Land: Indians and Empires in the Early American West*. Cambridge, MA: Harvard University Press, 2006.

Bolton, S. Charles. *Arkansas, 1800–1860: Remote and Restless*. Fayetteville: University of Arkansas Press, 2014.

Brack, Gene M. *Mexico Views Manifest Destiny, 1821–1846: An Essay on the Origins of the Mexican War*. Albuquerque: University of New Mexico Press, 1975.

Bradford, William. *Of Plymouth Plantation, 1620–1647*. New Brunswick, NJ: Rutgers University Press, 1952.

The British Critic. January 1823.

Brooks, Eugene C. *The Story of Corn and the Westward Migration*. Chicago: Rand McNally, 1916.

Brooks, Lisa. *The Common Pot: The Recovery of Native Space in the Northeast*. Minneapolis: University of Minnesota Press, 2008.

Brown, Matthew. *Informal Empire in Latin America: Culture, Commerce and Capital*. Chichester, UK: Wiley, 2009.

Brown, Samuel. *The Western Gazetteer; or Emigrant's Directory*. Auburn, NY: H. C. Southwick, 1817.

Brumble, H. David. *American Indian Autobiography*. Lincoln: University of Nebraska Press, 1988.

Buckley, Jay H. *William Clark: Indian Diplomat*. Norman: University of Oklahoma Press, 2008.

Burns, Louis F. *A History of the Osage People*. Tuscaloosa: University of Alabama Press, 2004.

Burns, Louis F. *Osage Indian Customs and Myths*. Tuscaloosa: University of Alabama Press, 2005.

Byrd, Jodi A. *The Transit of Empire: Indigenous Critiques of Colonialism*. Minneapolis: University of Minnesota Press, 2011.

Calloway, Colin G. "Neither White nor Red: White Renegades on the American Indian Frontier." *Western Historical Quarterly* 17, no. 1 (1986): 43–66.

Calloway, Colin G. *Pen and Ink Witchcraft: Treaties and Treaty Making in American Indian History*. New York: Oxford University Press, 2013.

Carter, John J. *Covert Operations as a Tool of Presidential Foreign Policy in American History from 1800 to 1920: Foreign Policy in the Shadows*. Lewiston, NY: Edwin Mellen Press, 2000.

Cass, Lewis. "Indians of North America." *North American Review* 22, no. 50 (1826): 53–119.

Catlin, George. *Letters and Notes on the Manners, Customs, and Condition of the North American Indians*. New York: Wiley & Putnam, 1844.

Cawelti, John G. *The Six-Gun Mystique Sequel*. Bowling Green, OH: Popular Press, 1999.

Chittenden, Hiram Martin. *The American Fur Trade of the Far West*. New York: Press of the Pioneers, 1935.

The Cincinnati Literary Gazette. Vol. 1, January 1824.

Clark, Edward. *Description of a Plan for Navigating the Rapids in Rivers: With an Account of Some Experiments Instituted to Establish Its Practicability*. Philadelphia: William Brown, 1823.

Clarke, Mary Whatley. *Chief Bowles and the Texas Cherokees*. Civilization of the American Indian Series, vol. 113. Norman: University of Oklahoma Press, 2003.

Copway, George. *Life, Letters and Speeches*. Lincoln: University of Nebraska Press, 2006.

Cramer, Zadoc. *The Navigator: Containing Directions for Navigating the Monongahela, Allegheny, Ohio and Mississippi Rivers; with an Ample Account of These Much Admired Waters, from the Head of the Former to the*

Mouth of the Latter; and a Concise Description of Their Towns, Villages, Harbors, Settlements, &C. With Maps of the Ohio and Mississippi; to Which Is Added an Appendix, Containing an Account of Louisiana, and of the Missouri and Columbia Rivers, as Discovered by the Voyage Under Capts. Lewis and Clark. Pittsburgh: Cramer & Spear, 1821.

Cronon, William. "The Trouble with Wilderness: Or, Getting Back to the Wrong Nature." *Environmental History* 1, no. 1 (1996): 7–28.

Crump, Richard S. "Twentieth Century Cherokee Property Claims: A Study Based on the Case Files of Earl Boyd Pierce." *American Indian Law Review* 19, no. 2 (1994): 507–41.

Dahl, Adam. *Empire of the People: Settler Colonialism and the Foundations of Modern Democratic Thought.* Lawrence: University Press of Kansas, 2018.

Davis, Jeffrey. "A Historical Linguistic Account of Sign Language Among North American Indian Groups." In *Multilingualism and Sign Languages: From the Great Plains to Australia,* Sociolinguistics of the Deaf Community, edited by Ceil Lucas, 3–35. Washington, DC: Gallaudet University Press, 2006.

Debo, Angie. *The Rise and Fall of the Choctaw Republic.* Norman: University of Oklahoma Press, 1961.

Deloria, Philip Joseph. *Playing Indian.* New Haven, CT: Yale University Press, 1998.

Deloria, Vine, and Raymond J. DeMallie. *Documents of American Indian Diplomacy: Treaties, Agreements, and Conventions, 1775–1979,* vol. 1. Norman: University of Oklahoma Press, 1999.

Dennison, Jean. *Colonial Entanglement: Constituting a Twenty-First-Century Osage Nation.* Chapel Hill: University of North Carolina Press, 2012.

Dickey, Michael. *The People of the River's Mouth: In Search of the Missouria Indians.* Columbia: University of Missouri Press, 2011.

Dippie, Brian W. *Catlin and His Contemporaries: The Politics of Patronage.* Lincoln: University of Nebraska Press, 1990.

Dippie, Brian W. *The Vanishing American: White Attitudes and U.S. Indian Policy.* Middletown, CT: Wesleyan University Press, 1982.

Dixon, Benjamin Y. "Furthering Their Own Demise: How Kansa Indian Death Customs Accelerated Their Depopulation." *Ethnohistory* 54, no. 3 (2007): 473–508.

Doolen, Andy. *Fugitive Empire: Locating Early American Imperialism.* Minneapolis: University of Minnesota Press, 2005.

Doolen, Andy. *Territories of Empire: U.S. Writing from the Louisiana Purchase to Mexican Independence*. New York: Oxford University Press, 2014.

Dowd, Gregory Evans. *A Spirited Resistance: The North American Indian Struggle for Unity, 1745–1815*. Baltimore: Johns Hopkins University Press, 1992.

Drake, Daniel. *Natural and Statistical View; or Picture of Cincinnati and the Miami Country, Illustrated by Maps: With an Appendix, Containing Observations on the Late Earthquakes, the Aurora Borealis, and the South-West Wind*. Cincinnati, OH: Looker and Wallace, 1815.

Drinnon, Richard. *White Savage: The Case of John Dunn Hunter*. New York: Schocken Books, 1972.

Dunbar-Ortiz, Roxanne. *Not "a Nation of Immigrants": Settler Colonialism, White Supremacy, and a History of Erasure and Exclusion*. Boston: Beacon Press, 2021.

Dunbar-Ortiz, Roxanne, and Dina Gilio-Whitaker. *"All the Real Indians Died Off": And 20 Other Myths About Native Americans*. Boston: Beacon Press, 2016.

Dunlop, Mary Helen. *Sixty Miles from Contentment: Traveling the Nineteenth-Century American Interior*. New York: Routledge, 2019.

DuVal, Kathleen. "Debating Identity, Sovereignty, and Civilization: The Arkansas Valley After the Louisiana Purchase." *Journal of the Early Republic* 26, no. 1 (2006): 25–58.

DuVal, Kathleen. *The Native Ground: Indians and Colonists in the Heart of the Continent*. Philadelphia: University of Pennsylvania Press, 2006.

The Eclectic Review. July–December 1823.

Edmunds, R. David. *The Shawnee Prophet*. Lincoln: University of Nebraska Press, 1985.

Eisler, Benita. *The Red Man's Bones: George Catlin, Artist and Showman*. New York: Norton, 2013.

Elmer, Jonathan. "John Neal and John Dunn Hunter." In *John Neal and Nineteenth-Century American Literature and Culture*, edited by Edward Watts and David J. Carlson. Lewisburg: Bucknell University Press, 2012.

Everett, Dianna. *The Texas Cherokees: A People Between Two Fires, 1819–1840*. Norman: University of Oklahoma Press, 1990.

Faragher, John Mack. *Daniel Boone: The Life and Legend of an American Pioneer*. New York: Henry Holt, 1993.

Fenn, Elizabeth A. *Encounters at the Heart of the World: A History of the Mandan People*. New York: Macmillan, 2014.

Fields, George W. *Texas Cherokees, 1820–1839: A Document for Litigation, 1921*. Edited by Jeff Bowen. Baltimore: Clearfield, 2012.

Fierst, John T. "Rationalizing Removal: Anti-Indianism in Lewis Cass's North American Review Essays." *Michigan Historical Review* 36, no. 2 (2010): 1–35.

Flint, Timothy. *Recollections of the Last Ten Years in the Valley of the Mississippi*. Edited by George R. Brooks. 1826; reprint, Carbondale: Southern Illinois University Press, 1968.

Foner, Eric. *Forever Free: The Story of Emancipation and Reconstruction*. New York: Knopf, 2013.

Foote, Henry Stuart. *Texas and the Texans: Or, Advance of the Anglo-Americans to the South-West; Including a History of Leading Events in Mexico, from the Conquest by Fernando Cortes to the Termination of the Texan Revolution*. 2 vols. Philadelphia: Thomas, Cowperthwait & Co., 1841.

Foreman, Grant. *Indian Removal: The Emigration of the Five Civilized Tribes of Indians*. Norman: University of Oklahoma Press, 1953.

Foreman, Grant. "River Navigation in the Early Southwest." *Mississippi Valley Historical Review* 15, no. 1 (1928): 34–55.

Fryd, Vivien Green. *Art and Empire: The Politics of Ethnicity in the United States Capitol, 1815–1860*. New Haven, CT: Yale University Press, 1992.

Fulford, Tim. *Romantic Indians: Native Americans, British Literature, and Transatlantic Culture, 1756–1830*. New York: Oxford University Press, 2006.

Gibson, Arrell M. *Kickapoos: Lords of the Middle Border*. Norman: University of Oklahoma Press, 1975.

Gilmore, Paul. "John Neal, American Romance, and International Romanticism." *American Literature* 84, no. 3 (2012): 477–504.

Goetzmann, William H. *Exploration and Empire: The Explorer and the Scientist in the Winning of the American West*. New York: History Book Club, 1966.

Goldstein, Alyosha. *Formations of United States Colonialism*. Durham, NC: Duke University Press, 2014.

Goslee, Nancy Moore. "Heman's 'Red Indians.'" In *Romanticism, Race, and Imperial Culture, 1780–1834*, edited by A. T. Richardson, A. Richardson, S. Hofkosh, and L. Doyle. Bloomington: Indiana University Press, 1996.

Green, Stanley C. *The Mexican Republic: The First Decade, 1823–1832.* Pittsburgh: University of Pittsburgh Press, 1987.

Greenberg, Amy S. *Manifest Manhood and the Antebellum American Empire.* Cambridge: Cambridge University Press, 2005.

Guarneri, Carl. *The Utopian Alternative: Fourierism in Nineteenth-Century America.* Ithaca, NY: Cornell University Press, 1991.

Gunn, Robert Lawrence. *Ethnology and Empire: Languages, Literature, and the Making of the North American Borderlands.* New York: New York University Press, 2015.

Gura, Philip F. *The Life of William Apess, Pequot.* Chapel Hill: University of North Carolina, 2015.

Halfmann, Ulrich. "In Search of the 'Real North American Story': John Neal's Short Stories 'Otter-Bag' and 'David Whicher.'" *New England Quarterly* 63, no. 3 (1990): 429–45.

Hämäläinen, Pekka. *The Comanche Empire.* New Haven, CT: Yale University Press, 2008.

Harding, Chester. *My Egotistigraphy.* Cambridge: John Wilson & Son, 1866.

Harrison, John F. C. *Quest for the New Moral World: Robert Owen and the Owenities in Britain and America.* New York: Scribner, 1969.

Harvey, Sean P. "'Must Not Their Languages Be Savage and Barbarous Like Them?' Philology, Indian Removal, and Race Science." *Journal of the Early Republic* 30, no. 4 (2010): 505–32.

Hasegawa, Guy R. "Quinine Substitutes in the Confederate Army." *Military Medicine* 172, no. 6 (2007): 650–55.

Henshaw, Henry Wetherbee. "Indian Origin of Maple Sugar." *American Anthropologist* 3, no. 4 (1890): 341–52.

Herrera, José María. "Vision of a Utopian Texas: Robert Owen's Colonization Scheme." *Southwestern Historical Quarterly* 116, no. 4 (2013): 342–56.

Herring, Joseph B. *The Enduring Indians of Kansas: A Century and a Half of Acculturation.* Lawrence: University Press of Kansas, 1990.

Herring, Joseph B. *Kenekuk the Kickapoo Prophet.* Lawrence: University Press of Kansas, 1988.

Hietala, Thomas R. *Manifest Design: Anxious Aggrandizement in Late Jacksonian America.* Ithaca, NY: Cornell University Press, 1985.

Hixson, Walter. *American Settler Colonialism: A History.* New York: Springer, 2013.

Hodge, Frederick Webb. *Handbook of American Indians North of Mexico.* Smithsonian Institution Bureau of American Ethnology Bulletin. 2 vols. Washington, DC: Government Printing Office, 1910.

Holt, Keri. "Double-Crossings: The Trans-American Patriotism of Francis Berrian." *Western American Literature* 44, no. 4 (2010): 312–41.

Horsman, Reginald. *Race and Manifest Destiny: The Origins of American Racial Anglo-Saxonism.* Cambridge, MA: Harvard University Press, 1981.

Hosack, Alexander Eddy. *A Memoir of the Late David Hosack.* Philadelphia: Lindsay & Blakiston, 1861.

Howe, Daniel Walker. *What Hath God Wrought: The Transformation of America, 1815–1848.* New York: Oxford University Press, 2007.

Hoxie, Frederick E. "Retrieving the Red Continent: Settler Colonialism and the History of American Indians in the US." *Ethnic and Racial Studies* 31, no. 6 (2008): 1153–67.

Humphreys, Charles. *A Compendium of the Common Law in Force in Kentucky: To Which Is Prefixed a Brief Summary of the Laws of the United States.* Lexington, KY: William Gibbes Hunt, 1822.

Hunter, John Dunn. *Memoirs of a Captivity Among the Indians of North America: From Childhood to the Age of Nineteen: With Anecdotes Descriptive of Their Manners and Customs.* Edited by Richard Drinnon. New York: Schocken Books, 1973.

Hyde, Anne Farrar. *Empires, Nations, and Families: A History of the North American West, 1800–1860.* Lincoln: University of Nebraska Press, 2011.

Hyde, George E. *The Pawnee Indians.* Norman: University of Oklahoma Press, 1988.

Jackson, Jack. *Indian Agent: Peter Ellis Bean in Mexican Texas.* College Station: Texas A&M University Press, 2005.

Jennings, Chris. *Paradise Now: The Story of American Utopianism.* New York: Random House, 2016.

Johnson, Victoria. *American Eden: David Hosack, Botany, and Medicine in the Garden of the Early Republic.* New York: Liveright, 2018.

Johnson, Walter. *River of Dark Dreams.* Cambridge, MA: Harvard University Press, 2013.

Jones, Landon Y. *William Clark and the Shaping of the West.* New York: Farrar, Straus and Giroux, 2005.

Keating, William H. *Narrative of an Expedition to the Source of St. Peter's River, Lake Winnepeek, Lake of the Woods, & C., Performed in the Year 1823.* Vol. 2. London: G. B. Whittaker, 1825.

Key, Joseph Patrick. "'Outcasts upon the world': The Louisiana Purchase and the Quapaws." *The Arkansas Historical Quarterly* 62, no. 3 (2003): 272–88.

Konkle, Maureen. *Writing Indian Nations: Native Intellectuals and the Politics of Historiography, 1827–1863*. Chapel Hill: University of North Carolina Press, 2004.

Krupat, Arnold. *The Voice in the Margin: Native American Literature and the Canon*. Berkeley: University of California Press, 1989.

La Flesche, Francis. *The Osage and the Invisible World: From the Works of Francis La Flesche*. Norman: University of Oklahoma Press, 1995.

Lay, Bennett. *The Lives of Ellis P. Bean*. Austin: University of Texas Press, 1960.

Lease, Benjamin. *That Wild Fellow John Neal and the American Literary Revolution*. Chicago: University of Chicago Press, 1973.

Lepore, Jill. *The Name of War: King Philip's War and the Origins of American Identity*. New York: Knopf, 1998.

Levasseur, Auguste, and John D. Godman. *Lafayette in America in 1824 and 1825: Or, Journal of a Voyage to the United States*. Philadelphia: Carey and Lea, 1829.

Lewis, James E. *The American Union and the Problem of Neighborhood: The United States and the Collapse of the Spanish Empire, 1783–1829*. Chapel Hill: University of North Carolina Press, 1998.

Limerick, Patricia Nelson. *The Legacy of Conquest: The Unbroken Past of the American West*. New York: Norton, 1987.

Lipton, Leah. *A Truthful Likeness: Chester Harding and His Portraits*. Washington, DC: National Portrait Gallery, Smithsonian Institution, 1985.

The Literary Gazette. April 19, 1823.

Lopenzina, Drew. *Through an Indian's Looking-Glass: A Cultural Biography of William Apess, Pequot*. Amherst: University of Massachusetts Press, 2018.

Macdonald, Donald. *The Diaries of Donald Macdonald, 1824–1826*. Indianapolis: Indiana Historical Society, 1942.

Manning, William Ray. *Early Diplomatic Relations Between the United States and Mexico*. Baltimore: Johns Hopkins University Press, 1916.

Matthews, John Joseph. *The Osages: Children of the Middle Waters*. Norman: University of Oklahoma Press, 1961.

May, Robert E. *Manifest Destiny's Underworld: Filibustering in Antebellum America*. Chapel Hill: University of North Carolina Press, 2002.

McCoy, Drew R. *The Elusive Republic: Political Economy in Jeffersonian America.* Chapel Hill: University of North Carolina Press, 1980.

McLaughlin, Castle, and Hillel S. Burger. *Arts of Diplomacy: Lewis and Clark's Indian Collection.* Cambridge, MA: Peabody Museum of Archaeology and Ethnology, Harvard University, 2003.

McLemore, Laura Lyons. *Inventing Texas: Early Historians of the Lone Star State.* College Station: Texas A&M University Press, 2004.

Meinig, D. W. *The Shaping of America: A Geographical Perspective on 500 Years of History.* Vol. 1: *Atlantic America, 1492–1800.* New Haven, CT: Yale University Press, 1986.

Meinig, D. W. *The Shaping of America: A Geographical Perspective on 500 Years of History.* Vol. 2: *Continental America, 1800–1867.* New Haven, CT: Yale University Press, 1993.

Mielke, Laura L. *Moving Encounters: Sympathy and the Indian Question in Antebellum Literature.* Amherst: University of Massachusetts Press, 2008.

Mitchell, Timothy. "Carbon Democracy." *Economy and Society* 38, no. 3 (2009): 399–432.

The Monthly Review. Vol. 102, November 1823.

Moseley, Edward H. "The United States and Mexico, 1810–1850." In *United States–Latin American Relations, 1800–1850: The Formative Generations*, edited by Thomas Ray Shurbutt. Tuscaloosa: University of Alabama Press, 1991.

Namias, June. *White Captives: Gender and Ethnicity on the American Frontier.* Chapel Hill: University of North Carolina, 1993.

Neal, John. "The Adventurer." In *The Token: A Christmas and New Year's Present*, edited by Samuel G. Goodrich. Boston: Gray and Bowen, 1831.

The New Monthly Magazine. Vol. 10, January 1824.

Nichols, David A. *Red Gentlemen and White Savages: Indians, Federalists, and the Search for Order on the American Frontier.* Charlottesville: University of Virginia Press, 2008.

Nielsen, George R. *The Kickapoo People.* 1975.

Norgate, Elias. *Mr. John Dunn Hunter Defended: Or, Some Remarks on an Article in the North American Review, in Which That Gentleman Is Branded as an Imposter.* London: John Miller, 1826.

Norton, John. *The Journal of Major John Norton, 1816.* Edited by Carl F. Klinck and James J. Talman. Toronto: Champlain Society, 1970.

Nunis, Doyce B. "The Sublettes of Kentucky: Their Early Contribution to the Opening of the West." *Register of the Kentucky Historical Society* 57, no. 1 (1959): 20–34.

Nuttall, Thomas. *A Journal of Travels into the Arkansas Territory During the Year 1819*. Edited by Savoie Lottinville. Fayetteville: University of Arkansas Press, 1999.

Occom, Samson. *The Collected Writings of Samson Occom, Mohegan*. New York: Oxford University Press, 2006.

O'Daniel, Victor Francis. *A Light of the Church in Kentucky: Or the Life, Labors, and Character of the Very Rev. Samuel Thomas Wilson, OP, STM, Pioneer Educator and the First Provincial of a Religious Order in the United States*. Washington, DC: The Dominicana, 1932.

Oglesby, Richard Edward. *Manuel Lisa and the Opening of the Missouri Fur Trade*. Norman: University of Oklahoma Press, 1963.

Oliva, Leo E. "Enemies and Friends: Zebulon Montgomery Pike and Facundo Melgares in the Competition for the Great Plains, 1806–1807." *Kansas History* 29, no. 1 (2006): 34–47.

Ostler, Jeffrey. *Surviving Genocide: Native Nations and the United States from the American Revolution to Bleeding Kansas*. New Haven, CT: Yale University Press, 2019.

O'Toole, Fintan. *White Savage: William Johnson and the Invention of America*. New York: Macmillan, 2005.

Owen, William. *Diary of William Owen from November 10, 1824 to April 20, 1825*. Edited by Joel W. Hiatt. Indianapolis, IN: Bobbs-Merrill, 1906.

Owens, Robert M. *Mr. Jefferson's Hammer: William Henry Harrison and the Origins of American Indian Policy*. Norman: University of Oklahoma Press, 2007.

Owsley, Frank Lawrence, and Gene A. Smith. *Filibusters and Expansionists: Jeffersonian Manifest Destiny, 1800–1821*. Tuscaloosa: University of Alabama Press, 1997.

Parks, Ronald D. *The Darkest Period: The Kanza Indians and Their Last Homeland, 1846–1873*. Norman: University of Oklahoma Press, 2014.

Pike, Zebulon Montgomery. *Journals, with Letters and Related Documents*. Edited by Donald Jackson. 2 vols. Norman: University of Oklahoma Press, 1966.

Pitzer, Donald E. "The Original Boatload of Knowledge down the Ohio River: William Maclure's and Robert Owen's Transfer of Science and Education to the Midwest, 1825–1826." *Ohio Journal of Science* 89, no. 5 (December 1989): 128–42.

Pollard, Sidney, and John Salt. *Robert Owen, Prophet of the Poor: Essays in Honour of the Two Hundredth Anniversary of His Birth.* Lewisburg, PA: Bucknell University Press, 1971.

The Port Folio. Vol. 18, 1824.

Pratt, Mary Louise. *Imperial Eyes: Travel Writing and Transculturation.* London: Routledge, 1992.

The Quarterly Review. December 1824–March 1825.

Raitz, Karl B., George F. Thompson, and Charles Walters. *A Guide to the National Road.* Baltimore: Johns Hopkins University Press, 1996.

Reed, Henry Hope. *The United States Capitol: Its Architecture and Decoration.* New York: Norton, 2005.

Rippy, James F. *Joel R. Poinsett, Versatile American.* New York: Greenwood Press, 1968.

Rockwell, Stephen J. *Indian Affairs and the Administrative State in the Nineteenth Century.* Cambridge: Cambridge University Press, 2010.

Rode, Silvia. "Johann Georg Rapp (1757–1847)." *Immigrant Entrepreneurship: German-American Business Biographies, 1720–Present.* http://www.immigrantentrepreneurship.org/entries/johann-georg-rapp/.

Rohrbough, Malcolm J. *The Trans-Appalachian Frontier: People, Societies, and Institutions, 1775–1850.* Belmont, CA: Wadsworth, 1990.

Rollings, Willard H. *Unaffected by the Gospel: Osage Resistance to the Christian Invasion (1673–1906): A Cultural Victory.* Albuquerque: University of New Mexico Press, 2004.

Rollings, Willard H. *The Osage: An Ethnohistorical Study of Hegemony on the Prairie-Plains.* Columbia: University of Missouri Press, 1995.

Rossi, Ernest E., and Jack C. Plano. *Latin America: A Political Dictionary.* Santa Barbara, CA: ABC-CLIO, 1992.

Rothman, Adam. *Slave Country: American Expansion and the Origins of the Deep South.* Cambridge, MA: Harvard University Press, 2005.

Ruby, Robert H., and John Arthur Brown. *Indians of the Pacific Northwest: A History.* Norman: University of Oklahoma Press, 1988.

Sabo, George, and James P. Harcourt. *Human Adaptation in the Ozark and Ouachita Mountains.* Fayetteville: Arkansas Archeological Survey, 1990.

Sands, Kathleen M. "Narrative Resistance: Native American Collaborative Autobiography." *Studies in American Indian Literatures* (ser. 2) 10, no. 1 (1998): 1–18.

Satz, Ronald N. *American Indian Policy in the Jacksonian Era.* Lincoln: University of Nebraska Press, 1974.

Satz, Ronald N., and Laura Apfelbeck. *Chippewa Treaty Rights: The Reserved Rights of Wisconsin's Chippewa Indians in Historical Perspective.* Madison: University of Wisconsin Press, 1996.

Saunt, Claudio. *Unworthy Republic: The Dispossession of Native Americans and the Road to Indian Territory.* New York: Norton, 2021.

Sayre, Gordon M. "Abridging Between Two Worlds: John Tanner as American Indian Autobiographer." *American Literary History* 11, no. 3 (1999): 480–99.

Sayre, Gordon M. "A Native American Scoops Lewis and Clark: The Voyage of Moncacht-Apé." *Common-place* 5, no. 4 (2005).

Scharf, John Thomas, and Thompson Westcott. *History of Philadelphia, 1609–1884.* Vol. 1. Philadelphia: L. H. Everts, 1884.

Scheckel, Susan. *The Insistence of the Indian: Race and Nationalism in Nineteenth-Century American Culture.* Princeton, NJ: Princeton University Press, 1998.

Schoolcraft, Henry Rowe. *Personal Memoirs of a Residence of Thirty Years with the Indian Tribes on the American Frontiers: With Brief Notices of Passing Events, Facts, and Opinions, A.D. 1812 to A.D. 1842.* Philadelphia: Lippincott, Grambo & Co., 1851.

Scott, Pamela. *Temple of Liberty: Building the Capitol for a New Nation.* New York: Oxford University Press, 1995.

Seville, Catherine. *The Internationalisation of Copyright Law: Books, Buccaneers and the Black Flag in the Nineteenth Century.* Cambridge: Cambridge University Press, 2006.

Shannon, Timothy John. *Iroquois Diplomacy on the Early American Frontier.* New York: Penguin, 2008.

Sheehan, Bernard W. *Seeds of Extinction: Jeffersonian Philanthropy and the American Indian.* Chapel Hill, NC: Institute of Early American History and Culture at Williamsburg, 1973.

Slotkin, Richard. *Regeneration Through Violence: The Mythology of the American Frontier, 1600–1860.* Middletown, CT: Wesleyan University Press, 1973.

Smithers, Gregory D. *The Cherokee Diaspora: An Indigenous History of Migration, Resettlement, and Identity.* New Haven, CT: Yale University Press, 2015.

Stirling, Anna Maria W. *Coke of Norfolk and His Friends: The Life of Thomas William Coke, First Earl of Leicester of Holkham.* London: Lane, 1908.

Sugden, John. *Tecumseh: A Life*. New York: Henry Holt, 1998.

Sundquist, Eric J. "The Frontier and American Indians." In *The Cambridge History of American Literature: Volume 2, Prose Writing 1820–1865*, edited by Sacvan Bercovitch. Cambridge: Cambridge University Press, 1994.

Supalla, Ted, Fanny Limousin, and Betsy Hicks McDonald. "Historical Change in American Sign Language." *Handbook of Historical Linguistics* 2 (2020): 423–46.

Sutton, John D. *History of Braxton County and Central West Virginia*. N.p.: n.p., 1919.

Taylor, Christopher. "North America as Contact Zone: Native American Literary Nationalism and the Cross-Cultural Dilemma." *Studies in American Indian Literatures* 22, no. 3 (2010): 26–44.

Timmons, Wilbert H. "Robert Owen's Texas Project." *Southwestern Historical Quarterly* 52, no. 3 (1949): 286–93.

Tinker, George E. *Missionary Conquest: The Gospel and Native American Cultural Genocide*. Minneapolis, MN: Fortress Press, 1993.

Tinnemeyer, Andrea. "Enlightenment Ideology and the Crisis of Whiteness in *Francis Berrian* and *Caballero*." *Western American Literature* 35, no. 1 (2000): 21–32.

Torget, Andrew J. *Seeds of Empire: Cotton, Slavery, and the Transformation of the Texas Borderlands, 1800–1850*. Chapel Hill: University of North Carolina Press, 2015.

Treuer, Anton. *Ojibwe in Minnesota*. St. Paul: Minnesota Historical Society, 2010.

Treuer, David. *The Heartbeat of Wounded Knee: Native America from 1890 to the Present*. New York: Riverhead Books, 2019.

Unrau, William E. *The Kansa Indians: A History of the Wind People, 1673–1873*. Norman: University of Oklahoma Press, 1986.

Valdés-Ugalde, Francisco. "Janus and the Northern Colossus: Perceptions of the United States in the Building of the Mexican Nation." *Journal of American History* 86, no. 2 (1999): 568–600.

Van Young, Eric. *The Other Rebellion: Popular Violence, Ideology, and the Mexican Struggle for Independence, 1810–1821*. Stanford, CA: Stanford University Press, 2001.

Vaughan, Alden T. *Transatlantic Encounters: American Indians in Britain, 1500–1776*. Cambridge: Cambridge University Press, 2006.

Vogel, Virgil J. *American Indian Medicine*. Norman: University of Oklahoma Press, 2013.

Wade, Richard C. *The Urban Frontier: The Rise of Western Cities, 1790–1830.* Cambridge, MA: Harvard University Press, 1959.

Wainwright, Nicholas B. "The Life and Death of Major Thomas Biddle." *Pennsylvania Magazine of History and Biography* 104, no. 3 (1980): 326–44.

Ward, Henry George. *Mexico in 1827*, vol. 2. London: H. Colburn, 1828.

Warhus, Mark. *Another America: Native American Maps and the History of Our Land.* New York: St. Martin's Griffin, 1998.

Warren, Harris Gaylord. *The Sword Was Their Passport: A History of American Filibustering in the Mexican Revolution.* Baton Rouge: Louisiana State University Press, 1943.

Warren, Stephen. *The Shawnees and Their Neighbors, 1795–1870.* Urbana: University of Illinois Press, 2005.

Warrior, Robert Allen. *The People and the Word: Reading Native Nonfiction.* Minneapolis: University of Minnesota Press, 2005.

Watts, Edward. *An American Colony: Regionalism and the Roots of Midwestern Culture.* Athens: Ohio University Press, 2002.

Weatherford, Jack. *Indian Givers: How the Indians of the Americas Transformed the World.* New York: Ballantine Books, 2010.

Weber, David J. *The Mexican Frontier, 1821–1846: The American Southwest Under Mexico.* Albuquerque: University of New Mexico Press, 1982.

Weber, David J. *The Spanish Frontier in North America.* New Haven, CT: Yale University Press, 1992.

Whitaker, Arthur Preston. *The United States and the Independence of Latin America, 1800–1830.* Baltimore: Johns Hopkins University Press, 1941.

White, Richard. *The Middle Ground: Indians, Empires, and Republics in the Great Lakes Region, 1650–1815.* Cambridge: Cambridge University Press, 1991.

White, Richard. *The Roots of Dependency: Subsistence, Environment, and Social Change among the Choctaws, Pawnees, and Navajos.* Lincoln: University of Nebraska Press, 1988.

Williams, Chris, and Noel Thompson. *Robert Owen and His Legacy.* Cardiff: University of Wales Press, 2011.

Winkler, Ernest William. "The Cherokee Indians in Texas." *Quarterly of the Texas State Historical Association* 7, no. 2 (1903): 95–165.

Wolfe, Patrick. "Settler Colonialism and the Elimination of the Native." *Journal of Genocide Research* 8, no. 4 (2006): 387–409.

Wong, Hertha Dawn. *Sending My Heart Back Across the Years: Tradition and Innovation in Native American Autobiography.* New York: Oxford University Press, 1992.

Wyss, Hilary E. "Captivity and Conversion: William Apess, Mary Jemison, and Narratives of Racial Identity." *American Indian Quarterly* 23, nos. 3–4 (1999): 63–82.

Yoakum, Henderson King. *History of Texas from Its First Settlement in 1685 to Its Annexation to the United States in 1846.* 2 vols. New York: Redfield, 1855.

INDEX